Arnulfo L. Oliveira Memorial Library

Inside the Red Mansion

Inside the
Red Mansion

ON THE TRAIL OF
CHINA'S MOST WANTED MAN

OLIVER AUGUST

HOUGHTON MIFFLIN COMPANY

BOSTON · NEW YORK   2007

For information about permission to reproduce selections from
this book, write to Permissions, Houghton Mifflin Company,
215 Park Avenue South, New York, New York 10003.

Visit our Web site: www.houghtonmifflinbooks.com.

Library of Congress Cataloging-in-Publication Data
August, Oliver, date.
Inside the red mansion : on the trail of China's most
wanted man / Oliver August.
p.   cm.
ISBN-13: 978-0-618-71498-8
ISBN-10: 0-618-71498-7
1. China — Description and travel. 2. Lai, Changxing, 1958–
I. Title. II. Title: On the trail of China's most wanted man.
DS712.A88 2007
951.05092—dc22 2006026930

Printed in the United States of America

Map by Jacques Chazaud

MP 10 9 8 7 6 5 4 3 2 1

FOR MILA,
who went everwhere but China

CONTENTS

If you had wanted to go to China it was too late. You would have to content yourself with reading books about it, and that was as much of the old, unrecognizable China as you would know. At this moment the scene shifters were busy and they might be a long time over their job. When the curtain went up again it would be upon something as unrecognizable to an old China hand as to Marco Polo. And when this day came you had a feeling that curious travelers might find themselves restricted to state-conducted tours, admiring the marvels of reconstruction — the phoenix in concrete.

— NORMAN LEWIS, *A Dragon Apparent (1951)*

AUTHOR'S NOTE

This book describes a journey, or rather two journeys — mine and that of the people I met along the way. On occasion I found it necessary to protect their identities. Where I've changed names I indicate my reasons for doing so in the text.

Quotes appearing in the book are taken from contemporaneous notes. In the few situations where I found it impossible to take notes openly I used the text message function on my mobile phone to write down snippets. From them I reconstructed quotes immediately after the event. Where feasible I then checked the notes with everyone present. In a few cases, assistants also took notes on conversations for me. I have generally used their translations of the Chinese to capture the tone of an encounter.

Furthermore, in a few instances I disguised my real purpose for engaging people in conversation. I did so as a last resort and only when in the public interest — these are the guidelines laid down by the UK Press Complaints Commission for justifiable misrepresentation. To me, the public interest seemed to be served by enquiries about dishonest and corrupt practices. For more information, as well as photos and video footage, please visit my website, www.oliveraugust.com.

Inside the Red Mansion

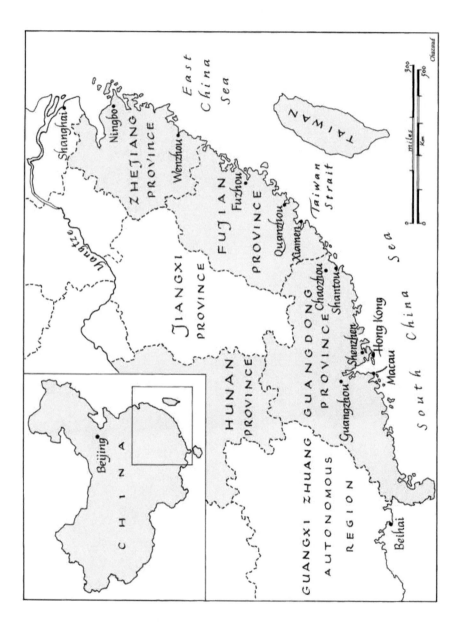

East China Sea

TAIWAN

Taiwan Strait

South China Sea

ZHEJIANG PROVINCE

FUJIAN PROVINCE

JIANGXI PROVINCE

HUNAN PROVINCE

GUANGDONG PROVINCE

GUANGXI ZHUANG AUTONOMOUS REGION

Shanghai

Ningbo

Wenzhou

Fuzhou

Quanzhou

Xiamen

Chaozhou

Shantou

Shenzhen

Hong Kong

Macau

Guangzhou

Beihai

Yangtze

CHINA

Beijing

miles

Km

300

500

Chazaud

PROLOGUE

THE SHAOSHAN, LAKESIDE DRIVE, XIAMEN CITY, FUJIAN PROVINCE

ELEVEN O'CLOCK on a Friday night, and the madam, or *mami*, at a private nightclub is waiting for the police. She straightens the nametag on her gray suit — it says "Lili" in Chinese and English — to avoid even the hint of impropriety. Dancers in sequined mermaid outfits are hidden away in a room to which only Lili has a key. She carefully counted in all seventy-six and ordered them dishes of five-spiced smoked fish and crushed cucumber with chili before locking the door from the outside. In a few minutes, blue uniforms with white rimmed caps will surround the klieg-lit stage where she has just turned off the last few bars of "Girl Across, Look My Way."

Lili started telling me the story of the raid right where it had happened. We were sitting below the same glittering stage where patrons had watched uniformed men wash in and then out again. "They will be back," she said, meaning the police, "don't worry, you'll get a chance to see for yourself." I hoped she'd be right, banishing worries I might get her in trouble.

The nightclub occupied a vast auditorium with blackened walls and distant rafters. It was large enough to accommodate a game of tennis, but guests expected nothing so predictable. They were seated on sofas of loamy upholstery like drivers of German luxury sedans. In front of them, waiters in tuxedos with elastic waistbands cowered on the carpeted floor, refilling glasses perched on low wooden tables. Beyond the tables was the vast spotlit stage that dominated the room. Flocks of sequinned mermaids waltzed past in merry circles, followed by operatic massifs of rouged Red Guards goose-stepping to "The Sound of Music." Willowy silk-clad maidens came next, kowtowing demurely then morphing defiantly into head-

1

tossing, stiletto-strutting mannequins. The club's nightly variety show was an elaborate homage to collective aspirations, equally indebted to China's past and sundry models of its future.

More remarkable still were the waiters who could occasionally be seen dashing onto the stage like kamikaze pilots. They would lunge forward, dodging dancers, swerving around formations of arms and legs swirling and flailing, accompanied by an offstage band. Near misses, last-minute course corrections, and blinding spotlights worthy of anti-aircraft batteries could not put them off, though their harried faces and sweat-stained uniforms hinted at the human cost of the endeavor. Eventually they would home in on one of the dancers and unload the cargo carried in their arms: bombastic garlands of plastic flowers, rings of green wire decorated with yellow, purple, and azure bulbs. The waiters, hardly slowing down, would throw the flowers around the dancer's neck and exit. Helpless in the face of unceasing floral strangulation, some dancers could barely continue. "Anymore and she won't be able to see," said a guest sitting behind me.

The garland ritual did not seem to be part of the regular stage program. The waiters were fiercely determined and lacked any sense of comedy or rhythm. The stage was a hostile high ground, to be stormed anew every few minutes. I wondered, could this be a promotion for a flower company? Chinese commercialism knew no bounds, I thought when Lili came back from her frequent rounds through the club, chatting at tables and settling bills. Sitting down, she tossed her black hair over her strong shoulders. Next to her bone-thin dancers she was sturdy and lump-kneed, yet her eyes moved faster than their limbs ever could.

I confided in Lili my guess that a flower company must be behind the garlands. She laughed and called over a waiter holding an order form. "Which of the dancers do you like?" she said.

"I think they're all wonderful."

"That's very polite, but which one do you like best?"

"Oh."

"Just choose one."

"But how?"

"By their numbers." She pointed out the small tags on their tasseled waists that were inscribed with three-digit numbers. "Tell me your number."

I did — by picking the one closest to us.

The waiter noted my choice and sprinted to the bar where he had the order form stamped. Triplicates were filed and registered — a bureaucratic ritual that might be the only Communist legacy here. The form was handed to another waiter who picked up a garland on his way to the stage. A well-practiced sports drill unfolded, like a relay run. The whole routine took no more than thirty seconds, from our table to the waiter hunkering down by the edge of the stage waiting for the right moment when the dancers were not gyrating or cartwheeling. Then he was off. He made eye contact with my choice, threw the flowers around her neck, and in the same motion swiveled around to point out our table in the dark auditorium before vanishing, replaced already by another waiter. The dancer nodded a midmotion thank-you in our direction.

"This is how the club makes money," Lili said. "You'll have to pay for the *hua* you just ordered for that dancer." Guests were charged $10 per reusable garland. You could send multiples, but Lili had been kind enough to put me down for only one. The dancers shared the fee with the club, she said.

"Is it a tip?"

"If you like."

"And do they make much?"

That all depended. When newly minted tycoons visited the club, the dancers could earn more in an evening than their parents did in a year. One such tycoon was Lai Changxing — the reason I had come to Lili's club. He was well known here, a regular. Everyone was familiar with his transformation from a rice farmer into one of the country's richest and most powerful men, all without joining the Communist Party. I had heard his story while traveling around China as a journalist in 1999, and it came to obsess me. My timing could have been better — Lai had just fallen out with the authorities and was a fugitive. Still, I sought out people who had known him. The first few I met by chance, mostly friends and associates of his. Soon I began to follow them across the country. They ascribed all manner of feats to him, thought him a visionary, a revolutionary even, or a crook of epic proportions, a bandit king. They could never quite agree.

On his first visit to Lili's club, she said, Lai had everyone's attention immediately. Before he ordered his first garland, the dancers knew he was no mere construction bureau official doling out *gong kuan,* public money, or a hinterland shopkeeper frittering away a meager inheritance. Lai asked

for a bottle of Hennessy XO cognac costing close to a thousand dollars —
an urban worker's annual salary — to play drinking games. He replaced
weighty decanters and polished beakers with Bourbon shot glasses, which
he filled until they overflowed, swallowing the mud brown liquor in one
and washing it down with Qingdao beer. The effect was even more electri-
fying on the wait staff, the management, or the dancers than the hangers-
on for whom he was pouring drinks. A sixth sense for money, which none
of their parents had had, trilled louder than the offstage band.

"Men like Lai always order Hennessy XO cognac," Lili said. In modern
China, the letters XO were synonymous with free-spending indulgence,
supreme wealth, and previously unattainable aspirations. Restaurants offered special XO soy sauces at stupendous extra cost; the hyperambitious
adopted X.O. as initials on their business cards; and companies incorporated XO into their name before listing on the stock market. For all this,
the French luxury group LVMH was responsible, owners of the Hennessy
brand.

When he came to the club, Lai sat on a sofa close to the stage surrounded by XO bottles, dressed in a XO suit, with his XO limousine outside
and XO aftershave in the air. There could be no mistaking his status. Lili
watched him from the back of the room. "He wasn't tall," she said, "but you
noticed him straightaway. He looked like money."

I asked Lili how much of it he spent. She whispered to a waiter that no
one should bother her for a while and settled into her sofa seat. After several rounds of cognac swilling, she said, Lai shifted his attention to the
stage, watching a dancer in a traditional dress. "He was ready for the *hua*,"
Lili said, "so I sent over a waiter." Lai ordered several garlands, then some
more, toasting the dancer with cognac watered down with Sprite. But when
he saw that she was also receiving *hua* from someone else, he became agitated, scanning the audience for his rival. Within minutes even more *hua*
arrived from the unknown suitor.

"Who was sending them?" I asked.

"It had to be another man in the audience, wouldn't you think?" said
Lili. Lai eyed the other guests but couldn't spot him. Propping himself up
in his seat like someone challenged to an arm-wrestling contest, he waved
his plump hands to attract the attention of a waiter. Lili said, "The waiters,
all of them, were already watching him like a gold coin dropped in the
street." Lai decided to sweep away his opponent by sending as many *hua*
as a waiter could carry. The elastic-waisted tuxedo disappeared under a

mountain of make-believe geraniums and roses swerving across the stage, and then so did the girl.

Lai sat back in his sofa. Ahh. He had a little belly, Lili said, you could tell. He looked around the room, surveying the vanquished. But his moment of glory did not last. Another waiter, equally obscured by *hua*, stumbled across the stage. "It was wonderful," Lili said. "It's such moments you wish for." Then the music stopped, the dance was over, and another group of performers came on. "I don't want our guests to be disappointed so I sent the young dancer over to greet her admirers. She knew exactly what to do. She thanked Lai for the *hua* and had a drink with him, but just one. Then she excused herself, saying she had another thank-you to say." Lili laughed. "Lai was very angry."

Lili's sly coquettishness gave her unrivaled authority in the club, as of course did the money she made. Lili was not the owner, not even the manager, more like a maitre d'. She inspected bills and ran the wait staff. One of the waiters came to our table now. She dismissed him with a nod. Meanwhile, a group of dancers dressed as swans passed the stage slowly in single file, adorned with flowery flotsam. Lili counted out of the corner of her eye.

"But that's not where story of Lai ends," she said. Except for when she mimicked Lai's peasant accent, her voice was clear and icy. "Later that night," she said, "Lai's favorite was back onstage, this time dressed in a full-length ball gown. Now the bidding really got out of hand." For special occasions the club had stand-up floral arrangements in various colors priced at $100 each. All of them made of plastic. Soon the front of the stage was lined man-high with fake shrubbery. You could barely see the dancers, yet everyone in the club crowded into the main auditorium to watch. Lili said, "I told the dancers and the band to repeat their routine again and again, and then I sat down next to Lai." He was enraged. His opponent had matched every offering. He must have spent thousands. Lili had a drink with Lai as his favorite flitted by on the stage, barely visible behind the floral wall. Then, suddenly, Lai got up without saying a word. He was gone for a while and no more *hua* arrived. Had he had enough? Had all this gone too far? Lili bit her lip. "Then I saw him," she said. "He stood in the corridor surrounded by security guards and other men who worked in the building." He had recruited them to his cause. He started marching toward the stage and they filed in behind him, carrying heavy pots filled with real flowers from the club entrance and foyer. Some were as tall as the room. There were small trees among them. He marched the men all the way to the stage and directed — arms waving — the assembly of his final offering. "He won his battle," Lili said.

Without interrupting her story, she had given orders to waiters, signed off on bills, and whispered instructions to passing dancers. Now she got up, but stopped and turned around. She stood still and tall, her muscular legs aligned like an Olympic diver about to plunge. "Of course, the other person who sent *hua* was not really sad to lose." She looked straight at me, her face breaking into a mock pout. "That was me. I sent the other *hua*."

I smiled. "That's not very polite."

"That's how we make money."

"Did Lai find out?"

"Yes, he found out."

"Was he angry?"

"Oh, no. I told him myself. He just laughed . . . since I had let him win."

༄

Later in the evening, I remember wondering as I unbuckled: is there a name for the attendants in the lavatories of expensive hotels who open the taps for you and hand out small, immaculately folded towels with the establishment's name monogrammed on them in italicized letters? I was standing in the gents of Lili's nightclub, when a short man approached me from behind. He was wearing a formal black waistcoat, a distinct contrast to the dancers in spandex trousers and sequinned ballgowns. I assumed he was the lavatory attendant and did not take much notice of him. With the music thumping, I did not hear him step right behind me until he placed his hands on my shoulders, his short arms raised straight up. He started to massage me, making it impossible for me to complete my *xiao bian,* or small convenience.

I fled into a cubicle, passing the attendant, who gave a little shrug. Now he pushed the cubicle door open. "Would you like a massage?" he asked. I slammed the door shut. When I emerged a minute later he seemed neither embarrassed nor offended. "It is a service we offer," he said. Diversion was the club's business and he made sure customers would not be bored for one moment. Beside him lay a small box for tips. Shamed by my hostility, I made a generous donation and Mr. Zhou, as he introduced himself, became talkative. He was a wrinkled, limping fifty. His hands and forehead were veined like a river delta. He had belatedly left his job in a state-owned factory to join the private sector. The hours and the social benefits were not as good in the club, he said, but the pay was infinitely better. In China today, one had to build one's own career. The iron rice bowl was broken and the cadres only looked after their own welfare. You had to help yourself. Street sellers were openly competing with the Friendship Store on the front steps of the old flagship chain, government chauffeurs used their official limousines to moonlight as taxi drivers, and Mr. Zhou gave people one-minute massages while they were busy with a small convenience, for which he usually received the Chinese equivalent of a dollar. The club didn't pay him anything. But the lavatory was a great business opportunity, he said, handing me a towel and asking for my business card. Perhaps there was more he could do for me. "You work for a company?" he said.

"Yes. A media company."

"And you have an office in China?"

"In Beijing."

"That's good. How many people in your office?"

"Two."

"You need a driver?"

"No."

"A cleaner?"

"We have one."

"A bathroom attendant?"

As I walked back into the club auditorium, I remember thinking, "now I know why I am still here." I had come to the club to learn about Lai, but it was late and I'd stayed beyond what prudent research demanded. What detained me were glimpses like this one, glimpses increasingly familiar, though rarely as unfiltered. I was still here because of people like Mr. Zhou, people who were reinventing themselves from the rubble left behind by Chairman Mao, driven by fantasies acted out on stages large and small, tempered only by occasional limits imposed from above.

Shortly after Mao's death in 1976, steps had been taken by his successors to liberalize the economy. Private business was brought back, social strictures eased. Chinese could once again travel and pick their own profession. In the two decades that followed, the country became driven by money and the desires it brought. Despite a continued shadow of repression, people like Mr. Zhou and Boss Lai and Lili reveled in the pursuit of wealth. One-time workers and peasants gloried in excess, thrived on rule-breaking, and turned established morality on its head. They planted skyscrapers by the bushel and overran entire global industries, chipping away at remaining strictures until and unless the government intervened. In this welter of change, their identities were at last their own. They could, or so it seemed, be anything.

~

Around two, Lili invited me for a late dinner at an outdoor food stall in the warm night air coming off the ocean. Container ships moved in a deep-water channel beyond the dead-end street that marked land's end by day. Illuminated with dim lights stacked on top, the clench-jawed hulls slid through the dark like apartment buildings venturing out for a wander while their inhabitants were asleep.

Dinner after closing the club was a ritual, the spicier the better, Lili said, and usually with a guest paying the bill. She scanned the menu for a worthy encore to the evening. Fire-exploded kidney flowers. Man-and-wife meat slices. Eight treasures wok pudding. Pockmarked Mother Chen's bean curd. Eating in China was entertainment as much as nourishment, maybe the best on offer.

Lili grinned when our oily red food arrived, packed tight on small plates like passengers in a "hard seat" train carriage. How many of the chilies mixed in with the dry fried chicken could I eat? The answer turned out to be one. And how about the dark, chewy strips of hot-and-numbing beef? Two chopstick-loads, maybe three if I hadn't already had the chilies. Lili ate the rest of both. Other diners crowded around to watch us, pushing closer. Most were white-helmeted men in soiled overalls, migrant workers on a break from an all-night construction site. The smell of fresh cement mixed with the fumes of distilled rice wine. They were listening to our conversation as if it was being televised. And how many *kuaizi* — wooden chopsticks — could I eat? Lili was asking me but she was looking at the crowd. The men burst into embarrassed giggles and returned to their tables. It was them she had challenged, gently, not me.

Lili's touch was so light, her control seemingly effortless. The authorities regarded her occupation as barely legal, raiding the club's premises at will. But she rode the free flow of money and people that coursed through Xiamen with the ease of a practiced casino dealer. At least for now.

"I once worked in a place like this, when I first arrived in Xiamen more than ten years ago," she said. At the time, tipping was unknown. Waiters would run after the occasional foreign customer who left a small gratuity on a table strewn with chicken bones and fish heads. Paying anything other than the exact amount stated on the bill was inconceivable. It never occurred to the waiters to pocket the change. "Except for me," Lili said. Salaries were fixed by the government, as were the prices on the menu. A decade later, she always checked restaurant bills. Waiters had learned to look out for themselves even if tipping was still rare. Those who did tip though were remembered for it. Lai, the flower-giving entrepreneur, had become famous among local taxi drivers for handing over hundred-yuan notes for six or seven yuan rides and refusing the change. At the Holiday Inn, waiters still talked about the time when Lai walked in with his entourage, straightaway signed a blank credit card slip, and asked not to be bothered with the total at the end of the evening.

Lili's pinched smile said she thought him a fool. But she liked to tell stories. This was her world. She knew every last *wulai* (ne'er-do-well), *xiao wang* (little dazzler), and *pizi* (ruffian).

After paying for both of us, I asked Lili what happened during the raid at the club she had talked about earlier. How did the guests react? Had there been guns? What were the police looking for? Events like the club raid seemed to hint at a central mystery in China — how could the government loosen controls and yet stay in control? Anarchic freedom and stately might seemed to coexist.

"The police were looking for our dancers," Lili said. "We're not supposed to have them. Apparently we commit *jingshen wuran* (spiritual pollution) with our shows. That's why I lock the dancers away, along with some food. It can take a while."

During the most recent raid, she said, all but the room with the dancers had been searched when an officer asked Lili what was in it. "Must you know all our secrets?" she said. He indulged her. She knew her cue. "To be honest," she said, "I know nothing about the room. The general manager would be in a much better position to answer your question. Let me take you upstairs."

The general manager, a shaven-headed man with a handshake cold as a hook, was waiting in his office. Teacups were assembled on his desk and a kettle was on permanent boil by the windowsill, leaving steam marks on the large windowpane overlooking the auditorium. They drank tea together and the general manager thanked the officer for making sure the club was in order. A man of such fine standing, he insisted, ought to be better remunerated. It was a shame the government could not afford to be more generous. A *hong bao,* a red envelope stuffed with what was essentially a tax payment directly from source to end recipient, found its way into a uniformed pocket. Then came the departure of the police, as quick as they had arrived though with considerably less fanfare, followed by the return of the seventy-six dancers in sequined mermaid outfits. "It goes like that every few months," Lili said, "especially before national holidays when the government likes to show off. But mostly we're left alone."

The government had parted from past fervor as if aging and mellowing like a person. Of course, its officers could still call on an illustrious heritage of class warfare, draping themselves in the mantle of moral guardianship. But unless fighting insurrection, their real interest could usually be expressed in an unspoken figure, the more zeros the better. Lili understood that. She offered compensation for the officers' magnificently diligent efforts to sustain the greatness of China's ancient civilization. Unstinting reserves of entrepreneurial ambition could tame the state machinery, a hopeful portent in a society nominally still Communist. Those who failed to finesse the authorities might even now end up in a labor camp. But having learned to steer around officialdom, Lili did not expect to be among them.

1

WRITERS

Beijing Bureau, the *Times of London*, Shenku Courtyard,
Ritan Park

MY INVOLVEMENT with China began quite by chance with a telephone
call in June 1998. At the time, I was a twenty-six-year-old reporter for a
British newspaper in New York. I had never been to Asia, and probably
never even thought about it. "We'll be looking for a new correspondent in
Beijing," the editor in chief of the *Times* told me on the phone across the
Atlantic. "When you next come by the office on a break, maybe over Christmas, let's have a chat about it." From my cubicle in Rockefeller Center,
where daylight was rationed even in summer, the chance of escaping to the
Middle Kingdom seemed a godsend. A few minutes after the editor in chief
rang off I picked up the handset again and dialed the number of a travel
agent across Sixth Avenue. Yes, there were still seats on the evening flight to
London. I booked a ticket and turned up the next morning in the teeming
office of the *Times,* unsure of my reception. "You said on my next visit I
should talk to you about the Beijing job." Well, there I was. I had joined
the paper less than three years before as a trainee and was undoubtedly
the least qualified of the candidates for the position. The editor in chief
laughed when he saw me standing in his office door. A brief interview concluded, and with no mention of the other candidates, he sent me off to
Beijing.

I had no idea what was involved in covering an authoritarian country, and the editor in chief had offered little advice. So, on my first morning
I did what journalists always do. With the help of Sophie, the twenty-five-
year-old daughter of Chinese diplomats, I read the local newspapers. Cornfields of newsprint opened up before us with not a cartoon in sight. The

stories, which Sophie translated for me, painted a picture even I could tell was grotesque. Happy one-child families lived in newly built modern high-rises, using ever more television sets and mobile phones while boosting the economy by buying their first private vehicles thanks to the government's glorious reform policies. Variations on this appeared daily. Half the stories were probably true, but the treacly prose was unbearable. Sophie and I decided to put the papers to better use. We cut out the obligatory front-page photographs of members of the politburo and stuck them on a dart board I had brought with me to China. From then on, we started the workday with a game of darts in the company of a changing cast of local dignitaries. Sometimes they were waddling along a fierce honor guard of bayonet-wielding soldiers; other times they gave speeches, looking alarmed and pointing rosy fingers directly at incoming darts. I memorized their names faster than expected.

My main job in the first few months in Beijing was to learn Chinese. At first it seemed a hopeless undertaking. I was studying Mandarin, the dialect of the Beijing region, yet there were dozens of other Chinese tongues, like Cantonese. Would I ever be able to speak to anyone but my neighbors? I need not have worried. Soon I met a man from the Mekong River near the Golden Triangle. His native dialect was closer to Thai than anything Chinese. But he, too, was learning Mandarin, along with his entire family, prodded by a central government keen to extend its reach to far-flung provinces. I told him I was impressed by his efforts. "Oh, it's normal. I know you foreigners all speak it," he said. "I've seen it on television." He had never heard of dubbing, and I did not yet have the vocabulary to explain the concept.

Initially when I met Chinese I tried to introduce myself using my Mandarin name. My teacher, the writer David Su, had chosen one for me. "What does 'Oliver' mean?" he had asked during our first lesson, when I was still unaware of his peculiar sense of humor. I said that since a man who worked on a farm was a farmer, a man who harvested olives was an "oliver." This made eminent sense in Chinese, the language of the world's biggest farming population, said Teacher Su, as I addressed him (professional titles like Teacher, Driver, and Lawyer having replaced the once ubiquitous "Comrade"). He went on to cull the first character from the word for olive and the first character from the word for farmer and put them together. Gan Nong, he declared proudly.

I have been the laughingstock of acquaintances ever since. Nobody in their right mind in China today called themselves a farmer. Millions were fleeing the land to become city dwellers, to partake in the industrial revolution, to become rich. When I introduced myself, people guffawed to each other, "a foreign farmer has come to our China." Friends of Sophie, the office assistant, would ask on the phone, "how is your farmer?"

There were more setbacks and soon they threatened to overwhelm my enthusiasm for learning Chinese. Teacher Su had a fondness for obscure phrases and aphorisms. *Tuo you ping,* I would repeat after him, or carrying a bottle of oil. I was learning to describe the circumstances of a widowed woman who brings children into a new marriage. We moved on to *zhua xiao bian zi,* or seizing the short pigtail, meaning to pick on someone's weaknesses or mistakes, something I would most likely be expressing in the passive form. Most of the sayings I learned were derived from ancient parables and made references to animals or an emperor. They were rooted deeply in the past, bringing unexpected color and earthiness into the present. *Sha ji yan yong niu dao?* Why use a butcher's knife to kill a chicken?

I was fascinated, but nonetheless decided to find a new teacher. Once again I ended up with a writer. Xu Xing wore leather jackets and long hair that came down to his turtleneck sweaters. His eyes were round and bright like polished apples, searching and yet trusting. The inside seams of his trousers were stained from riding a Flying Pigeon bicycle long after his friends had switched to taking taxis.

Xu Xing had the infidel air of the formerly exiled. Following the 1989 democracy protest in Tiananmen Square he fled the country and took up residence in France, where he published novels about rootless men roaming the land on metaphysical journeys of discovery and evasion. His works sold well in French translation, but he decided to return to Beijing after fathering a child in Paris, preferring the bonds of authoritarian government to the strictures of parenthood.

He started teaching in the hope of meeting western women, an orientation reflected in our lessons. Most of our early tutorials revolved around *guniang,* girls, and the first thing I learned from him was *bai bai,* a Sinified bye-bye used when breaking romantic engagements.

Xu Xing's pedagogy was on a par with Teacher Su's name-giving. We used no textbook for he believed all one needed to learn Chinese was self-confidence and a bit of practice. In a typical lesson, he would lean back on the sofa in my office and command me to pick up the phone. "Dial this," he'd say, and dictate a string of numbers.

"Who am I calling?" I asked the first time.

"A friend of mine."

"Does he speak English?"

"Of course not."

"And he has no idea who I am . . ."

"No."

"So why am I calling him?"

"Just explain who you are and that this is a teaching exercise." Seeing the panicked look on my face, he added, "please, talk about anything." He was grinning. "I will watch how long you can keep going."

Another day, Xu Xing walked into the office and said, "What's the most difficult subject we could talk about in Chinese?" I looked up from my desk, buried in newspapers, and gave him an answer I would regret for the next hour. "Wittgenstein. The philosophy of Wittgenstein."

"Good. I might find that useful one day. You will explain Wittgenstein to me."

In later lessons, Xu Xing attempted to teach me snippets of China's highly stylized official language. The Communist Party often referred to itself as the "great, glorious, correct Communist Party." Yet, according to Xu Xing, a mere switching of adjectives could undermine any sense of greatness, glory, or correctness.

China's official language consisted of hundreds of sculpted phrases and slogans. They were not mere leftovers from the Mao days. New slogans were still coined every month, and repeated endlessly at official functions. They were important tools of control. They allowed the party to nudge public opinion in this direction or that. Their genius lay in their vacuity. "Seek truth from facts." Who could object? The slogan committed the party to nothing, yet most Chinese understood its coded meaning. To "seek truth from facts" was the opposite of Maoist mania. It was a reassuring message, an allusion to fairness, while allowing the party to choose exactly which facts to seek truth from.

Once in circulation, however, slogans could take on a life of their own. "Seek truth from facts" was a subtle but effective weapon to anyone who picked it up. "Seek truth from facts" — so dissidents challenged government officials claiming China had an enviable human rights record.

Official language was a perfect target for subversion and corruption. Xu Xing recalled singing the Chinese national anthem, written in the days of Communist revolution four decades earlier, with students on Tiananmen Square during the tumultuous spring of 1989. No official could object . . .

> Rise up, you who would not be slaves,
> Let us build our flesh and blood into a new great wall.
> The Chinese people have reached their most dangerous hour.
> The very last scream has been forced from each of us.
> Rise up, rise up, rise up.

Xu Xing eventually became a friend. More even than linguistic subtleties, he introduced me to the little shortcuts of life in Beijing. Over two decades, and all through his stay in France, he had kept the same basement apartment in a prime Beijing location. Books lined the walls and varying girlfriends half his age ate bowls of homemade *suanla* soup while listening to his favorite Mozart. Although property prices were climbing across the city, Xu Xing could not recall ever having paid rent. The apartment was given to him in the 1970s when he was a soldier in the People's Liberation Army, and so far nobody had asked him to give it back. "Maybe I am not supposed to be here anymore," he said. "But sometimes you just have to take what you need, even if it belongs to someone else."

As Xu Xing saw it, China was stuck in a state of armchair tyranny. The two dozen elderly members of the politburo, staring down from my dart board, were all-powerful. Yet they maintained a watchful distance and let you abuse their picture. They relied on slogans ("It is good to have just one child") and occasional crackdowns to maintain a sense of order. The rest of the time they appeared to be hidden, looking on as two decades of economic reforms took hold.

How to report on a country like that? Framed on the walls of my office hung yellowing copies of the front-page dispatches sent by my predecessors at the *Times*. Mao meeting Nixon in 1972. The Chairman's death in 1976. Tanks ordered onto Tiananmen Square in 1989. Nothing similarly iconic was happening now. China was changing but it refused to do so in neat or pronounced steps. There was no overall plan, much as my editors would have liked to see one. "Are there any events or diary dates next week," they asked in one email, "which could be used to create a news story?" Frequently I disappointed them. Press briefings seemed uneventful to me, public debates meaningless, protests soon died down, and political figures were uniformly dull. In any case, access was limited and interlocutors were far from frank. Journalists were treated like historians, expected to rely on written reports and the published views of known experts, rather than speak to participants in the events we reported on.

To their credit, most of my colleagues did not go along with this. They went back to their original training, in some cases rediscovering a craft they had learned decades earlier. Leaving behind comfortable offices in Beijing, they became eyewitnesses again, like cub reporters on the police beat. The result was a good deal of original reporting from little-known places like Qinghai and Yunnan and Jilin, much of it vivid and insightful. There was only one problem. The reporting seemed to be describing different countries. In some stories, labor camps were overflowing, in others citizens enjoyed previously unheard-of choices, in yet others the system of erratic autocracy was about to collapse, while in others yet it was soon to trump the west.

Modern China was a magic mirror. You could see whatever you wanted to see, and whatever you said would never be entirely wrong. There really were bloated labor camps, even as people outside the gates won new liberties, and of course none of this could guarantee the stability of the wobbly-kneed gerontocracy — as it nimbly raced ahead of economic competitors in the west.

Being a newcomer, I carefully read my colleagues' stories during my first few months in China, hoping to glean what I should be reporting on. The result was a case of newsprint-smeared whiplash, one that *Times* readers must have felt. My stories tried to take in all sides of everything. Only slowly did I learn to follow not my colleagues' writing but their example and ignore the work of others. The only way to report modern China was to get out and rely on what you saw yourself, even if it contradicted what you'd seen or read yesterday.

I began to travel, often for weeks at a time. I crossed grasslands, hiked remote gorges, slept on overnight trains, and rented cars with monks as drivers. And yet, even then I felt I was falling short. I was witnessing something extraordinary, but to describe it in newspaper terms was to both exaggerate and belittle it. "New China" revealed itself in sideways glances and overheard conversations, not increases in mobile phone ownership. Editors' requests for factual indicators of how the country was changing were justified, to be sure. This was a unique moment in history. A new, or rather a very old, superpower was rising. But even the best newspaper fare seemed to miss much of what was happening around me. The "New China" known to readers had even more clichés than people. What was most remarkable got lost. The country I lived in was both free and oppressed, at once anarchic and authoritarian, totally chaotic yet highly regulated. It was changing completely while staying very much its ancient self.

If any one story could embody these contradictions, I came to feel, then it was the story of Lai Changxing. I started out knowing little more than rumor, but over the years his story filled out, and I came to think of him as emblematic. His bent business practices were both the trigger for brutish crackdowns and for some of the most momentous changes in China. Arguably, no individual did more than Lai to bring the country into the World Trade Organization. Men like him are transforming the system from below. Their actions give the country a new direction. By testing the limits, and breaking them, the outlaw entrepreneurs are converting China to no-holds-barred capitalism.

Born one of eight siblings in Fujian province at the time of the disastrous Great Leap Forward (1958), Lai knew near starvation and received almost no formal education. During the Cultural Revolution (1966–76), he tended fields and dug ditches. When he turned twenty and the government moved toward economic liberalization, he started a business making simple car parts. The business took off and soon turned into an empire. Within a decade, Lai was the country's biggest private car importer and one of the main distributors of foreign cigarettes as well as an oil trader responsible for one sixth of national imports. Every door seemed open to him. He moved to Xiamen, a nearby port city pronounced *scia-men,* and started building hundreds of high-rise apartments. For himself he erected a replica of the Forbidden City, the imperial residence in Beijing. He copied the design of the red walls, the moat, the vast courtyards. He was modest enough — and wise enough — to keep the picture of Chairman Mao that adorned the original. Still, he styled himself a dirt emperor, or *tu huangdi,* entertaining lavishly. His favorite guests were officials of the Communist Party, especially those who could aid his business. Central Committee members arrived from Beijing, including the party's soon-to-be-anointed number four, the deputy police minister and the head of military intelligence. They had appetites Lai never knew as a child. Fish flown in from Tokyo. Modern-day concubines in private chambers. Red envelopes stuffed with cash. Lai provided it all.

Then, one day, his good fortune ran out. On August 11, 1999, less than three months after I arrived in China, the government staged one of its occasional crackdowns. Warrants were issued and homes raided. Lai was accused of an enormous fraud. He had apparently smuggled goods worth $6.4 billion into the country, evading $3.6 billion in taxes, aided by a legion of associates and corrupt officials. Some of them were regular recipients of Lai's largesse. Others he met only once. He would, so it was said, visit their offices, holding a briefcase filled with cash. After explaining what he needed, he would depart, leaving behind his briefcase as if he had forgotten it.

Beijing's response was harsh. Detention and torture for hundreds of Lai's associates, and eventually fourteen death sentences in show trials — the government had not forgotten its old repertoire. Lai himself managed to get away though. He slipped out of Xiamen and went into hiding.

Traveling around the country, I would hear Lai being mentioned. People became agitated when discussing his feats or the government's response. The more I heard, the more I became curious. How had he been able to slip away? And how could he have risen so far in the first place? How could the son of a penniless farmer have transformed himself so thoroughly?

I looked at old photographs of Lai. I saw his features evolve from childhood — his short frame filling out, limbs turning into sausage tubes, a parade of changing hairstyles. Yet in all the pictures the expression on his face was the same. Trusting, awkward, toothy. Aged forty and very wealthy, he seemed the same as he was at twenty, a country boy. His transformation, however, was real, if perhaps incomplete. Lai's business ventures betrayed an ambition different from anything attempted by his ancestors, who lay buried on a muddy hillside behind the family village, having lived and died right where they were born.

Not surprisingly, the authorities regarded Lai's flight as sensitive. Senior Communist leaders were involved. To protect them, and out of reflexive stealth, the case was hushed up. Enquiries were met with silence. Domestic news media was censored, foreign media warned against delving in too deep.

The effect on me was electric. My interest grew. I wanted to know more. In any case, defying limits imposed by the authorities — even if in a minor way, or perhaps only then — held its own attraction.

I had got my first taste of this when I went to see the Great Hall of the People in Beijing, the cavernous palace overlooking the Mao mausoleum. Foreign journalists were invited to go there once a year for the opening session of the National People's Congress, China's quasi parliament. Having been warned of bad traffic, I decided against going by taxi and put on my in-line skates, skating all the way down the Avenue of Eternal Peace, across Tiananmen Square, and past the mausoleum and the official slogans ("Only socialism can help China"). A policeman tried to stop me. But I was late. I couldn't stop. I headed toward the entrance of the Great Hall. Suddenly a mob of Chinese press photographers surged forward. A foreigner on wheels appeared to be more interesting than the arriving delegates. To escape the snapping lenses I headed straight to the Great Hall entrance and through it without taking off my skates. The security guards looked stunned but didn't object. I was inside. I was free to skate around miles and miles of smooth marble floors and an auditorium that seated five thousand. I talked with a Chinese colleague and listened to a speech by the prime minister. Then I went back home on my skates.

The next day's Chinese papers carried pictures of me taken by the photographers outside the Great Hall, along with stories interpreting my skating as an impertinent protest. A government-run news agency quoted an outraged security officer as saying, "This is too unserious."

I liked the way my skating was being read. I was thrilled. The authorities gave me more credit than I deserved.

Yet when it came to Lai, the authorities were harder to defy. Nominally, coastal cities like Xiamen, where Lai was based, were among the freest places in China. Residents could make fun of Communist leaders, as long as it was in private. Business associations were tolerated if they were apolitical. Watching foreign television channels and receiving foreign visitors drew little attention. People even discussed politics — and yet, discussing Lai was cumbersome. Domestic newspapers took half a year to even mention his name following his disappearance. When they finally did, it was in identical notices that answered few questions. Follow-up reports were heavily censored. Private websites could be more informative, but their sourcing was dubious.

The official silence was compounded by Lai's relative obscurity. He may have been the most powerful man in Xiamen, but residents knew surprisingly little about him. Of course they knew his name. It was synonymous with wealth and influence. But the source of his wealth and his influence were obscured. Like most successful Chinese entrepreneurs, Lai had avoided publicity. He never named a building after himself, a prudent choice. Private wealth was still politically sensitive. To flaunt capitalist success was to challenge the government's continued nominal support for "Marxism-Leninism-Mao Zedong Thought." Like most rich Chinese, Lai never drove around in sports cars. They were deemed too flashy, a sign of nonconformity — not a good image. Lai preferred a black Mercedes with tinted windows.

What ordinary people knew about Lai was mostly myth. In the absence of facts they spun dreams into stories attributed to him, some of which appeared on the Internet. According to one, Lai often stopped his black Mercedes at the Xiamen train station — among the *lanke* (hotel touts), *piao fanzi* (ticket scalpers), and *piao tuo* (bus company pushers) — to hand out one-hundred-yuan notes to newly arrived migrants. He was passing money swindled from the government onto the deserving poor. He was styled a Robin Hood.

To hear about the real Lai, one needed to talk to people close to his case. Only his associates and those in contact with the authorities knew details. Yet they rarely agreed to interviews. Government crackdowns were delicate. Only personal trust could overcome reluctance, and that took time. The pace of my search thus stood in marked contrast to the hectic tempo of the region. I ended up traveling along the southern coast for seven years, far longer than any editor could wait. On occasion, my search yielded newspaper stories, mostly about people I met along the way. But Lai himself only came into focus bit by bit. The crabwalk nature of my journey is reflected in what follows, an account of a world — Lai's world — that slipped its moorings with no firm bearings and all too many destinations.

2

PETITS BOURGEOIS

Dining Room No. 6, Hao Qing Xiang Restaurant,
Lakeside Drive, Xiamen

THE FIRST TIME I heard of Lai was from a man called Fangmin. He was sitting behind the wheel of a parked sedan. I told him I was looking for a driver to hire and he invited me to get in the back seat where the windows were so dark I could barely see out.

Fangmin was forty, with a puckered face and a cigarette in his mouth. When he smiled his nose turned into a shriveled berry. He was jangling a key in the ignition and complained, unprompted, that addiction to nicotine was the fault of government officials. They demanded small gratuities like cigarettes whenever you wanted to talk to them. You always had to carry smokes around with you, he said, lighting one more for himself. "The biggest problem in China are the corrupt officials and the *hei* (black) bosses behind them. They should all be punished."

We were on familiar territory. Nobody liked corruption.

"Have you seen this happen?" I said. "*Hei* bosses paying corrupt officials?"

"Yes, many times. I have seen them drinking together. They talk and enjoy themselves, watching show girls dance onstage."

"That doesn't sound very *hei* to me."

"It's very *hei*, I'm telling you. People like that don't just drink together because they are friends. They do business."

"In a nightclub?"

Well, usually they went to the car park to hand over money, he said. Once, there was a boss who put half a million yuan in the trunk of his car parked outside a club in Xiamen. The boss went in to meet an official whom he wanted to give the money to. But the lock on the trunk didn't close properly. A problem with the remote control. One of the security guards in the parking lot saw it and once the boss was inside he took the half million and disappeared.

"And then?" I said.

Fangmin smiled and slowly turned the key in the ignition to power up the spring-loaded cigarette lighter on the dashboard. "Everyone expected the boss to get very angry," he said. "Maybe he would beat up someone. But he didn't. When he heard what had happened, he said the guard had got lucky. He told the official he would get his money next time and forgot about the whole thing. At least that's the story."

And what, I asked Fangmin, do you get from a *hei* official for a sum like that? I did a quick calculation. Half a million yuan was the equivalent of an annual salary for a western office worker.

The lighter popped up and Fangmin lit another cigarette, filling the car with smoke. The outside world shrunk to cardboard box dimensions. "You get very useful help whenever you need it," Fangmin said. "This same boss I mentioned, he asked officials for help all the time. Once he wanted to leave a nightclub with a beautiful woman. But she belonged to another group of men. The boss insisted she come with him and the other men started to attack him. So the boss called friends in the police. When the police arrived they didn't just stop the fight but they beat up the boss's enemies. They went to the hospital. He left with their woman. She really was very beautiful."

Fangmin sounded envious, as if he might consider trading in his high moral tone of earlier for a slice of the good life. (I did not yet know him as a man of different wants. The pots of flesh he desired were made of clay and came filled with carrots, onions, and seafood.)

With smoke wafting across the back seat, I climbed out of the car. Fangmin offered me a pack of cigarettes as a gift. I declined.

All this took place soon after my arrival in China. I had flown two hours from Beijing to Fujian province, together with Sophie, the office assistant. Fujian was on the southern coast, closer to Hong Kong than Shanghai. We traveled overland to the provincial city of Xiamen, which faced the renegade island of Taiwan. If China were ever to invade Taiwan, as it had threatened, Xiamen would be the main staging post. My editors had sent me here to ask residents about recent military exercises. But the residents had little to say on the subject. They did not talk about war — for three days they talked about construction materials. They were preoccupied with converting their factory wages into new homes. I learned how to say "wall-paper adhesive" (hu bi *zhi* jiao) before mastering the past tense. One man told me he was the first person in his family to use a spirit level. "My father and grandfather built houses, but they only ever had strings with weights to keep things straight."

✍

The day after talking to Fangmin in the back of his car, Sophie and I were scheduled to return to Beijing. We walked into a hotel to hire a car for the ride to the airport. We pushed past half a dozen workmen changing light bulbs in the glum but busy lobby. Maybe the hotel staff could call a car. Yet before we had reached the reception desk, a man stepped in front of us. The blue of his jacket matched his creased trousers. The braided epaulettes and the peaked cap extinguished all doubt as to who he was. Politely he asked whether we would mind answering a few questions. He stood erect with the manicured confidence of a general manager. Next to him, a gangly plainclothes colleague gave me a "and-*you*-thought-we-wouldn't-catch-you" look.

They wanted to see my passport, which I handed to them. If there was to be an encounter with the authorities it might as well be over quickly. While they leafed through pages of smeared entry stamps and expired visas, I cursed myself for deciding against the long-distance busses we had seen outside — they were slower than a cab but not as slow as this.

Epaulette man held up my passport and said, "Are you a foreign journalist?" Then he pointed at my Chinese visa, which prominently bore the letter J for journalist. I said nothing. Like men in uniform everywhere, he took my silence to be an admission of guilt. With what sounded like mechanical creaking, he and his colleague moved on to the next stage of their procedure. Why are you here? When did you come? Whom have you met? How many interviews have you conducted? You must tell us who you have talked to. It is the law in China, or are you not familiar with Chinese laws? They wanted to know the names of all the people I had met. When I refused, they started asking more specific questions. Had I met a man with such-and-such a name? He was the boss of a certain big organization. They gave me details. Had I heard of him? Had I met any of his associates? I answered no to all the questions. To half of them I didn't even know the answer. I would have had to check my notebook, but that I kept firmly tucked in my pocket.

It was Lai the officers were asking me about. It was his name they kept repeating, and his associates I was suspected of having met. The officers were part of the largest task force ever assembled in modern China, roaming the coast between Hong Kong and Shanghai on the lookout for him. We had become caught up in their manhunt. None of this was apparent to us at the time. Nor did we understand the interest in Lai.

Eventually the officers withdrew to a corner of the lobby to confer. We knew we had a problem. Foreign journalists needed official permission to travel outside their place of residence. You had to ask a few days or weeks in advance and sometimes they agreed to let you go. If they did, a government minder accompanied you most of the time — and charged up to a hundred dollars a day for the privilege. In Beijing, a certain amount of surveillance was inevitable — my mail often arrived delayed and unsealed — but it rarely hindered my work. To travel with a minder, however, was a different matter. Which Chinese would talk when the government was listening in? I had therefore traveled to Fujian as a tourist who happened to be taking notes. Most of my colleagues did the same when they left Beijing.

Ten minutes later we were still in the lobby, waiting for the officers to return. We could see them huddle around a ring binder, maybe a manual for interrogating foreigners, subsection journalists. Next to the officers we could see five clocks, each with its own label. Beijing. Tokyo. Moscow. London. New York. They were all set to the same time. I took this to be a touching belief among the hotel staff that the world outside the People's Republic was really not so different. Beyond the clocks we could make out an engraved sign giving room prices for singles, doubles, twins, and suites, as well as an hourly rate for an unspecified room. I really did not want to spend the night here. Our flight was leaving in two hours.

Sophie, who had worked for the *Times* for three years, was unruffled. She said not to worry when the officers came back across the lobby. There were four of them now. "Do you have official permission to travel to Fujian province as a foreign journalist?" they asked. I knew the question was coming. But the insolence of it, the sheer obnoxiousness of having a separate set of rules that only applied to journalists, not to all foreigners or all people, was infuriating. I tried to calm myself. All you want to do is get out and go home. Don't tell them anything you shouldn't. But I did. "I don't need permission," I said. I offered no reason to back up this contention. After a pause for breath, I simply stated it again and added what I hoped would be a little insult. I didn't care that it might delay us further. "I don't need permission, comrades." They tittered. No foreigner had called them comrade for a long time.

They walked back across the lobby for more conferring. I watched them assemble tools of bureaucratic torture. The clipboard. The two-way radio. The form in triplicate. The stamp with matching ink pad. The officer who had first approached us was supervising the procedure. He was a master of the economic yet authoritative gesture, calling someone over with his raised index finger while holding a pen in the same hand. Handing documents to an underling behind him without looking up. Petting the black rubber truncheon on his belt during casual conversation. He made it seem like the matter of my unauthorized presence was as complicated yet unambiguous as the Taiwan question.

We watched a hotel waiter bring him a cup of tea on a tray. He took it and walked over to us. "Please drink some tea," he said and gave me the cup. "It is for you."

"I guess I can go now," I said.

"Sorry, but no." He took off his peaked cap with a sigh. "If you don't have permission you cannot stay in Fujian. It is impossible." I thought about telling him I didn't want to stay in his province anyway, not one minute longer than I had to. But something held me back. I listened to him say, "We will have to transport you to the airport and put you on the next flight to Beijing." Then he explained the details of the procedure. For a few minutes I protested vigorously against this unfair deportation — just in case he might change his mind. The officer insisted and insisted. Finally he commanded one of his men to take us to the airport and left.

Sophie said the situation was as awkward for him as it was for me. The rule book clearly stated there shall be no unauthorized travel by journalists, but it did not specify what to do with someone like me who was inexperienced enough to let himself get caught traveling without a permit.

On the way to the airport, Sophie befriended the police driver. Soon, his investigative zeal gave way to curiosity. He wanted to know how much Mercedes limousines cost in the west. A lot. And how fast did they go? Very fast. Then Sophie told him the departure time of our flight. The driver switched on the siren and sped up, passing other cars in the emergency lane. We were all grinning. Neither side knew what the other was really up to, but everyone got what they wanted. We were going home and they were rid of us. At the airport, the driver walked us to the gate and when we boarded the plane he waved like a relative from behind a barrier.

⌇

"Better not to return" was the last thing the officer had said. But of course I did. I was drawn back as if by a rubber band. I kept wondering why I had been questioned. What was going on here? More than anything I was intrigued by how seemingly different this patch of China was from the rest. I thought I had glimpsed a more open future of the country, regardless of my police questioning. The nightclub culture, the frenzied construction work, the stories of the legendary entrepreneur — they hinted at a whole community on the march, testing the limits.

Back in Beijing, I tried to learn more about Xiamen. It was perched on a rocky island of the same name, ten miles wide and beached in shallow water just off the coast. According to the guidebooks, the island was connected to the mainland by a causeway and two bridges. Out to sea there were smaller islands, some though not all under Chinese control. On a map, they seemed to be reaching out to the world, their shorelines jutting into the Pacific Ocean, pointing toward a gap between Japan and the Philippines. Behind them on the mainland stood a tall semicircle of mountains, cutting them off from the rest of China, thrusting them out to sea, to new destinations, new ideas.

On Xiamen Island, an uninhabited peak was covered with tropical vegetation. The rest was filled with factories, including ones belonging to Kodak and Dell, who had their China headquarters here. Xiamen offered them ideal conditions. It had two million inhabitants, a tenfold increase since Mao's death. About half were registered with the government. The other half were hungry and unregulated migrants, *mingong* from the hinterland — short on roots and high on aspirations.

One of these ambitious migrants was Fangmin, the driver who first told me about Lai. I remembered how shamelessly he had combined a claim to moral rectitude with an instinct for personal pleasure. He was a secular man's tippling priest. He became as much a reason for my return to

Xiamen as Lai himself. Over time he grew to be a friend as well as something of a counterpoint to Lai. I would watch him fail where Lai had succeeded.

The first time I went back — a few weeks after my first trip — I looked for Fangmin straightaway. Finding him in the maze of factories proved easier than expected. He had given me his mobile phone number and when I called he suggested we meet immediately. I declined to be picked up and asked him to come to the lobby of my hotel. Over cups of tea brewed in a pot filled with sliced tropical fruit, Fangmin told me he was looking for a new business idea. He had stopped driving taxis and wanted to start out on his own. Every day and all around him new shops were opening. Outfitters, chophouses, fry kitchens, department stores. Money was as plentiful as dust. He couldn't let others take it all. The only problem was picking the right idea. He needed to think of something different. Perhaps I could give him advice. He looked up hopefully.

What type of business was he thinking of, I asked. He wasn't sure. I said there might be opportunities in manufacturing. Chinese exporters made a life cycle worth of goods from baby toys to coffins. But my suggestion did not elicit much enthusiasm. To actually make something rather than just flog it seemed to intimidate him.

After an awkward pause, I told him how much I was enjoying the tea. By the time it was poured into our cups, the steaming infusion had taken on the creamy yellow and biting orange of the fruit. "What about tea as a business?" I said. I was thinking of a café or a teahouse. Fangmin could rent a small space and serve overpriced teas. But that was not how he understood me. His spirits suddenly restored, he pointed at the teapot. "A great business idea," he said. "Selling tea. From foreign countries." I had difficulties imagining Fangmin at the head of a revamped East India Company, and said as much. "Isn't the tea trade the business of the last rather than the next century?" He ignored me and proceeded to recount a newspaper article he'd read that said tea pickers in India earned even less than their counterparts in China. A lot less. Perhaps not even half as much. Fangmin's idea was as simple as it was epochal. After centuries of competing with Indian tea plantations for export markets in the Old World, China was ready to import tea, in effect joining its former colonial masters. "Buy tea in India where people are paid less than one yuan an hour," he said, "and sell it here where people earn many times that." He didn't bother with

even the back of an envelope. And never would. The next time I saw
Fangmin, he had already forgotten the idea. But for a moment, it gave us a
glorious tickle. The region around Xiamen had once been the heart of
China's tea trade. The hillsides had been filled with bushes, not cranes. Tea
coolies carried bamboo poles on their shoulders slung with bales of re-
deeming leaves and carried them on foot all the way to Guangzhou and
Hong Kong, from where the leaves were shipped to Britain as fuel for the
Industrial Revolution. Doused in hot water, they were welcome relief for
workers in mills and mines.

Leaving the trade in tea where it belonged, I went on to ask Fangmin
about the conversation about Lai we had when we first met. "That man you
mentioned," I said, "he sounded very interesting."

"Huh . . .?"

"The boss who paid off officials."

" . . . ?"

"You remember . . . he was in a nightclub . . . he called the police to
help him with a dispute over a woman."

" . . . ?"

I paused. "A beautiful woman."

"Oh, I remember," he said. But instead of taking up the story where he
had left off, Fangmin started looking for a pack of cigarettes.

"You remember," I said. "That's great. You know more about him?"

"I think he is not very interesting."

"That's not how it sounded when you talked about him before."

"Maybe it's not convenient at the moment."

To say something was not "convenient" was to politely deny a request.
But Fangmin's behavior seemed so odd, I pressed on.

"I wouldn't mind meeting him." I said.

"Impossible."

"That's too bad. Why?"

"He's not here anymore."

"Well, maybe he'll come back."

"Maybe."

"And where is he now?"

Fangmin said he didn't know. His name was Lai Changxing. He was a
fugitive, and it would be better if I stopped asking.

I wondered why Fangmin had talked so openly about Lai when we first met. Later I realized it had been right at the time when Lai fled Xiamen and he was not yet known to be toxic.

In the months that followed, Fangmin and I saw each other several times. We shared meals whenever I came to Xiamen. After he had ordered for both of us, we would discuss ideas for new business ventures. Sourcing bricks from the countryside. Selling television rights to cricket fights. Combining a plastic surgery clinic with a tailor shop to adjust patients' existing wardrobe to their new body shape. Much time was spent discussing names for these businesses. I favored old staples like "Bumper Harvest" and "Serve the People," while Fangmin leaned toward salad-style combinations of hibiscus, phoenix, dragon, pearl, and yellow springs.

〰

During one of my visits to Xiamen, Fangmin invited me to join a dinner he was hosting at a seafood restaurant. As instructed, I arrived ahead of the other two guests and waited just inside the door of a private dining room on the second floor. The carpet felt soft and spongy beneath the soles of my shoes as if to underline this really was private, if a little sinister. Under an unlit chandelier of uncertain origin stood a single table set for four. Sitting down, Fangmin was going through a large-leafed menu with a group of waiters. They were recommending lobster to him. The Hao Qing Xiang Restaurant was known for its lobster, but Fangmin had different ideas. He insisted on crab for dinner, preferably still muddy. From a tank in the kitchen, waiters brought a selection of live crabs with their pincers tied for Fangmin to choose from. The crabs hammered dully against the polished tabletop. *Tock-tock-tock.* Fangmin inspected them much as he might have a secondhand car. After checking the short hairs on the back of the shells, he searched for plastic identity tags typically clipped to the boxy crab claws, and found one. This was a genuine hairy crab from Jiangsu province, it said. Fangmin asked a waiter how he could be sure the tag wasn't a fake. The waiter said there was a phone number on the back — he could call to check with the delivery company. The whole company could be a fake, Fangmin said, and turned another page on the menu. In any case, he said, he needed more crabs.

For most of the hour before the other guests were to arrive, I was no more visible to Fangmin than a waiter hovering to refill glasses of water. On past occasions when ordering food, I had tried to help. But Fangmin had a fondness for eating well that could only be satisfied by giving unusually personal and specific instructions to waiters and often involved trips to the kitchen for further direction to chefs. He said, by way of explanation, that eating made him happier than anything else. It was the equivalent of sex for him, he said, reiterating a common belief among Chinese that intercourse was a national pastime in the west. *Zuo le ma?* Have you done it yet? did not strike Fangmin as an odd way to greet me. Others he addressed with *chi le ma?* Have you eaten? instead of, how are you?

Fangmin was a man who could silence you with his appetite, who could relegate you to a dark corner by enumerating all that he intended to consume, a man worth watching, I had decided. Fangmin operated on the principle that two Beggar's Chickens cooked in mud casings or two Hair Pin Prawns speared with bamboo shoots tasted twice as good as one. True satisfaction always appeared closer to him than it really was, within easy grasp, yet still beyond it. I rarely heard him recall past meals, but often he talked about the next. Fangmin did not like looking back — not because he wanted to avoid drawing attention to a dark past, or his growing belly, but because it meant losing time that could be spent looking ahead. You might call Fangmin an optimist, if only he weren't so suspicious.

Today, he was even more difficult than usual. He told the headwaiter the crabs ought to be served whole rather than broken up in the kitchen and then reassembled on a plate. The Hao Qing Xiang Restaurant preferred the latter. It wanted to spare its guests the effort of having to pry open the shells of the females to get at the prized roe, a buttery orange glob that was to caviar what crack was to cocaine. But Fangmin worried some of the roe might be removed in the kitchen. He didn't quite accuse the chefs of cheating yet insisted they leave the bone crunching to him. Meanwhile, the crabs brought out from the tank were still sitting on the table, staring at us with keen eyes. Fangmin didn't notice. His order finally complete, he was inspecting his wallet with quiet zeal. It seemed he was pondering the dinner ahead, perhaps reminding himself not to give his guests the chance to *mai dan*, or "bury" the bill. On the pretext of going to the washroom, he would slip out to the front desk and pay before anyone else could. He would not be beaten at this game. (Only once had I been able to.) Afterward, he'd come back and wait for his moment of triumph. A dining companion would eventually make his own disguised attempt to pay and return with a rainy mien. Such was friendship — a string of small betrayals. Fangmin excelled at it. Then, after almost an hour of overlooking me by the door, he turned around. "We're ready," he said, "don't you think?"

↝

Food is serious business in China. It reveals plenty about an eater's identity. "You are worth what you eat," read a newspaper headline I saw once. This is especially true in seafood restaurants, the most expensive segment of the Chinese culinary universe. Rare crustations are prized for their cost as much as for their taste. Invariably they are ordered when entertaining benefactors. The higher the bill, the greater the credit in the favor bank. Equally, the type of rice grain one eats is an indicator of class. Lowly tricycle riders described themselves as "sandy rice eaters."

Food is a status symbol more potent than, say, the car one drives. And just as Chinese identify each other by what they eat, so they do with foreigners. A man I asked about his views on President Bush told me, "Everyone says the United States is good. But their chicken is terrible. To eat American chicken is no different from chewing wood shavings. Look at their chicken wings and legs. They taste no better than machine parts."

China's obsession with food is reflected in plenty of neologisms. A small newspaper article is called a *doufu kuai,* a bean curd cube. Yet to eat bean curd, *chi doufu,* means to cheat on one's wife. To eat soft rice, *chi ruan fan,* was to mooch off a woman. To eat vegetarian, *chi su de,* is to be easygoing. To stir-fry, *chao,* is to speculate. To have one's squid cooked, *chao youyu,* is to get fired, while someone who doesn't want to leave his job with a state-owned enterprise is a *guotie,* a pot sticker.

Of course, food metaphors are not new to Mandarin. "Sow melons, reap melons," went an aphorism I learned in language tutorials. Impatient people are "rice pullers" — after a farmer who tugged at his grains to make them grow faster. And there is the now famously broken iron rice bowl, as the socialist welfare state is known.

Food is — and always has been — not only a key to identity but a signpost to power. Many Chinese remember their first dining-out experience like Americans do the Kennedy assassination. Where were you when . . . ?

In 1976, at the time of Mao's death, there was only one restaurant for every three million Chinese (reserved for a smug elite publicly railing against bourgeois dining pleasures). With the onset of economic reforms that changed. Many of the first private businesses to open in the late 1970s were places to eat. Today there is one restaurant for every four hundred Chinese and eating out is the number one leisure activity. No birthday bash is complete without a display of gastronomic opulence, and guests tell each other — with pride — that of the four thousand imperial staff who once worked in the Forbidden City, almost 60 percent handled the emperor's food and wine . . . a stark contrast to the deadly famines of the Mao years that many can still remember.

∽

Fangmin came over to the doorway of the private dining room and stood next to me as we waited for his two other guests to arrive. The live crabs — having completed their beauty pageant on the table — were back in the kitchen. About now cooks should be manhandling them into bubbling vats of gingery broth. They would be ready in a few minutes. Fangmin had asked for our food to be served as soon as we sat down. He had also selected two waitresses to be present in the room at all times to respond to additional requests. One fitted perfectly into her long embroidered *qipao* dress; the other was so tall her calves were showing. Positioned by Fangmin, they stood in the far corners of the room. Like that, we waited in silence.

The walls were covered with faux stucco and shuttered air shafts. In between hung prints of smoke-blown European sea battles. The room reminded me of something. I wondered what. It didn't just look like the inside of a submarine from a Jules Verne novel, I wrote in a small notebook I held in my hand, it looked like a Jules Verne submarine that was about to encounter the mechanically operated giant squid from the 1954 film version of *Twenty Thousand Leagues Under the Sea* that won an Oscar for its special effects including the squid's fight with James Mason and Kirk Douglas in a special studio tank. Well, maybe.

Fangmin was happy for me to take notes as long as we were alone. Once the guests arrived, though, I would have to stop. He asked me to not even tell them I was a journalist. I agreed unthinkingly and quickly regretted it. Journalistic convention demanded that I identify myself unless I had very good reasons not to. He tried to reassure me, telling me the two men we were expecting both worked for the city government and they wouldn't mind. As long as they could deny to their bosses they had knowingly met a foreign journalist, all was fine. "In any case, it is me they are coming to see, not you," he said. Fangmin had a new business idea for which he needed the support of the officials. He wanted to open a taxi company using imported vehicles. He required a government license, he said, and the officials could help him get it. Unfortunately, they could be quite difficult. We would have to try hard to charm them. Maybe I could tell them a bit about business in the west. And be respectful. They were known to walk out if a meeting wasn't going well, he said.

A few minutes later, after renewed silence, Fangmin clumsily grasped one of my hands. He said he wanted to thank me for helping him. My presence was a great show of friendship, and very useful. "In China it is very important to have friends," he said. "We all have to help each other. Thank you." There was a pause. Then I said it was the same where I came from. Friendship mattered a lot.

This was the sort of conversation Fangmin and I normally never had. It was stilted and uncomfortable. Too many encounters in China went likewise — painful silences brought to an end by proclamations of friendship. But in a way, and despite this little interlude, I realized Fangmin was right. We had become friends. It was a strange friendship but, unlike some, it worked. Other Chinese friends would invite me to share meals with them during which they desperately searched for common ground. Usually, they would profess eagerness to learn about life outside China. But there was a limit to how far they would reveal themselves, how deep I might delve into their lives. I rarely visited their homes or saw their parents or met their bosses. Something was holding them back. I couldn't pin it down but whatever it was, Fangmin didn't have it. He happily took me along.

Eventually, hearing the two officials coming up the stairs, we stepped out of the dining room. Fangmin greeted them and introduced me with a mumble. I didn't quite understand what he introduced me as but they seemed happy enough to see me. The first official introduced himself as Bureau Chief Wang and the second was his assistant. I took Bureau Chief Wang to be that invaluable breed in Chinese government — the relationship man. Relationship men talked party vernacular and inhabited the same dimly lit offices as career functionaries and showed the same disregard for traffic rules when they were in a rush. They laughed with supreme confidence and studied every speech of the General-Secretary like the rest of them. But they were also the sort that foreign investors fearful of red tape praised as someone "you can do business with." Rightfully so, for their allegiance was not to ideology. They had a healthy respect for ideologues, perhaps even shared an office with one. But they were primarily interested in getting things done. And if you had a relationship with such a man, for they were almost always men, you could too. The ablest among the relationship men rose high up in the Communist Party. They became trade negotiators or governors of rust-belt regions. Wherever cogs in the bureaucracy were stuck, they could be found. In a decade or two, foreign multinationals were sure to ask them to join their boards of directors. Bureau Chief Wang for one already looked the part. His pitch black hair was combed back across his head, each gelatinous strand aligned in parallel.

As soon as we were seated, the waitresses started putting food on the table. Fangmin hovered halfway up in his chair to serve us. He ladled out single dollops of each dish, holding a small serving spoon with both hands in a gesture that was both respectful and comical. He introduced each dish by name and which part of China the main ingredient had come from. Fish from Shanghai, mushrooms from Yunnan, lamb from Inner Mongolia. Only the crab from Jiangsu was missing. After the food was served, Fangmin busied himself with drinks. He filled four glasses with beer, Bureau Chief Wang's choice, and passed them around. We toasted. Once glasses had been refilled, Fangmin drank with the bureau chief alone. Then he drank with the assistant, and encouraged me to do the same. The two officials were not nearly as difficult to please as Fangmin had suggested. They seemed delighted with the food and soon proposed a return round of toasts.

The conversation we struck up was the equivalent of weather talk. Shanghai had the best fish. No, Hunan. Doesn't Hunan have the spiciest food. No, Sichuan. Eventually, conversation drifted away from food. People from Sichuan are short but their women are quite pretty. Maybe it has something to do with the heat in Sichuan. Yes, Sichuan is the hottest place in China. But isn't Hunan hotter? And so on. Mostly it was the bureau chief who talked.

Eventually, we moved on to western countries. The Germans built the best cars. The English played the best football. The French were the best lovers, and the Americans the best businessmen. Bureau Chief Wang had never been outside China but that didn't stop him. "I must disagree," I said. "Germans also play good football and Americans make great cars." They looked at me in surprise. "Of course Americans make great cars," the bureau chief said. "They are great businessmen."

Fangmin said the Jiangsu crabs were still missing. "Where are they?" One of the waitresses went out to check. Fangmin followed her, threatening to strangle the cook. I guessed he would be paying the bill.

Left alone with the two officials, I proposed another toast. The bureau chief followed up with one of his own. When would Fangmin be back? We desperately needed a new topic of conversation. But what to talk about? There was one thing I was dying to ask them — Fangmin was refusing to discuss Lai Changxing, pleading ignorance. But surely these two would know more about him. So I asked. They appeared comfortable enough with the topic. "The matter of Mr. Lai is a small one," Wang said. "The authorities are looking into it." Looking into what? "Nothing more than tax issues." And didn't everyone have tax issues, he seemed to imply. So where was Lai now? That he couldn't tell me — it sounded more like wouldn't — but Lai should be back soon. "How very interesting." I needed to ask more innocuous questions if I wanted to continue. "What line of business was Mr. Lai in?" Mainly shipping, the bureau chief said. "He ran several docks and container yards. They had been part of the import trade and helped to make Xiamen into a major city with fast economic growth." It seemed odd that the bureau chief was talking about Lai and his businesses in the past tense. Had he been gone long? When his assistant pitched in, calling Lai a model worker, the bureau chief shut him up.

Returning to the room, Fangmin was followed by three waiters carrying plates piled high with crabs. Their gray shells had turned a rosy red. Following a short tutorial on how to open them, Fangmin placed one specimen on each of our plates. The officials called the oily roe "delightful."

For the rest of the meal, we then talked not about but around the subject of Fangmin's new venture. The fact that he was applying for a license never came up. The bureau chief merely agreed with Fangmin that taxis were a good business. He inquired what companies Fangmin had run in the past. It was important, he added, for companies to have international partners, someone who could help Chinese apply for special loans from foreign embassies. We discussed the taxi business in other countries. I was invited to give my views on taxis in the United States. I said I had lived in New York and there were many taxis, mostly yellow ones, but I didn't know much more about it. They nodded, and after one more round of toasts they got ready to leave. Standing by the door, the bureau chief sent off his assistant to get his car. Then he suggested we exchange business cards. This was awkward. Fangmin clearly did not want me to hand out my *Times* card. But

I would have to offer something. I hesitated, looking at the card of the bureau chief. Oddly, he was from the agricultural department of Xiamen Municipality. What good could he possibly do for someone applying for a taxi license?

While I studied his card — a respectful gesture in China — Fangmin reached into his jacket pocket. "You forgot your cards when you came to my office," he said. "I brought them along for you." From a stack in his pocket he handed a card to the bureau chief and gave the rest to me. It took me a moment to realize what had just happened. The topmost card on the stack I was holding read:

OLIVER AUGUST
FIRST SECRETARY
COMMERCIAL AND TRADE SECTION

Above my name were an eagle and the Stars & Stripes. Below it said in capital letters AMERICAN EMBASSY, next to what I knew to be the correct address and phone numbers of the U.S. embassy in Beijing. I read the card again. Then the next and the next. They were all the same. *Fangmin, you bastard.* By the time I looked up again, the bureau chief was already out the door and down the stairs.

৶

China has always been obsessed with names and labels. Imperial roll calls were exceptionally cumbersome affairs in the Forbidden City, even a mere century ago toward the end of the Qing Dynasty. Following the Communist takeover, a new system evolved, one no less pedantic, from *tongzhi* (comrade) and *dangpiao* (card-carrying party member) to *ganbu* (cadre) and *zhuxi* (chairman, Mao's title). Today, the less ideological *guanyuan* (official) is commonly used, but in daily interaction, the *guanyuan* matter less and less. Livelihoods now depend on private company owners who offer better-paying jobs. This shift in power has led once again to the creation of new names and labels. Private company owners are *getihu*, or self-made rich. Those spending their wealth wildly are *baofahu* (explosive rich), or *dakuan* (big spenders). Those merely aspiring to such a status are *xiaozi* (petits bourgeois) or *xingui* (newly expensive).

Labels have also changed inside families. Spouses are no longer *airen* (lovers), a term favored by Maoists. Old forms of address such as *lao gong* (husband) and *tai tai* (wife) returned, as did Mr. and Mrs., previously deemed bourgeois. Other forms of address soon followed. A *chuang tou gui* (nightstand) is a henpecked husband. A *cu tanzi* (vinegar jar) is a jealous husband. A *yazi* (duck) is a gigolo. An *er guo tou* — a term that sounds similar to a fiery liquor — is a woman who got divorced to remarry.

As more and more rules have melted away in China, people at all levels define new roles for themselves and attempt to name what they find unfamiliar all about them. At times the new names can be confusing. For the position of commercial middleman, something nonexistent before, there are at least four novel terms: *daoye, zouhede, xuetou,* and *erdao fanzi.* Over time, new hierarchies emerge. Profiteers are ranked from the lowly *chaoyou* (stir-fryer), to *daor* (speculator), *fang daor* (property speculator), *guoji daoye* (transnational goods speculator), and finally *yang daor* (foreign profiteer).

Most of all though, the obsession with names has manifested itself in the cult of the *ming pian,* or name card. No encounter between strangers is complete without an exchange of cards, whether out of curiosity, or a penchant for networking, or fear of associating with the wrong type.

Whatever the reason, Fangmin knew that a name card was essential. The right name card.

3

The Landlord

Fifteenth Floor, International Trade Ocean View
Apartments, Lujiang Road, Xiamen

I started to think of Xiamen as a woman. She wasn't dark-haired and slender like the ones on the street. Xiamen was a blonde — tall and fleshy and permed like they appeared in Raymond Chandler books. She was a broad. She lulled around, saying my name between puffs on long-tipped cigarettes. She drove her daddy's sports car, too fast, and her lipstick always ended up on my collar. At least that's what I told friends when they asked me why I spent so much time in Xiamen. To say the city had white, palm-fringed beaches wasn't enough. Everyone knew typhoons disturbed the sunny breeze. I found myself forever making excuses.

My editors had given me enormous freedom, allowing me to travel for months on end. I focused on stories from the fevered region around Xiamen, and even when reporting elsewhere I would come back on weekends. Eventually, I decided to rent a place in the city. Perhaps I could claim a piece of it for myself.

Chandler had said: Don't mess with broads. I didn't want to know. The alternative was too glum. In Beijing, I lived in a fenced-in ghetto guarded by armed police. It was called a diplomatic compound but there was nothing diplomatic about it, unless you counted the view of the Iraqi embassy from my kitchen window. Chinese citizens were banned from living in the compound, and on visits they had to show their papers at the front gate. My apartment was in a 1970s tower block built by a B-team of Russian engineers. Russian cars and planes appeared limber by comparison. The apartment walls were two feet thick and unreceptive to nails and picture hooks despite repeated attempts. The British defense attaché told me he had put a metal detector to the walls of a similar apartment, discovering enough wire and microphones to record a symphony orchestra.

Xiamen at least *felt* different. With a twinkle in her eye, she cast a spell on me. Here, hopes and riches bubbled up like they once did on East Texan oil fields. Private interests fused and sometimes clashed with state priorities. High-tech plants mingled with sweatshops while legions of migrant workers, known as the Blind Tide, or *mangliu,* poured in from the hinterland.

Xiamen is an archetypal Chinese boomtown, one of several that have sprung up along the balmy coast between Shanghai and Hong Kong. The boomtowns lay comfortably far from the capital ("Heaven is high and the Emperor is far away" — another of Teacher Su's phrases) and close to international shipping lanes. By my count, there are at least nine of them: Ningbo, Wenzhou, Fuzhou, Quanzhou, Xiamen, Shantou, Chaozhou, Shenzhen, and Zhuhai. Further north there are also Qingdao and Dalian, but they are late bloomers. Near the border to Vietnam one might have counted Beihai and Haikou before they started withering.

Xiamen shares several traits with the other boomtowns. Access to trade through a port is one, past occupation by colonial powers another. In the contentious settlement of the Opium Wars in the mid-nineteenth century, most of the towns became "treaty ports" exposing them to modern commerce. Foreign traders occupied them for almost a hundred years, yet none attained the exulted status of a Shanghai, Guangzhou, or Hong Kong. When Mao died, this turned out to be a plus. Less rigorously policed than their bigger neighbors, they soon became the furnaces of China's newly inflamed economy.

Output doubled roughly every three years and millions of farmers arrived to take jobs in factories. The boomtowns still make up only a tiny part of the country, much of which remains poor. But the coastal migration — more so even than the economic growth — is remarkable. It signals a break with the past. Over millennia Chinese have been wedded to ancestral lands. They tended tombs and passed down traditions from generation to generation. When they moved, it was usually in clans. In Book II (Li Ren 19) of his *Analects,* Confucius had laid down this reasoning: "While parents are alive, one must not travel afar. If one must, one's whereabouts should always be made known." Filial piety dictated that grown children care for elderly parents. In the boomtowns, however, there is no room. Workers sleep in dormitories next to their sewing machines and assembly lines. The millions who moved to the coast in the 1980s and 1990s did so alone, in rare cases with siblings or spouses. Everyone else was left behind, awaiting remittances.

Chinese have of course long been going overseas on their own. They have become laborers in the west and traders across Asia. But domestically migration had been more common in family units. Until now. The change gave rise to a riotous spectacle. During Spring Festival, when factories closed down briefly, some one hundred million migrants tried to go home for their once-a-year chance to see family. Roads were blocked, trains overflowed, stations closed down. Many migrants had to travel thousands of miles to the mountains surrounding the Tibetan plateau, the deserts bordering central Asia, the steppes of Manchuria. When they got there, families barely recognized them. Former farmers and herders, rootless and tossed together in the coastal cities, they had reinvented themselves, talking of new foods and following new fashions.

Alas, it isn't just the farmers who were changed by migration. The coastal towns were too. They adapt to the needs and preferences of new arrivals, shaped by successive waves like sandbanks in tidal seas.

The results could be confounding. When I traveled to a boomtown, I would buy a map on arrival, and then throw it away as soon as I left. Maps were out of date within months. Publishers printed new editions four or six times a year. Towns were changing that fast. A year on, whole districts were unrecognizable.

Holding on to an old map meant risking disaster. A new map was essential. Travelers mostly avoided asking for directions on the street. Someone a block from my destination in Xiamen once told me, "Oh, that's a department store, the really tall building? I never looked at it." People worked too hard or were just too new to know their surroundings. They had not yet made the towns their own.

I liked that. It put me at ease. The migrants were just as alien as I was here and knew each other no better than I did. Perhaps it was preposterous to think so — they were, after all, Chinese. Yet their Mandarin was no better than mine. They spoke in simple sentences, having only just left behind their local dialects. We could understand one another, and with time I was able to learn about them. They were full of murky tales and untapped resentments, a good reporter's crop: monies lost in get-rich schemes, marriages lived thousands of miles apart for the sake of betterment, children invested with more hope than they could ever repay.

But that came later. In the beginning they were just wide-eyed.

⌒

Officially, I continued to live in Beijing. But over the next few years, I stayed in Xiamen as much as I could. In good years, three or four months.

My double life began in earnest with a trip to a housing agent. "I need an apartment that's cheap and quiet," I told the mop-haired and unusually candid Mr. Chen from the "Fast Help Convenient Agency." I hoped he would understand. Chinese rents were low. I could afford to live reasonably without relying on the *Times*. "Cheap and quiet" was meant to convey "not one of those garishly painted, horrendously overdecorated tower blocks," something I struggled to express in Chinese. "Very cheap, very quiet, please," I said on the way to our first appointment. Mr. Chen shook his head. "I'm not sure that exists."

We were crossing a multilane highway on foot in jet-fueled afternoon traffic when a car missed us by an inch. "Don't be afraid," Mr. Chen said. "If a driver hits you, he will have to pay extra because you are a foreigner." We avoided the highways after that.

Mr. Chen wore a cream suit that was crumpled and stained and beaten into submission. He was one of the few locals who was actually from Xiamen. His parents and grandparents had spent their whole lives here. For a while, they had struggled to compete with the new arrivals, the country migrants, but now they were comfortably well-off. They had become part of an urban middle class that was rapidly emerging — and with it the standard trappings of newfound affluence.

"You know the theory of the Two Musts?" Mr. Chen said.

The Two Musts was a bit of Maoist dogma that most Chinese laughed at now. "The masses must be prudent, and they must preserve plain living," I said.

"Right, right. But that's not what I meant. We have our own version . . . must have an elevator, and must have a swimming pool."

Just as I had feared, we went to see apartments in newly built towers. They were very much not "cheap and quiet." They had names like Leisure Heaven, Luxury Garden, Dynasty Territory, Forever Rising Tower, and

Home of the British Monarch. The modern Chinese penchant for aspirational models was much in evidence. Mr. Chen led me through an entrance hall decked out like the Moulin Rouge complete with imitation windmill, red curtains, and an empty cocktail lounge in the foyer. Next we passed green-tinted bay windows in a mock Victorian penthouse and went on to see a cupola roof modeled on the U.S. Capitol perched on top of a twenty-story building. At least the view here was good. Xiamen sprouted in manic bouts of concrete and sparkled with slapdash puddles of color. From above the city resembled a furious sea of cement and marble, wave upon wave of high-rises rippling out, strips of tarmac submerged at bottomless depths. Earlier, at street level, there had been reminders of Old China — laborers carrying burlap bags holding all their worldly possessions, live chickens rolling off long-distance buses — but up here I only saw cornfields of spiky towers nibbling at the horizon.

Mr. Chen pointed out a boxy building with a cream-colored roof that seemed to tower above all others. He called it the Banana Split Building with a Vanilla Hat. It was a typical moniker. Residents liked to think of opulent symbols of progress in terms of food. There was also the Stack of Pancakes Building. It did very much look like a tall stack of brutishly hewn pancakes. Then there was the Chocolate Tower, as solid a brown pillbox as could be found in any Chinese city. And across the city we could see the Sliced Cucumber Building, sporting layers of roofs, sundecks, and decorative flourishes, piled high and painted green. Xiamen mixed the delicate with the bombastic, the modern and the monumental, a concrete hell made worse by an orgy of overstimulation, its crassness written in large-lettered neon. But only those lacking sympathy for the dream of personal reinvention would think it soulless. Most residents had come here to start anew, and the city was following suit.

"None of this existed when I was a child," Mr. Chen said. "It was much less crowded." Did he not miss the old Xiamen? "Not at all. My parents, though, they do. Especially the cemeteries." To make room for new buildings, ancient burial grounds were often moved or built over, he said. "My parents believe it's terrible because our ancestral spirits rest in the graves. To disturb them will bring harm to the family. It worries them constantly. My mother rarely goes out for fear of ghosts."

"And your clients?"

"Well, few people want to live over an old cemetery."

"How would they know?"

"Not from me."

Sometimes, he said, relatives excavated their ancestors before the diggers and cranes arrived. Especially rich overseas Chinese liked to come back to Xiamen to perform the ultimate act of relocation. Urns were emptied into plastic bags, packed as carry-on luggage, and ancestors delivered to the New World never seen during their lifetime. Somewhere near a Chinatown in New York or London, a reburial awaited them. No wonder the spirits were a little disturbed.

At last Mr. Chen showed me an apartment I liked. It overlooked a narrow wharf where wooden junks departed for the mainland. The view from the fifteenth floor was magnificent, though the interior was less so. There were three bedrooms, two bathrooms, and one shrine with incense sticks smoldering among offerings of apples, almonds, and bananas on a copper plate. The cupboard-sized red box towered over the rest of the furniture.

The landlord, Mr. Huang, was delighted when I said I had no furniture of my own. "I brought new apples for the shrine today," he said.

"Yes."

"You like it?"

"I prefer it to windmills."

Mr. Chen and Mr. Huang launched into contract negotiations while I watched the incense burn. A silky thread of smoke rose like a foreign object among the apartment's plastic sofas and gilded mirrors. As I followed the path of the smoke I forgot to ask what might be lurking in the ground below.

⟍⟋

Thus I became a resident of Xiamen, at least unofficially. I did not have a residence permit. But then neither did half the population. The old *hukou* registration system had withered in a dusty place on the statue books, mummified beyond recognition. Most months I traveled back and forth to Beijing and across China. When I returned I found that no matter how short my absence, I had to discover Xiamen anew. Familiar streets were foreign within weeks. Clusters of houses vanished along with their inhabitants, entire blocks of Mao-era dwellings disappeared overnight, replaced by skyscrapers and shopping malls erected in just weeks. Whole boulevards were moved and public parks came and went seemingly at a whim. Right in front of me, a vast urban experiment was being conducted, all ardor and annihilation. Over the years, I felt I never saw the same city twice. Xiamen was a perpetual frontier, a mixed metaphor come true. Just add water while you dance on the volcano.

However, when I asked ordinary residents about this revolution in their midst, many just shrugged. It was of no great concern to them. They did not rejoice in their city as I did. Approvingly, I would describe Xiamen as wild, dishonest, and dangerous, even a little mad. They would give me blank looks. That was not the sort of place they would want to live in. When asked, they had little to say about what sort of place they preferred. Instead they talked about their families. Would their children have better lives than they had? That mattered. They also talked about history. The past seemed very much present to them, even as they reinvented every last scrap of their physical surroundings in the pursuit of betterment. Some still used prerevolution, pre–reform era street names. Others reconstituted old or demolished neighborhoods in modern surroundings, social networks intact. They prided themselves on the fact that their civilization, though hurt severely, marched on with the walking wounded. Mao had tried to erase large parts of it. Millions had suffered. But, so it seemed to me, he had only been able to scratch the surface. The hard-wiring survived. From history's depths now reemerged a reverence for learning, a focus on family, and a predilection for expressing personal ambition through wealth.

"Are you from here?" I once asked a woman in the lift of my apartment building. "No. Nobody is really from here," she said over rhythmic pinging floor by floor. "I was born in Sichuan. My son was born here though, last month. He will go to university." Before I got out on my floor, I told her my brother would be having a child soon too. His son was to be born any day now. "I will become an uncle for the first time," I said. The woman from Sichuan was delighted. "Wonderful," she said. "You will get a promotion."

In Xiamen that seemed a perfectly normal thing to say. The city's inhabitants may be beaten by bosses and cheated by crooks. Their muscles, lungs, tendons, and brains may fray in industrial plants. But not before they had secured betterment for their families. Nothing could shake that aim. Nobody would die like their parents. They would all get promotions, no matter how hard they had to work. They would *wen qian*, make money, *yezihuo*, get rich, and *lai cai*, bring vegetables.

Two miles from my apartment stood Xiamen's main "Employment Center." The building on Forever Green Street looked like a cross between an airport arrivals hall and a stock exchange. Behind a seamless glass dome, a vast electronic board flashed up job notices. Sugar boiler, cement tube maker, forklift driver. Call this number. Thousands of job seekers crowded around the board, mobile phones at the ready, sure to reach prospective employers quicker than the next guy. There was no filling in of forms in triplicate, waiting for bureaucrats, sending in résumés, or sitting for aptitude tests. All one needed to get a job was stated on the board. The notices specified gender, height, and maximum age. Tall people appeared to be in particular demand. Height equaled good health. The stunted and malnourished need not apply. The first five jobs I saw scrolling up on my first visit were:

1. Sewing machine repairer, younger than 29, taller than 1.60 meters, $80 per month
2. Fabric dye merchant, female, younger than 35, no color blindness, $100 p/m
3. Water meter installer, 20–45 years old, male, not a local, $3 per day
4. Security guard, younger than 25, $110 p/m, demobilized woman soldier wanted
5. Telephone operator, English speaking, taller than 1.62 meters, $105 p/m

Forever Green Street is close to the long-distance bus station where the countryside unloads its daily cargo of willing labor. The new arrivals are the sharpest, keenest, and best-looking . . . the most ambitious, hungry, and fierce . . . the most desperately optimistic and highly driven newcomers from backwater villages across the country. Only those with bottomless appetites for hardship and reinvention embark on journeys like this. Out of China's gigantic population, Xiamen gets the best raw material, honed by decades of scarcity. The city's newest residents, cheeks still sun-burned from farm work, are relentless seekers of opportunity. Uprooted and as good as naked, they are driven to subversive industriousness. Every day they come by the thousands, every one a potential Lai Changxing. The more of them I met, the more I was convinced — to know Lai I had to understand them.

౿

Along with the shrine in my new home in the International Trade Ocean View Apartments, I acquired a roommate. Kim wore black corduroy trousers, a camouflage fishing vest, and hair shorn to within a pencil's width of her skull. Hairless and bulbous, her head loomed over her short frame. She had changed her Chinese name to Kim, she said, because boys as well as girls might be called that. Nobody would be able to tell her gender by looking at a form or nametag.

Kim had been a student at Xiamen University in 1989 but stopped attending classes during the student protests. Since then she had dedicated herself to liberating her *tongzhi,* her comrades, as she said with a fleshy pout. Even I could tell Kim was not a Communist Party member. Being *tongxinglian,* gay, was still a taboo in China, Kim said. But she was hopeful. Two "comrades" had recently managed to get married, she said. After the betrothal, they had both flung their bouquets behind them, clutched their white dresses, and jumped into a waiting limousine. "Should we wait for the groom?" the driver asked. The women laughed. "He's in the other car," they said and drove off.

Kim was born in the Yangtze River delta and had come to Xiamen in the late 1980s following a million-strong trek. She was out to reinvent herself but not quite like the other migrants. One of Kim's friends, Mian Mian, later wrote a novel about vagabonds like her. The back cover of the book talked of "love like poison, evenings filled with music and girls who need chocolate to live as if it was air." Within three days of publication the book was banned by the censors for its explicit content. Kim thought it the best thing that could happen. "You never make money from books here, but foreign publishers love it when they can advertise something as banned in China." She was right. *La La La* was soon sold at airport bookshops across the western world. It struck a cord despite the fact that — or perhaps because — it portrayed China as vastly different from common perceptions. The insatiable appetites of people like Kim had created a society that was suddenly decadent, unruly, intrigue-ridden, and yet remarkably sensual and attuned to spiritual currents. This awakening of desires seemed like a good explanation for why China was changing so quickly. Might unceasing hunger and boundless enterprise fuel the country's breakneck transformation, rather than a fuzzy "reform process" directed by octogenarian leaders in Beijing?

A few weeks after we started living together, Kim took me to one of Xiamen's hidden nightclubs for comrades. There was no sign outside, just an all-night fruit stall at the bottom of an unlit staircase in a residential complex. Two flights up, through an unmarked door, we slipped into a regular apartment with blacked-out windows. Strobe lights cut through thick smoke. She ordered coconut milk heated in a microwave. There may have been alcohol in it. I couldn't tell.

"Are you married?" a man asked me at the bar. Another asked again a little later. "Why do they want to know if I am married?" I said to Kim. "Is that code for something?"

"No, no. They just want to know if you are married."

"Does it matter what I say?"

"They're just being polite." She laughed. "Maybe they are married themselves and want to talk to you about their children."

She said many gay men *were* married — with children. Never to wed invited stigma. Hence they crafted new shells for themselves, a straight identity. They married and produced heirs as was expected of them. During the day they were fathers and husbands, and by night they came here to talk about what men around the world discussed while propping up bars: pesky wives, blaring children, haughty in-laws.

If you knew how, you could now choose your own destiny in China, right? Kim thought so. But you had to be careful. A few years ago, she said, she was detained by police in Beijing for organizing a gay and lesbian conference. She had moved to the capital to campaign for civil rights. But to do so, even if peacefully, was not welcomed. Detention did not frighten her much, yet nor had she done much campaigning since. Now back in Xiamen, she said, "it was fun being a rebel, but my wild days are over."

I had my doubts. On our way home from the club we passed a chained dog. It snarled at us through a wire-mesh fence. Kim stopped and growled, then bent down and barked back at it.

꒰ꔠ꒱

The most frequent, and perhaps most hapless, visitor to our apartment was standing in front of the living room shrine. "Why do you keep this anyway? Are you superstitious?"

Andy was a student and lived on the nearby campus of Xiamen University. I first met him in a restaurant that served, by universal acclaim, the best *xiaolongbao* soup dumplings in Greater China. During our meal we were so preoccupied we hardly talked. You had to be careful with these dumplings. They were scalding hot. However, if you bit into one to let the insides cool, precious drops of soup might spill. Yes, the soup was inside. How it had got into the dumplings was a subject of lingering fascination to me (did they wrap ice cubes made from stock into the dough?) but not to Andy. I leaned over to ask.

"Don't know," he said.

"But you've eaten here before?"

"I guess it's tricky" was the furthest he would venture.

Like the dumpling recipe, Andy was originally from Taiwan. He had decided — rather to my surprise — to leave the island. Plenty of adventurous Taiwanese of his generation did. They saw home as cramped and stifling. China was different. It was the reincarnation of the booming American West of the late nineteenth century whereas Taiwan was troubled Ireland, but closer, separate by a strait rather than an ocean. Across it the same language was spoken and the prospects for the bold were limitless.

Andy, however, did not strike me as bold. To ease his passage west, he had decided to go to university rather than find a job. Campus would offer a secure perch, he hoped, giving him room to find an adult self. He enjoyed visiting Kim and me in his first few months after his arrival, at least most of the time. Kim would tell him she liked his broad shoulders and shiny black hair. "So cute," she would coo, feeling his muscles. "You work out?"

He would wince but not reply.

One day Andy came over and saw me inspecting a black Sichuanese wok from a street market. I found it hidden among electric rice cookers and power steamers. The wok was the only used thing in the market. Factory new was the norm. Goods were so cheap — why bother with secondhand? The old men who had long made a living from fixing tools, fitting plugs, and rethreading wires on street corners looked ancient now.

I put the wok on the gleaming kitchen counter between the microwave and a paper bag from an American fast-food restaurant near the university in which Andy had brought his lunch. I knelt down to inspect the wok. One handle was missing, the other worn thin from years of use. Ruts and scratches ran through the blackened pan like creases in the parchment paper face of a shaman. I mentioned being surprised to find something so wondrous among the electric jumble in the market.

"It's dirty," Andy said. "You should to wash it."

"Of course it's dirty. It's probably a hundred years old."

"No, look. It's really dirty." He ran a finger across the wok and held it up. Grease glistened dully.

"Well, it's an original."

"It's disgusting." Andy ran water in the sink to clean the scarred wok.

Kim, who had silently followed our conversation, pushed Andy aside. "Don't do that," she said. "Wash it and it becomes useless." Sichuanese chefs believed the age of a wok determined the quality of their food, Kim said. Pots and pans were never properly washed in order to harness decades of flavor accumulated in scratches and dents. You could — nose to the pan — still smell chicken fried fiercely with mounts of red chilies, beans blistering with heat, and tofu buried under whole peppercorns that crackled when chewed. Chefs in Sichuan used exceptionally fresh ingredients and incinerating spices, but so did their colleagues in other regions. Their real trick was the wok. It explained the superiority of the Sichuanese cuisine. Even today.

Kim lifted our specimen out of the slowly rising foam and placed it back on the counter. I rejoiced — hail the trophy — even while I wondered if she had just made that up. Kim did not like washing up or cleaning. She never even tried while we lived together. She liked eating, and not just Sichuanese, but always in restaurants since she didn't like cooking either. She preferred her kitchen to remain untouched. If nobody else toiled there, she would not be expected to join in.

Andy shrugged and said he was hungry. He reached for the fast-food bag on the counter. Burger grease and condensation from a carbonated drink had soaked through the paper skin. When Andy lifted the wet bag, it ripped and spontaneously disemboweled, spilling its oily and tangy contents across Kim's kitchen.

❧

Another frequent — and usually unannounced — visitor to the apartment was the landlord. The delivery of new offerings for the shrine was his usual excuse for wheedling his way through the front door, which was triple locked on his instruction. When we didn't open up quickly enough, he pounded on the door as if we were squatters rather than tenants.

In his hand, Mr. Huang typically held a sheaf of paper money. It came from a local shop, which I thought of as the central bank for the afterlife. The tatty branch office around the corner sold all manner of denominations. Yellow notes with wise men highlighted in gold. Red sheets the size of government bonds imprinted with dueling lions. And, my favorite, a thousand dollar bill showing the face of Confucius in place of a U.S. president on the front and "heavenly voucher" written on the back. The bank did brisk business.

Mr. Huang said he first came to Xiamen as a day laborer in the early

1980s. He was the third of five sons in a family of rural coffin makers. Now, he was sixty-six years old, "closer to the end than the beginning," he said. He wore clunky gold rings, two-tone black-and-white loafers, and chino trouser legs rolled up to the knee for ventilation. The lid on his gimpy left eye was permanently cocked. He said he belonged to the "four bad categories," as Maoists used to call landlords, criminals, rich peasants, and counterrevolutionaries.

Immediately after his arrival at the apartment he would remove a metal bin from behind a set of doors at the bottom of the shrine. Going on to the balcony he scattered paper money inside and lit it. Later he emptied the bin and returned it to the shrine. Then he offered nourishment for the spirits. At one point, I counted one pineapple, two oranges, four pears, a morphing mess of soft-skinned tomatoes, a dust-covered cup of honey, a half-empty pack of cigarettes (had Kim borrowed the other half?), and a vacuum-sealed pack of Uncle Ben's rice all stacked on the shrine.

Having successfully tended to the next life, he turned to this one. From our sofa, a polyester three-seater, he commanded Kim to draw the heavy curtains to keep out the afternoon sun, and sent Andy to sweep the floor.

"I only let you move in here," he said to me, "because you agreed to keep the shrine. You are the forth person to come to me about the apartment. I rejected the first three."

"Why?"

"One wanted to remove the shrine."

"And the other two?"

"The first wanted to take down the curtains, and the second was chewing betel nuts. He was probably spitting on the floor when I wasn't looking."

"You're a cautious man, Mr. Huang."

"To do business you have to have an alert mind."

He had paid more than a hundred thousand dollars for the apartment, not a big sum for a millionaire like him, he said. "I decorated it myself. I have more time now since my two sons took over the business. Interior decorating is my hobby. I did my own apartment first, two years ago. And then this one. Looks good, don't you think?"

I asked him about the business now managed by his sons. Reluctantly he gave up on interior decorating. "Stones," he said.

"You are in the construction business?"

"No, gravestones."

One morning a few weeks later, Mr. Huang invited us to visit his workshop. He boasted about paying none of his workers more than a hundred dollars a month. Standing among them, we were dwarfed by piles of burial stones in various hues. Persia beige, desert brown, pearl blue, china black. For a city so full of life Xiamen seemed in startling need of gravestones.

Andy asked Mr. Huang, "Have you chosen your own for when you die?"

You never mention death in China, not directly. At least that was the custom. But Andy did not seem to know that. Kim looked over to me, her eyebrows arched.

"Of course I have," Mr. Huang said. "I will show you." Kim's brows dipped with relief.

I liked having Andy around. He asked questions I didn't dare or never thought to ask. Away from home, he was acquiring a sense of curiosity.

Mr. Huang's final resting place, we soon learned, was to be no mere grave. In death, he would complete the change of identity he had begun when he came to Xiamen. The former day laborer showed us plans for an imperial tomb covering half a tennis court. Dragons watched over a double-story pagoda roof resting on Ionic columns. Carved from Irish diamond green, the tomb included benches for mourners to sit on, even coat pegs. I recognized the taste in interior decorating. Except for a legion of Terracotta Warriors, Mr. Huang had thought of everything an emperor would need on his final voyage. Soon the tomb was to be assembled at a hillside cemetery with good views. Mr. Huang seemed to be looking forward to that. "The tomb will cost me more than your apartment," he said with evident pride.

"But why . . . why such a big one?"

"I want my sons to remember how rich I made them," he said, "and to make sure they don't give me a cheap funeral."

༄

Kim, Andy, and I left Mr. Huang's workshop and went to lunch. Over bowls of fried rice, I witnessed a small shift in the tectonic foundations of our friendship. For the first time, Andy robustly fended off Kim's bark. He began by saying our landlord reminded him of his relatives. They had migrated from Fujian to Taiwan generations ago but would still fit in here.

Kim thought this preposterous. "Taiwanese don't understand China," she said. "You have become too American." Like many Taiwanese, Andy had studied in the United States and preferred people to use his English rather than his Chinese name.

"Taiwanese companies are doing pretty well here," he said.

"But they don't understand the mainland. Their policies are too soft."

"Really, like what?"

"Like giving out free T-shirts to customers and offering free shuttle buses to shopping malls."

"What's wrong with that?"

"Everyone will take the free stuff and not buy anything. Outsiders get cheated."

"No."

"Yes. Customer service, that's an invitation to cheat. People will just buy a pair of trousers from Gap or Armani, wear it for three months, then return it. And then keep on doing so."

Kim elaborated on her vision of the anarchy that would ensue once foreign retailers were fully set up — a consumerist paradise for poor Chinese, like the ones overseas they had heard so much about, but without the cash registers. Andy patiently explained these were growing pains of transformation. In other countries, few customers returned three-month-old trousers. They preferred spending time with family to driving an hour to a shopping mall and an hour back, even if the shuttle bus was free, just to return something. Kim still didn't believe him. But she stopped arguing and focused on eating.

After lunch, we took a taxi to the beach. We went to a place where the sea curved around Xiamen's south and east. The waves were small; the tide was low and the sand smooth. Palm trees shaded a gravel path where men with beards grilled meat skewers, baskers with guitars awaited diners, and a steady breeze took away the heat of the midday sun.

Kim said this part of Xiamen had changed more than any other in recent years. Where we walked — a manicured lawn set back from the beach — had been inaccessible except to soldiers. The whole area had been mined and the beach filled with landing barriers. The dunes had been studded with lookouts and foxholes. "It was like that for a long time," Kim said. "I never came here as a student."

Xiamen Island lay at an unenviable intersection of history and geography. In 1841, during the Opium War era, a heavily armed British flotilla of thirty-eight ships had occupied the bay. A year later, Beijing signed a much despised treaty, ceding control to western powers, led by Britain, over many of its ports. They included Hong Kong and Shanghai as well as Xiamen, known then as Amoy. The island got its own colonial administrators, embassies, gentlemen's clubs, opium dens, and a string of foreign ships that came to ply trade.

After the Chinese civil war ended in 1949, Xiamen found itself in the hands of the victorious Communists. Yet the neighboring island of Jinmen, which we could see from here, remained under Nationalist control. When the two regimes formally separated, Jinmen became part of the rump state of Taiwan. Tensions remained high though. In 1958, Communist forces started shelling Jinmen to drive out the Nationalists, who replied in kind. The two sides traded volleys daily (at the time Jinmen was known as Quemoy and as such it entered the history books). Soon, the little fistfight escalated. For a while it looked like China was making full-scale invasion plans. Bound by a "Mutual Security Pact" to Taiwan, Washington became involved. A rerun of the Korean War loomed. Hostilities were barely averted when Beijing backed down. Still, the trading of artillery fire continued. Shells rained down sporadically until the 1980s. Damaged houses still stood along the coast.

Only in the 1990s were most mines and landing barriers removed from Xiamen's beaches. By then Taiwan had withdrawn its troops from Jinmen to concentrate on defending the main island further offshore. Both sides now converted their beaches into propaganda zones. They erected slogans visible across the narrow strait. Where Kim, Andy, and I walked it said in hundred-foot-high lettering, "*Yi guo, liang zhi. Tong yi zhong guo.*" "One country, two systems. Unify China."

Behind us, overgrown hills rose up, filled with listening posts. Antennae twisted in the breeze. Not so long ago they had played a part in another superpower tussle. In 1996, Beijing surprised Washington by conducting missile tests on Taiwanese territory (which of course it didn't recognize). Washington protested. When the tests continued, the United States dispatched two aircraft carriers from the Seventh Fleet based in nearby

Japan. Beijing backed down, following a by now familiar if humiliating pattern.

✍

The more time I spent in Xiamen, the more I saw Amoy. The old colonial town poked through in unexpected ways. Modern façades were no mirages, to be sure. But what mattered was often what was old. People wanting to redress the humiliation of the Opium Wars and the imposition of foreign "treaty ports." People obsessing about shrines and tombs. People holding on to hundred-year-old woks. People discovering an interest in traditional Chinese medicine — though this could create its own problems. I knew a man in Xiamen, a schoolteacher, who was convinced of the healing powers of tiger carcasses. The tail remedied skin disease, he said. The whiskers cured toothache. The bones were good for fighting rheumatism. And a tiger penis was apparently an excellent aphrodisiac. The teacher said the recipe was ancient, still handed down from generation to generation.

"Until there are no more tigers," I said.

"Yes. But bears and rhinos have some of the same qualities."

For decades, Mao had preached disdain for the past (as well as for the environment). His fervent political campaigns had aimed to bury what Chinese had accumulated over millennia. His Cultural Revolution was to be the start of a permanent holiday from history. Temples were closed, scriptures burned, traditions vilified. Eventually, when Mao died, the blind fervor began to wane, soon followed by full retreat (as well as a cover-up of his crimes and a ban on researching Cultural Revolution history).

Now at least the more distant past is coming back. It looms large especially in spiritual matters. There is much in addition to tombs and shrines. Millions of Chinese follow the teachings of Li Hongzhi, the leader of the Falun Gong group (who was persecuted when he threatened to eclipse Mao's popularity). Others prefer to believe in ghosts and other earthly demons. Gambling, though prohibited, is popular once again. The cult of the lucky — or unlucky — number enters all parts of modern life. In new high-rise buildings there are no fourth, fourteenth, or twenty-fourth floors. The number four in Mandarin, *si,* sounds similar to the word for death. Equally, the number eight, *ba,* sounds similar to fortune, *fa.* Telephone numbers with fours are shunned, while those with lots of eights are in high demand. (When the state phone company sold the number 8888-8888 at public auction, Sichuan Airlines paid three hundred thousand dollars to use it for a customer hotline.)

Alas, the return of pre-Communist history is limited. Bulldozers, for one, do not observe it. Cemeteries are razed and built over. So are imperial-era buildings. Leftovers from the founding of Xiamen in the fourteenth century were destroyed to accommodate new construction. A similar fate befell structures from the seventeenth century, a time when the last court of the Ming Dynasty escaped to Xiamen.

The boomtown flattens everything in its path. Everything physical that was. Old China's infrastructure is decimated daily and by the square mile. Yet its traditions, often older still, prove more resistant. In many cases they thrive in adverse conditions. When I began visiting Xiamen, I was astounded that most migrants were arriving without their parents. This seemed such a severe break with traditions of filial piety. Now I saw them sending for their parents as soon as they could afford to. Many were building extra bedrooms to accommodate them. The Confucian focus on the family was alive. Indeed it flourished, one of the few exceptions — according to Kim — being the customary three-year ban on sexual intercourse after the death of a parent. "That would be rather long," she said.

4
BOATMEN

Junk 1141, No. 1 Wharf, Bay of Xiamen

WHERE WAS LAI? Not any place I had visited in Xiamen. Still he was present all around. His construction projects shaped the city even now. Buildings along main roads recalled the grandness, and the poor taste, of his ambitions. Near the Marco Polo Hotel stood residences he had decorated with medieval lookout towers done in pink marble. They might have been a challenge to authority. Or they might have been rococo flourishes. Meanwhile, other structures announced Lai's sudden absence. On a plot next to my apartment gaped an enormous hole. From the kitchen window I could see it reach five floors below ground. The walls were clad in smooth concrete like an Olympic diving pool with most of the water drained. When Lai fled, the site was abandoned. Rather than becoming one of his high-rise legacies, it was now just another dead-end lead, another empty glimpse of the man.

I felt stuck in my search. Reflections alone would not bring me closer to Lai. I decided to seek help from Kim and Andy. Might they look through library and newspaper archives, I asked, not realizing such records were restricted in China? Might they have useful contacts in the city, and were I to stumble, might they assist me in Mandarin? I offered to pay them whatever they earned in other jobs. After a moment's hesitation over the attention we might draw from the authorities, both agreed.

"Maybe we'll get put in the cell next to Lai," Andy said and grinned. We were standing on the balcony of the apartment, looking at a banner below ("Advance law and order: no cursing"). Beyond the banner we could see the narrow quay, known as No.1 Wharf, lined with trim wooden junks.

Every few minutes a junk steamed across the water to the nearby mainland. It would sound its horn, a sonorous *ah-tooooom*. Beyond it was the shoreline, and beyond that mountains rose like stately fortifications, walling freewheeling Xiamen off from China proper.

I told Andy I wanted to speak to people who knew Lai personally. He nodded. I said Lai was trading oil and other commodities, or at least he used to. Andy looked down from the balcony. He suggested talking to boatmen on the passing junks. They flitted between container barges and oil tankers all day. If Lai was in shipping, they would know him, would they not?

Later, when the sun started to set, we watched the boatmen tie up their junks. They lashed bows and sterns together, buffered by rubber tires fixed to their hulls. When they were done, they lit incense sticks on shrines in their wheelhouses. Like my landlord, the boatmen filled their shrines with fruit offerings and paper money.

Andy watched them with a sneer. "The ghosts must be really stupid here," he said.

"Why?"

"It's paper money."

"Well, it's a symbol . . ."

Andy shook his head. During festivals, he said, local people lit firecrackers to drive out bad ghosts. "What kind of a ghost is scared of firecrackers?"

"Elderly ones?"

"And then there is this thing people do with their doors."

"Yes?"

"Some have a big step at the bottom of their door to keep out ghosts. Can't the ghosts climb over the step?"

I liked my conversations with Andy. He saw such different things in Xiamen. To him, the port and all the other ports along the coast were places of departure. From here his ancestors, and those of millions of Chinese, had gone overseas. He struggled to view the ports as anything but places to be left behind, places that were outmoded and stuck in the past. To me, they were places of arrival. From across the water came what was familiar and what fueled and renewed a city like Xiamen. The importation of goods brought in new ways. Here migrants from the hinterland made precious connections to the outside world — now more than ever.

Yet I had to agree with Andy. The city's ghosts did seem rather faint of heart.

⟆

Over the next few weeks, Andy rode on dozens of junks, crossing the Bay of Xiamen like a water dervish. He became fascinated and his attitude began to change. Often he brought back stories. One boatman had said Andy's family and his may have been related a thousand years ago. Another boatman performed an elaborate tea ceremony for him, and told him things like "Advanced science equals wealth, wealth equals advanced science." Andy scribbled such maxims in a small notebook. Later he repeated them to me.

Often Andy rode with the same skipper. Old Ye plied the route to Haicang, site of a new deep-water port. "I've spent my whole life on boats," he told Andy, although on another occasion he told Andy he had been a farmer until the government requisitioned his land. Old Ye wasn't quite sure where or what he wanted to be. He dyed his gray hair black and liked to complain that the ferry business was no good anymore. Passengers were switching to the new Haicang Bridge that connected Xiamen to the mainland. "I've only been up there once," he said, pointing at the cars passing overhead. "I hate that bridge."

Andy sometimes rode the ferries instead of attending classes at Xiamen University, asking the boatmen questions about Lai, but nobody he talked to knew him personally. They knew Lai's name, Andy said, but little more. "Or they don't want to tell me." Andy was frustrated. For weeks, the only useful information he found was the name of a film studio owned by Lai. "It's on the mainland," Andy said. "The entrance is near an industrial park a few miles from the coast."

While Andy rode more ferries, Kim looked for and found the studio's address. We went off the next day, crossing the bridge in a taxi, then passed green hills studded with canneries and brick makers. For half an hour we saw a different Xiamen. Streets were deserted here. Sheep clambered along. When we reached the studio, the front gate was wide open. In the middle of the squat red gate hung a portrait of Chairman Mao. I recognized the wan smile. The white stone bridge in front of it I recognized too. We were looking at an exact replica of the Tiananmen Gate in Beijing, from the top of which Mao had proclaimed the People's Republic in 1949. A red banner declared, "Strengthening Socialist spiritual civilization is the great strategic goal!"

We walked through an opening under the Mao portrait and emerged in a large inner courtyard, a replica of the Forbidden City. "This is unbelievable," Kim said. "Who does Lai think he is, the emperor?"

Courtyard after courtyard was decked out in imperial regalia. Costumes were stacked on sound stages for the filming of period dramas. Feuding concubines mingled with scheming eunuchs and kung fu fighters. On television, such dramas outshine contemporary fare. The more China modernizes, the more ravenous its appetite for the past becomes. "You're history" could never be an insult here. Interest in old ways of life might be crude — the very sophistication admired in Old China is glaringly absent from the filmed reproductions. Nonetheless they are watched with real passion, and supported by the government. The period dramas are regarded as politically useful. They stir nationalist fervor and crowd out opposition voices. They also deflect attention away from more recent history. The Cultural Revolution is still a taboo, and accounts of the Long March are heavily censored. Few Chinese know Mao had not marched with his followers across the country in 1934–35 but was carried in a litter like a feudal landlord. The government wants to keep it that way. History is coming back, but in restricted form.

At the far end of the Forbidden City we found the studio manager's office. "Sorry, you can't come back here," said a man in a suit and a peachy shirt. "This is for production teams only."

I was about to turn around when Kim replied, "We are a production team."

"Which production?"

Kim said, "We have come here to arrange a new production."

"From which company? Who is the director?"

"Why, that's a lot of questions. Are you in charge here?"

The man said he was the assistant to the *laoban*, the boss.

"Well, then get us your *laoban*."

Another man arrived. He was out of breath and his shirt was too tight, like dumpling skin tossed in boiling water.

"Before spending a lot of money here," Kim told him, "we need to see the facilities."

"Very well."

"And you are really the boss here?"

"Yes, I am."

"Mr Lai's not around, is he?"

"Ehhm, no."

We started walking. "But he has been here?"

"Yes, he has."

"Regularly?"

He pointed to our left. "There is a small Ming Dynasty courtyard where he kept a room to rest in. He used to stay quite often, sometimes overnight. But now he is no longer here."

Could he show us the room? No. He said the Forbidden City had only just been built and the room was still not quite finished. The studio's total cost had been twenty million dollars and it would one day be part of a large entertainment park. Lai had plans for hotels, fairground rides, and a conference center twice as big again.

We climbed up stone stairs to a lacquered pavilion and found ourselves by a gold bedecked throne next to a beer company umbrella. "This is still here from when the studio was opened. We had a big party."

"I am guessing it was Mr. Lai who sat on the throne?" Kim said and laughed. Our guide did not.

⌇

In the weeks that followed, Kim introduced me to a local journalist who had worked in Xiamen her entire career. I asked her whom in the city I should interview about Lai. She suggested an elderly man by the name of Huang Zhongxian. He had gone to Indonesia when he was fifteen in the 1940s. A few years ago, now a retired banker, he had come back. There were plenty of people like him in Xiamen, the journalist said — wealthy Chinese who finally thought it safe to return. They were known as *hai gui*, or sea turtles who brought home their nest eggs. They also brought with them a greater openness. Huang Zhongxian would be happy to discuss anything. "He thinks like a foreigner now," the journalist said.

On a day arranged by her I rode up to the thirty-second floor of a new office tower, a *motianlou* — a building that scratches the sky. I was shown to a large room by an assistant. On a wooden desk I found dozens of different business cards with Huang Zhongxian's name. While waiting for him, I flicked through the stack. Chinese, Japanese, Dutch, English, French, and

Indonesian. Banking, insurance, industry, hotels. An extraordinary memoir of sorts, a lifetime of identity markers. The oldest cards were printed in black and white, the newest thickly embossed in three or four colors.

When Huang Zhongxian came in, he walked straight toward me and said, "How do you like my tower? I built it with my own money." He was barely half my height but walked fast. His hands were large-boned and calloused. Huang Zhongxian had gone into the construction business upon return to China and was his own best customer.

"It's a *da mianzi dasha,* a Big Face Building," he said, referring to the tower we were in.

"What kind of building?" I asked.

"A building that gives the owner a lot of face."

It was taller than the ones surrounding it, he explained. In the mid-1990s Xiamen had scrapped regulations on maximum building heights. Soon a race was on to build the biggest, tallest, most impressive tower. Many a sea turtle joined in. He walked me across the room to a window and pointed out skyscrapers owned by Lucio Tan, the richest Filipino-Chinese, and Chris Wong, the scion of a wealthy clan from Taiwan. "Big Face Buildings," he said.

"What about Lai Changxing?"

"He wanted to build one too. But look what happened." Huang Zhongxian walked me to a window on the other side of the room. Far below gaped a waterlogged hole much bigger than the one next to my apartment.

"That was going to be Lai's," he said. "Lai wanted to build a tower with eighty-eight floors, higher than any in China." Huang Zhongxian said he had watched the groundbreaking ceremony from up here. It was attended by more than two thousand guests. Every one of them was apparently given a *hong bao* (red envelope) containing 3,000 yuan ($375). But after the hole was dug everything stopped. "Lai had near-limitless access to capital. But one day the money just stopped coming in."

Huang Zhongxian, who worked for decades as a banker, would know. He said the proceeds and outlays for Lai's ventures all flowed through China's age-old underground banking system called *fei qian,* or flying money. Since the state strictly controlled banks and offered little interest on deposits, the wealthy had long sought alternatives. Syndicates, or what used to be called secret societies in imperial China, funneled money to borrowers. When Lai had spare cash, he lent it as *fei qian*. It allowed borrowers to get loans that banks would never approve. And when Lai needed money, the borrowers repaid the favor. That was how he had planned to finance the tallest building in the country. "But then he disappeared suddenly."

Had Huang Zhongxian ever met Lai? "No. I knew it would be a mistake," he said and fetched a half-empty bottle of wine from a cabinet. He invited me to lunch at a seafood restaurant at the bottom of his building. There he poured each of us a glass from the bottle. "You should marry a Chinese woman," he said. "They are hardworking and don't spend so much of your money." I promised I would. At the end of lunch, he recorked the bottle and carried it back up to the thirty-second floor, not having ordered any drinks in the restaurant.

Following lunch, I went to see Lai's hole in the ground. It was big enough to fit a sports arena. It was also deserted, except for a couple of ripped red banners ("Earnestly struggle to accelerate development" and "Bring forth new ideas"). I walked along a fence and reached another building site, this one still in operation. I wanted to talk to the workers but could think of no good reason for interrupting them. Then I saw a roadside restaurant. Tables stood around a tank with live fish. I walked back to the building site and asked the first two workers by the entrance if I could buy them lunch. It was perhaps the strangest thing anyone had ever asked them. I hadn't thought of that. Briefly, I imagined roles being reversed. But too late.

Coaxed by me, they chose a fish. It was served with onions and they devoured it. I told the men I had already eaten lunch, which must have confused them further. First a foreigner invites them to possibly the most expensive meal of their life, and then he refuses to join in. But my not eating gave me time to think and talk.

"Where are you from?" I said. In developed countries, people ask, "What do you do?" Occupation is a shorthand to identity. Not so in China. Geography is key. The hinterland lags the coast and cities outpace the countryside. It is a merciless but usually accurate calculation.

Mr. Wu and Mr. Yao, both in their thirties and dressed in loose-cut, sweat-stained coveralls, told me they were from farms in Jiangxi province south of the Yangtze delta, a tobacco-growing region. On China's social scale, that meant bottom rung.

I asked if they knew the name Lai Changxing. Of course they did. "One day I want to be rich like Lai."

"Yes, we all say that. Rich like Lai."

"It's everywhere in Xiamen."

"Rich like Lai."

"If you worked on a construction site you'd understand."

The men showed me scars sustained in work accidents. They recounted how colleagues regularly fell to their deaths, some entombed in freshly poured concrete. Others died in clashes over withheld wages or stolen tools. All year, they said they ate filthy rice and worked in shifts around the clock, sleeping in shacks made from stolen building materials. When Mr. Wu's wife came to visit once a month, Mr. Yao spied on them through a hole in the plywood partitioning, he said without embarrassment. "I have no wife of my own."

In this world of have-nots, Lai was a hero. Bosses like him were responsible for the terrible working conditions. Yet his wealth was so fantastic that feelings of resentment were seemingly overlooked.

"Rich like Lai," we toasted.

"Rich like Lai."

"Rich like Lai."

৩

My apartment was a short taxi ride from the construction site. When I arrived there I found Kim asleep on the polyester sofa. She was curled up with an arm cradling her shaven skull. Andy was in the apartment too. He had taken over the dining table. Handwritten homework sheets covered the glass and plywood surface. I left my research assistants undisturbed and went to the balcony where we kept two plastic chairs. Accompanied by honking horns from junks at the wharf below, I stretched out and began to read.

When I moved into the apartment I had limited myself to a single paperback. Literature could wait for Beijing, where the winters were long, I told myself. One book, however, I wanted here with me, *The Gilded Age* by Mark Twain. On the back cover of my Penguin edition, it was described as "a revealing portrait of an age of corruption, of national optimism, and of crooked land speculators, ruthless bankers and dishonest politicians." The original had been published in 1873 at the start of America's rapid industrialization between the Civil War and the Great War. Along came the railways and the meat markets and the steel-frame towers. Twain's book soon lent its name to an era. Reading it, I would sometimes think of Lai as a character from *The Gilded Age*. He'd fit right in, as would a whole lot of characters from the streets of Xiamen. They shared a cage-rattling hunger and the means to satisfy it. They would understand instantly what Twain meant by "going into something." In an early passage set in New York, he wrote:

> If there be any place and time in the world where and when it seems easy to "go into something" it is in Broadway on a spring morning, when one is walking city-ward, and has before him the long lines of palace-shops with an occasional spire seen through the soft haze that lies over the lower town, and hears the roar and hum of its multitudinous traffic.
>
> To the young American, here or elsewhere, the paths to fortune are innumerable and all open; there is invitation in the air and success in all his wide horizon. He is embarrassed which to choose, and is not unlikely to waste years in dallying with his chances, before giving himself to the serious tug and strain of a single object. He has no traditions to bind him or guide him, and his impulse is to break away from the occupation his father has followed, and make a new way for himself.

It was tempting — but treacherous — to draw analogies more generally between Gilded Age America and boomtown China. Both saw an influx of migrants that fueled an economic transformation. Unceasing streams of cheap labor from Sicily and Sichuan filled manufacturing plants. In the space of a few decades, both societies turned from preindustrial nations into dominant global traders.

Interestingly, both transformations began with violent social cataclysms, the Civil War and the Cultural Revolution. Both were also aided by revolutions in ground transportation — the railways in America and container shipping in China. And both saw massive inflows of foreign capital. Today's rush on Wall Street to invest in China would be familiar to speculators in the City of London a hundred years ago raising funds for dubious American railway ventures.

And yet there were obvious limits to what comparisons might be drawn. The America of the nineteenth century was a democracy. Free expression was guaranteed. Private property was an inalienable right (at least to white males). Not so in modern China. What select liberties its citizens have can be revoked at a moment's notice. There are no secure legal foundations, and the economy, though no longer directed by the state, is only in a superficial sense free.

Private choices reflect this. Many Chinese are seeking what Twain called "making a new way," to reinvent oneself like European arrivals had done in the New World. Yet a complete break with the past is a risky and unsettling thing. Chinese have only just been given back part of their past, and the government is offering no firm guidance as to what new selves will be tolerated.

৵

I was woken up the next morning not by the horns of the junks outside but by the sound of my neighbors decorating next door. I heard crates of tiles being moved into their bathroom. Every few minutes a new stack would be set down with a crash. After an hour of lying in bed sleeplessly I switched on my computer. Little by little at first, then with increasing frenzy, I searched the Internet for news of Lai's whereabouts. This was a weekly task. Today I was presented with 1,376 reports on his exact location and what precisely he had been doing since his disappearance. Rattling through an ocean of websites, my search dredged up news stories, private postings, and bulletin board messages. Lai was hiding out with associates in the Philippines. Lai had slipped across the border to Burma. Lai had had plastic surgery to change his appearance. Lai was in secret detention in Hebei province. Lai was staying with his wife's brother in the United States. These reports could not all be true. Perhaps none of them was. With truths hard to come by, myths ruled. Some myths may have been informed by truths, but more often the improbable crowded out splinters of truth.

Still, the Chinese Internet had a distinguishing characteristic that could be a blessing in grim disguise. Censorship. All websites are monitored to some degree, the most popular ones intensely so. Specially trained police block or delete sensitive information. The trick is to see what information is allowed to stay up and for how long. False statements are less likely to arouse the ire of censors than true ones. Lies stay, at least for a while. Truths are deleted sooner.

Generally, the authorities try to discourage people from posting any kind of sensitive information regardless of veracity. The Chinese version of Yahoo! warns users against providing content that "divulges state secrets, subverts the government, or undermines national unity." Nevertheless, in the lifestyle and sports sections unwelcome news can be hidden. The same is true for the online chat rooms affiliated with universities. The more obscure the subject, the more likely it is political. "Foreign country ideas" might hint at subversive content, while postings with "freedom" or "democracy" in the subject line elicit a standard error message: "You must enter a subject for your posting. The subject must not contain prohibited language, such as profanity. Please type a different subject."

In the search for Lai, among the most useful sites I found were www.muzi.com and www.fubai.spedia.net. The latter called itself an online guardian against corruption and carried colorful accounts of criminal cases involving government officials. Among the users were aggrieved victims, rumormongers, and enterprising citizen reporters. They sent in material that would never have made it into state media. They did so regardless of a warning from the host. "Please do not post any reactionary statements," he wrote. "This is a big issue for the site's development and survival. We plead with you."

I tried going to bed again at seven. But I could still hear the neighbors. They were no longer moving tiles. Now they were drilling. With no more sleep to be had, I went back to the computer.

Applying the censorship test to sites like this one (i.e., the longer news stays up the less likely it's true), a few things could be deducted with regards to Lai. For one, he probably hadn't been caught yet. Reports about his secret imprisonment, if true, would undoubtedly be deemed sensitive and quickly deleted. Suggestions that he had changed his appearance also sounded unconvincing. There was too much information — descriptions of his new face were placed next to adverts for plastic surgery clinics. If true, the doctors would have been arrested and their names taken off the Internet. Hence Lai was still on the run. But where? Where?

In recent weeks, the government had begun posting its own reports on Lai's trading schemes on the Internet. Lai had apparently bought goods on the international market — cigarettes destined for the Philippines, cars for Korea, oil for Japan — and then sent them to Xiamen for storage. While they awaited onward transport, parts of the shipments were removed. Containers and tankers eventually steamed out of port half empty. Lai paid no customs duty on what stayed behind. Instead he made private payments to customs officers to look the other way. The going rate was between 30 to 40 percent — expensive, but still cheaper than government tariffs.

One report said Lai notified associates in the customs office before his shipments arrived. They, in turn, told him how to bring the goods ashore without inspection. One day, Lai called them to say he had a problem. A shipment was declared as raw materials. But it was actually cars. And the cars were visible on the deck. The ship would sail past the main customs building the next morning. Lai knew the customs officers would be holding a meeting in their offices at the time. Maybe they should move the meeting to another location to avoid seeing the cars, he said. They did.

The government's reports never flattered Lai. They called him "China's most wanted fugitive" and admonished readers to "strike hard at piracy." But they did accord him a certain respect. They made his manipulations seem effortless. Lai was good at hiding things, they suggested. Such attribution of talent was convenient. It excused the government's failure to find him. Lai had disappeared more than a year ago, and none of the reported sightings of him were credible. Lai appeared to have hidden himself away like just another shipping container.

How could he do that? It was easy enough to adopt a new identity in China. Many people did. But it created a new set of problems. Where reinvention was the norm, trust in identity documents waned. Just obtaining a new piece of paper would not be enough. And yet for the authorities perhaps it was. I thought of the officials at Fangmin's seafood dinner who had taken me for an American diplomat. A business card had been enough. Even though identities had little permanence, officials clung to them. Bureaucratic tradition ran deeper than common sense. Lai must have known that.

⌇

On the invitation of an American professor, I went to speak to students at Xiamen University. The professor had suggested that I discuss journalism. It seemed an unusual choice. The students were mostly graduates from the business school. But they listened attentively as I talked about the importance of integrity. It was common for companies in China, I said, to pay for attendance at press conferences. Along with a press release, reporters were handed an envelope containing usually about fifty dollars. Grandly I insisted this undermined society itself. Journalists should be paid by their editors and nobody else. At the end of my little lecture, the students put down their pens and applauded. Bill Brown, the American professor, gave a short thank-you speech. Then he handed me an envelope containing about fifty dollars.

After the students had left, the professor invited me to his home. We sat on his breezy balcony overlooking a sunless Strait of Taiwan, gilded with fog beams. Bill Brown knew the view from both sides. He had been an American intelligence officer posted to Taiwan in the 1970s. A decade later, after a stint back in the United States, he came to China as a private citizen. He took a twenty-five-thousand-mile road trip with his wife and two children, he told me. Coming to Xiamen, they settled down. In addition to teaching, Bill Brown wrote English-language guidebooks. In one, he claimed it was the high price of Chinese food in America that had brought him here. In another, describing his childhood, he wrote, "I knew nothing about Chinese people, except that most were either cooks called Hop Sing or laundry men chanting *no tickee, no laundree.*"

Bill Brown had a fleshy mustache and spoke enviable Mandarin. It was his English that made him stand out. He called friendly locals "saucy rascals" and cultivated a peculiar sense of humor. "The history of this region extends well back beyond the dawn of Chinese civilization five thousand twelve years ago." Huh? "I was told China has five thousand years of history and that was twelve years ago."

Bill Brown may have seemed a dupe, but he was better informed than most diplomats surveilling China from behind embassy walls. He understood intimately how Xiamen worked. The city's wealth and extravagance, he said, could be traced back to a single bureaucratic decision. In 1979, the central government chose a few coastal cities including Xiamen as experimental hothouses for economic reforms, later to be repeated elsewhere. The local authorities were given unprecedented liberties to try out market capitalism. In these "special economic zones," the rules Chairman Mao had insisted on until his death were suspended. Taxes and tariffs were lowered or scrapped, business licenses made freely available, and trade encouraged. Mao's successors wanted to see what would happen. They had their reasons for choosing Xiamen as one of the billion-dollar lab rats. If the capitalist experiment went wrong it would be easier to contain the damage here than in, say, Beijing.

"This is one of the most remote cities on the southern coast," Bill Brown said.

"And where do people like Lai Changxing fit in?"

He hesitated a moment. "Some officials felt they needed people like him."

"For the money?"

"Not just."

"What then?"

"Xiamen has been growing fast. In 1996 it built the biggest airport in the country. If you want to keep growing you need people who take risks."

"And Lai did that?"

"More than once."

"And that's it?"

"No. He also gained stature. In 1997, Xiamen's party secretary made him an honorary citizen. Not many people get an award like that. All the senior officials attend the ceremony."

"And you know that how . . . ?"

"I got my own award."

✍

Before leaving, Bill Brown told me Lai had aided the city in many unexpected ways. In 1998, for instances, he gave it a first-rate football club. He spent two million dollars to purchase a team based in Foshan near Guangzhou, then disbanded it and transferred all the players to Xiamen. They won promotion to the top national league the same year, possibly thanks to more money changing hands. No wonder Lai was liked across the island.

The next time the team played a game in Xiamen, Andy and I went along to watch. This was my first football match in China, and one of the most memorable I have seen anywhere. What actually happened on the pitch that afternoon I cannot recall in detail. But the spectacle all around us on the terraces was a revelation. The crowd showered the referee — and his mother — with more abuse than seemed linguistically feasible. Emotions flowed like I had rarely seen in China. The fans could be angry and jubilant and angry again all in a matter of seconds, switching back and forth between shouting *xiongqi* (erection) and *yangwei* (impotent). At the first hint of defeat, they deserted their team, delighting in its misfortune almost as much as in its success. Conceding a goal, their roar was as loud as when scoring one. There was real, thousandfold anger in these screams of disappointment. It was an anger not borne solely of the game. People shouted out everyday frustrations, whatever they might be. There were no rules or controls on the terraces, and people clung to that freedom.

We were seated in a flag-waving, jersey-wearing block of diehard supporters. Andy tried talking to one of them, a man with spindly arms and a manic grin, but the roar and abuse proved too loud. Andy agreed to meet him after the match at the nearby shop where he worked. Later, when we went to see him on the third floor of a mall, his shop turned out to be what Chinese called an "adult health store."

"Come in, come in," he motioned from behind a glass door, surrounded by rubber toys and lubricants.

"Are we really going in there?" Andy asked.

I said we would.

"You need something, anything?" the fan greeted us.

"What, like Viagra, or something?" said Andy and stayed close to the door.

"I have many different Viagras," he said, holding up packs of herbal products. There was *weige*, or Viagra, meaning Great Elder Brother in Mandarin, and other "male power enhancers" including something called Turtle Deer Magical Elixir.

〜

Andy's mobile phone rang. He talked for a few seconds, then hung up. "We've got to go," he said. "Old Ye found someone who knows Lai. As a favor he has asked him to come to his junk. He is there now."

When we arrived at the No. 1 Wharf, Old Ye was waiting for us in his wooden wheelhouse. There he introduced us to a man whom he called Atou, or Big Head. He was in his thirties and dressed in a suit. His face had the smooth sheen of an oilstone — it didn't glisten so much as slip past the eye with a fine-grained menace.

Together we steamed away from the dock to find a quiet fishing spot. Old Ye handed each of us a rod. Big Head said he was a boatman too, but had recently sold his junk. His shirt was clean and his dark trousers were freshly pressed. Old Ye wore a stained overall.

It seemed the two barely knew each other. They didn't talk. Instead Big Head offered us cigarettes and shook our hands. "Let's just be friends," he said. "Maybe I can buy you dinner later."

"Thanks," said Andy, "and you're really called Big Head?"

"I've had that nickname since I was young and it stuck."

"But your head's not so big or anything."

We tied up at a pontoon in shallow blue water by an oil storage tank on the mainland. Big Head reeled in a fish, then looked at the taut line on my rod. "Yours is caught under a rock," he said. "Let me help you." He took the rod and started tugging gently. "If I pull, the hook will come off," he said. He pulled and the hook came off. He looped the loose line several times around the base of a new hook and tied it off.

A nervous hush lay over our fishing outing. Old Ye and Big Head both knew we were keen to hear more about Lai and his business practices. But neither of them dared to mention his name. So in the end I did.

"Lai's a good man, right?" I said. "You've worked with him?"

"He's okay," said Big Head.

"Just okay?"

"Okay. He got us the diesel for our boats. That's good."

"How did he do that?"

"He imported diesel."

"That's before he went away?"

"Yes. Diesel. Oil. Everything. He kept prices down."

"How was he able to do that?" Big Head looked uncomfortable. "Did you know him personally?" I said.

"I did some work for him. Not much," said Big Head. Then he got up from the plastic stool he was sitting on. He wandered off to the far end of the pontoon and spoke into his mobile phone for several minutes. When he came back I tried again. "So what kind of work did you do for him?"

Reluctantly, Big Head talked about Lai's business. Tankers and freighters came into the Xiamen port, he said. They were from Hong Kong, Singapore, or Yokohama. Sometimes they docked in Haicang. Most of them carried oil but some also shipped cars or containers. Big Head said he had worked for many shipping companies. "You never know who you're dealing with. Just like right now. I don't know if you are a bad person or not. I have just met you. How can I really know?" He was agitated. "Someone says to you he wants to meet you and maybe rent your boat and you go out to somewhere offshore to do something. I only helped Lai's company like this two, maybe three times. That's all. They never said anything about who they were or what they were doing and I never asked."

A second, smaller junk pulled alongside the pontoon and Big Head got up. "I have to go," he said. "My friend is picking me up." I assumed it was the friend whom he had called on his mobile phone. So much for our dinner.

Of course there were lots of people who didn't want to discuss Lai. My friend Fangmin was one of them. He would change topic whenever I tried. But Big Head was different. As soon as I mentioned Lai, he had become uncomfortable just being around us.

Old Ye started his diesel engine for the journey home. Loudly it came to life, rattling a stack of plastic stools on the foredeck. The water running past the hull turned opaque and then to fathomless dark as we left the mainland shore and reached the shipping lanes. Xiamen slowly came into view. Glass towers shone green and blue in the sinking sun. It would be evening soon.

5

DANCING GIRLS

Room 42, the Shaoshan, Lakeside Drive, Xiamen

FOR THE DANCERS at Lili's nightclub, workdays began with a business meeting. Several hundred of them sat on sofas in the auditorium freshly made up and dressed in costumes while neon light fell from the ceiling, weighing on them like an overnight snow dump.

Looking down at them from the stage was Lili, holding a microphone. She stood erect but at ease. She expected no problems with the police, she said, her amplified voice filling the room. "Everything is okay. But stay alert and react quickly if there is a raid. You all know where to go." While she spoke, stacks of plastic flowers were positioned on the side of the auditorium, right where Andy and I had snuck in. We tried to get a drink but it was too early. Waiters in tuxedos were still preparing order forms as barmen hauled in crates of XO cognac.

"Today is Army Day," Lili said, "a day to celebrate our glorious liberation from Nationalist forces. Let us unite to complete a historical task and an unfailing struggle." Amplification gave her voice an excited rattle. She was mimicking Communist propaganda broadcasts. "Today's show will have a military theme," she said. "You have all prepared new dance routines for this show. You should know the order in which you will perform." The dancers listened silently. It was August 1, the day when official China celebrated its armed forces. Since morning, state television had been showing footage of parades and maneuvers. In keeping with the spirit of the day, the club was putting on a special Army Day variety show. The dancers were dressed in uniforms and campy marching songs had been added to their repertoire.

From the back of the dark auditorium, the club seemed a microcosm of Lai's China. Authority was uncertain. The forces of the state were simultaneously praised in kitschy songs and evaded by hiding away dancers during raids. Patriotic posturing was mixed with blatant rule-breaking. It worked because the state was happy to collude. Police officers took their bribes and so did their political masters. Bribery rather than entertainment was the club's real business. Entrepreneurs came here to host government officials. In between glasses of XO cognac they offered cash-filled envelopes and paid companionship. For the right price, one of the dancers would be available for the night. The women were for sale just like the officials. Send enough plastic flowers at ten dollars each and one turned up at the table.

⁓

Andy and I left the club and went home to change. A few hours later we came back with Kim. The sofas in the auditorium were empty now. The dancers were gone, Lili's speech-making was over, and the neon lights were turned off. This was the club's witching hour — guests were about to arrive. "Your dancers are waiting for you," Lili said and led us through a warren of corridors and up a stairwell. We passed several dozen private rooms that could be rented by the evening. Some of the club's guests preferred to be sheltered from the bustle of the auditorium. Others wanted to mix with the dancers who lingered here between stage appearances.

"There they are," Lili said. "A bit nervous." She opened a door to a small room lit by a low-hanging chandelier. Five young women sat on sofas lining the tatty stuccoed walls. They looked up at us. Five pairs of wide eyes under sparkly blue caps that matched their dresses. The women were a team. They danced together and lived together. Whenever we came to the club Lili would arrange for us to sit with them. We would buy them rounds of drinks and talk about life outside and where it might lead. After the show we sometimes bought them snacks. It was a friendship of sorts. They called us *dage*, big brother, or *dajie*, big sister. We called them *meimei*, younger sister. Other guests called them *xiaojie*, little older sister, a term interchangeably used for waitresses and prostitutes. Lili called them *xiaomei*, little younger sister.

On our most recent visit the women had invited us to see the Army Day show. It was a big test for them, they said. All five were recent arrivals at the club and this was their first themed show. They were expected to earn several flower rings each.

Kim took a seat and said to the dancer next to her, "Will you be in the military show too?"

"Yes."

"Then how come you're not wearing a uniform?"

"Our part in the show is at the end. We'll change later."

"You won't have to kill anyone for a while then," Kim laughed. The dancer did not.

I sat down in between two of her teammates.

"We thought you might not turn up tonight," said Dilinor.

"I didn't think that," said Maria.

The girls — they were both seventeen — sat on the edge of the sofa, their legs tucked under the table in front, sipping red wine watered down with lemonade. They kept their hands in their laps, as they had been trained to do by Lili. But every so often an impetuous arm would rise into the air.

"You'll soon be drunk if you don't add more lemonade," said Maria.

"That's my problem," said Dilinor.

"If you're drunk we can't do the show."

"If you don't add more red wine to your lemonade you'll annoy me to death."

Dilinor's hair was red and her lips plump. Maria's arms were covered in dark fuzz and her long eyelashes real. Neither looked Chinese. They came from the far west of the country. Their home province of Xinjiang bordered Pakistan and Afghanistan, a six-hour airplane ride from Xiamen. They were members of a Muslim minority and their appearance was almost Persian.

Maria had chosen her name when she came to Xiamen. Though not a Muslim name, it fit her. She was capable of deft motherly care. During meals she ladled food onto others' plates while eating very little herself. She weighed less than most twelve-year-olds but was by no means fragile. In one of our early conversations, Maria recounted leaving home a few months earlier. She and the other four rode a train for almost a hundred hours sharing a single cot in a "hard sleeper" compartment. By turns, two of them would nap sitting up. The others would stand in the crowded aisle.

Maria described the journey to Xiamen without complaint. She seemed to be made of steel-reinforced porcelain. She never slept later than nine, she said, even when she had gone to bed at four or five. For breakfast she drank a cup of herbal cold medicine to prevent sickness. Then she read a chapter in a business book, which she kept in a locked trunk. In the afternoons, she made telephone calls to club regulars to encourage them to turn up in the evening, and soon she would be starting afternoon English lessons. "It is important to learn skills," she said. One day she expected to run her own business, perhaps a clothes shop or a hair salon.

In my notes I referred to Maria as Miss Ambition. While hardly imaginative, the name captured what I found most remarkable about her. Similarly, Dilinor was Miss Adventure. She was broad-shouldered and fond of talking up the small triumphs she accomplished in Xiamen. There was her first meal at McDonald's, and drinking alcohol, and seeing an African with pitch black skin. Receiving five flower rings during a stage show, her record so far, came lower down on the list of triumphs. At the very top was seeing the ocean for the first time. Her home on the edge of the Gobi Desert was further from the sea than any other spot on earth. Before she came here, the only beaches and ships she had seen were on television.

Dilinor's most cherished possession was a laminated photograph she carried in her wallet. It showed three of the five dancers sitting in a studio in their hometown. None of them wore makeup then and their arms were locked boyishly around one another's shoulders, not placed in their laps. Having been passed around again and again, the photograph was dog-eared like a favorite book.

Every evening, the five Muslim dancers performed on the club stage. Their short blue dresses with matching caps were part of an Arabian Night segment in the club's regular show. They weren't, to be sure, one of the highlights. The five had only very recently learned to belly-dance. Hired for their supposed exoticism, they had yet to win favor with guests. Their earnings were minimal.

"Everyone is getting more flower rings than us," Dilinor said.

"Don't fuss," said Maria. "You'll be a concubine soon enough."

The women sometimes called their more successful colleagues *qingfu*, concubines. They said so coyly yet with a certain coquettishness. The more successful dancers all had regular admirers who sent them flowers. After the show they would go off to a hotel together. Maria and Dilinor shied away from calling their colleagues prostitutes. Prostitution was illegal, but concubinage was familiar from historical dramas. All day long, television channels showed imperial courts filled with concubines dressed in colorful costumes.

To the dancers the concubine label was more than a euphemism. It legitimized and shielded them. They were merely borrowing an identity from the past, so they seemed to be saying to one another. Of course they knew that traditional concubinage worked differently. A hundred years ago, a concubine would have been procured in a teahouse, a forerunner of today's nightclubs. But there parallels ended. A traditional concubine became a permanent part of a man's household in full view of his wife. She was not snuck off to a hotel for a few hours.

∽

In addition to quasi concubinage, the club offered two forms of diversion. One was the stage show. The other was *ka la OK*, karaoke, done in private rooms. Every one of the rooms was equipped with a television, a microphone, and a computer loaded with thousands of prerecorded tracks. Many guests spent their evenings singing along to them.

"Karaoke was Lai's favorite," Lili said.

"Why?"

"It was private. In a room like this he was safe."

"But why sing?"

Lili thought for a moment, then she said Lai had been a farmer. "Maybe he still felt like a farmer even when he was rich. Many people are like that. They stay farmers no matter what clothes they wear." She leaned back in her seat and adjusted her gray suit. "Maybe he didn't like being a farmer. When you sing, you are not a farmer. You are someone else."

A large television screen towered over our heads like an exam monitor. It showed music videos with superimposed song lyrics. The videos were not the sort broadcast on state television. They had been filmed especially for the club — soft-focus footage of galloping horses and classic car races and roller-coaster rides. And always casinos. There were endless shots of blackjack tables and slot machines. The wide-eyed camera panned across western gamblers in evening gowns and linen suits, and back across. All the while, song lyrics scrolled along the bottom of the screen, the clumsy shorthand to new identities.

Dilinor picked up a microphone. "Everyone, how are you?" Electronic reverb turned her mutter into a buoyant stage greeting. The other dancers cheered. "Start my song then," Dilinor said. "This one is for my rich husband." The dancers giggled. Then lyrics appeared on the screen. *Ai bu ai ni*

. . . Do I love you or not . . . Dilinor held the microphone with her right hand and balled up her left against her chest. Her head rolled back, as if giving herself up to a stadium-sized audience. Meanwhile pictures of motorcycles and the Statue of Liberty flickered across the screen. When the song ended, Dilinor said, "I feel like I've lived through a plane crash." The microphone was passed around the room and the others took turns. Each of their songs had its own coded video message from an alien civilization. There were lovelorn young women walking along Dutch canals, free-spending shoppers in Paris, the lights on Broadway.

Then Maria said to me, "It's your turn." This was the moment I had dreaded. On a previous night she had told me my voice sounded "like you haven't eaten in four days." But that appeared to be no reason to stop calling on me. She said there were hundreds of English songs on the database. I felt like a penny being shaken out of a piggy bank.

Whenever I was pressed to sing, my default choice was "Sailing" by Rod Stewart. Not because it was easy — uh, the crescendo on "Can you hear me . . ." — but I found consolation in the fact that the accompanying video was even worse than my singing. I went over to the computer to key in the five-digit number code for "Sailing."

The screen filled with panoramic views of the snow-covered Alps.

Mount Blanc comes into focus.

Zoom in on a mountain village with pleasant gabled roofs.

A cow trots into the foreground, grazing on a sloping meadow.

Cuckoo clocks, Swiss chocolate, smiling skiers. I am skiing, I am skiing . . .

Next, the computer played Simon and Garfunkel's "Bridge Over Trouble Water" while the screen showed smiling pine-sprung families in modern apartment blocks caught in careless abandon.

Around eleven the dancers filed out of the room. They said it was time to change into their uniforms for the show. None of them seemed keen. I wondered what gruesome goose step they had been taught, but it was too late to ask. They were gone. Except for muffled sounds coming from the auditorium, it was quiet. Kim and Andy had joined Lili downstairs a while ago, and all the waiters were busy.

I sat back in my sofa seat and watched karaoke videos with the sound turned down, feeling like I was spying on a nation's private fantasies. I thought about how far the five dancers were from home. In my head I calculated the distance they must have traveled from the central Asian border to Xiamen. It took five, maybe six hours to fly from here to their home, the same distance as across the North Atlantic. The five women had traveled as far as nineteenth-century European migrants who boarded ships in Bremerhaven on the German coast to head for Ellis Island in New York — all just to go from a dusty Chinese forecourt to a crowded balcony. And unlike early migrants in the United States who found wide-open prairies, they arrived in boomtowns that were far from fenceless and abundant. Xiamen was filling up. Those who failed here had to go back home. There was no room to idle, no second chance. The migrants' vulnerability is reflected in the names more established city folk give them (many of them once migrants themselves). They call the new arrivals *tubie* (beetles), *xinlimei* (turnips), *youhulou* (field crickets), as well as *amulin* (wood-headed people), *lao maor* (Old Closed Eyes), *erduo genzi ruan* (soft ears, i.e., pushovers), *yashimin* (inferior market people), and *waigua liezao* (crooked melons and split-open dates, meaning people who are earnest but unattractive).

≈

When the band began to play *tam-ta-tam* marching songs and the start of the military gala seemed imminent, Kim, Andy, and Lili returned to the room. Lili picked up a remote control and set the television to a channel showing a closed-circuit feed from the stage. A heavy curtain went up. Dim klieg beams flickered into life. The stage — wide enough to accommodate a battalion — slowly became visible like a photograph in a developing tray. We saw banners and ammunition belts, then mockups of armored personnel carriers. Camouflage netting had been draped over loudspeakers. An announcer mouthed patriotic slogans ("People, you must be vigilant"), then battle commenced. A group of ten dancers performed with plastic hand grenades and rocket tubes, followed by a group in pleated skirts and white navy uniforms with tin medals pinned to their chests, followed by a succession of dancers gamely saluting and sword-wielding.

They all performed to revolutionary songs from the Mao era played by the band. One could read this as either patriotism or parody, or both. The Communist revolution was still an important touchstone, and yet it could also be exploited in the search for profit. Waiters were sprinting onto the stage delivering plastic garlands, while the band played "Even My Parents

Aren't as Dear as the Party and Chairman Mao" and "Red Flowers Are Blooming Everywhere."

In the languid fatigue of late evening I imagined for a moment a future war where men in bulletproof tuxedos raced across the battlefield to drape flowers over combatants.

The five Muslim dancers were among the last to appear in the show. They wore red tasseled dress uniforms with pink bobbles in place of epaulettes. In their hands they held batons. Lili sat up in her seat. She was about to find out the troupe's value to the club. She said anything fewer than ten flower rings would be a disappointment. The band struck up a marching song and the batons rose above clouds of dry ice. Arms and legs swirled. Pairs of feet struggled to keep up.

A few minutes later and the dancers still hadn't garnered any flowers. Once again they were also-rans. They would finish long after the applause had died down.

"I knew it," Kim said and shook her head.

"It must be because they wear ugly uniforms, don't you think?" Andy said.

Kim didn't reply.

"Couldn't we send flowers from here?" Andy said at last.

"There might be a way," Lili said, and she picked up a house phone in the corner of the room. Kim nodded. We agreed to send the dancers two garlands each. We also agreed not to tell them who had sent them. We grinned at each other in a moment of uneasy complicity. We wanted success to feel real to them even if we had conned them. Then we wondered if it might have been they who had conned us.

〰

A few weeks after the Army Day show I came across a publication run by the foreign affairs office of the Fujian provincial government. It was the size of letter paper and comprised only a few pages. Each of its stories reported on an event involving the foreign affairs office: a visit by an African agricultural delegation or the signing of a scholarship agreement with an American university. Among the stories was also one that mentioned me. It said that the "correspondent for *The Times of London*" had "slandered Fujian province." It went on to mention allegations of corruption and deception that may or may not have taken place in the area around Xiamen. Lai was not mentioned by name. But some of the material sounded familiar.

A month later, the same story on "slandering Fujian province" was re-printed by the *People's Daily* newspaper, the official organ of the Communist Party. It appeared on the back page, prominently displayed above a picture from a propaganda event at the Beijing Children's Hospital.

Few outsiders appeared in the *People's Daily*. Or if they did, it was rarely in a positive light. I felt I needed advice. I called Mark O'Neill, a veteran reporter. After poring over the calligraphic jumble while we were on the phone, he said: "You have to understand how Chinese will interpret this. If the *People's Daily* says you are wrong to suggest in your articles that there is corruption in Fujian province, then many will assume that Fujian is totally corrupt. Chinese have learned to believe the opposite of whatever is in the official media." I could hear Mark fold the paper. "During a trip to South Africa sometime in the eighties I happened to meet a jolly man from Poland," he said, slipping into a Polish accent. "At the time, few Poles able to travel abroad, so I asked what he doing so far south of equator. He said he had been sailor and one day when ship on high seas entire crew decide to defect. But why choose South Africa? Well, he said, we have read in Polish press that Apartheid regime human hell on earth — random detentions, torture, death squads. That's all we need to know. We convinced South Africa is paradise." Mark laughed and said, "In China, you will find the press is read in much the same way."

A few days later, I called Tim Collard, a senior UK diplomat who made a living out of decoding messages from the Chinese government. He was a connoisseur of propaganda of any imprimatur. When we first met he had been holding a brochure sent over from London titled "British diplomacy in action." Tim said, "Some of us think the last two words should be written together." As for the *People's Daily* article, he thought it was a clever piece of Chinese media manipulation. "It is certainly an attack on you," he said. "But it's also an attack on Fujian and its problems with corruption. The *People's Daily* doesn't rebut and hence repeat many allegations made in the foreign media. When it does it indirectly slaps down those whom you attacked. It's a warning, if you like, that Beijing is keeping an eye on corrupt businessmen and officials."

The article fueled my interest in Lai and Xiamen. But it also made me wary. Like most foreign journalists in China I lived in perpetual fear of causing contacts grief. The paranoia was probably overdone, but who wanted to take chances?

I worried that Lili had put herself in danger by telling me about her club. I had noted down details of her involvement in bribery. To protect her and her dancers, I decided to refer to the club in writing as Shaoshan — after Chairman Mao's sleepy hometown, which still occupied a sacred place in Communist Party mythology. "Shaoshan is one of the most raucous and rambunctious places I have visited." I would grin when I wrote down sentences like that, imagining a baffled or perhaps livid reader in a police uniform. Paranoia had its own subversive rewards.

☙

When I went to the Shaoshan it was usually in Kim's company. Andy might trot along too, but it was Kim who really took to the place. And it to her.

One evening not long after the Army Day show, Kim was sitting on a sofa in a private room flanked by several dancers. She was wearing frayed leather trousers and a collarless shirt. Her head was freshly shaven and her ankle-high studded boots rested among wineglasses on the table in front of her.

"How old are you?" one of the dancers asked her.

"Thirty."

"And you're not married?"

"Too much trouble."

"What about a boyfriend?"

"I have had many lovers but I'm still a virgin," she teased them.

"You were never a concubine?"

"No."

"So what kind of boys do you like?"

"Quiet ones. Who don't talk too much."

"No such boys exists . . . only girls can be quiet."

A waiter came into the room to deliver drinks. Kim's legs, propped up on the table, were blocking his path. "Excuse me, little brother," he said trying to pass her. The women laughed.

They wanted to know if Kim had a job. "No," she said, "I prefer traveling."

"But how to afford it?"

"You have to find someone to pay for you. A rich friend or a university or a journalist. Tonight, Oliver is paying."

They nodded. "And where have you traveled?"

She said she had been to Tibet where she hiked around a glacial lake.

The area was off-limits to tourists and she was detained by police who suspected her of being a Japanese spy. But she charmed the police chief, she said, who was bored and lonely, and for the next week he showed her around the region as his personal guest. He also introduced her to lamas at nearby monasteries. They were "very cute," she said.

Sitting next to Kim, Lili said, "You can always make something even bigger out of everything." It was a compliment. Kim was younger than she, and unemployed. Yet Kim was the only woman here free to shave her head, curse as she pleased, and travel far from home for mere pleasure.

6

THREE HANDS

Hole 1, Dong Fang Golf Course,
Haicang Main Road, Xiamen

IF LILI EVER had a regional accent it was gone now. Her Mandarin placed her nowhere. It was effortless and flowed in an even stream. Throaty rasps were swallowed, sharp-toothed hisses smoothed out. She might stumble on a foreign name, but it wouldn't detain her. Conversations with her were like that too. Every so often I would bring up Lai. I'd ask what she was hearing about him. Sitting between dancers, she would talk, her bearing one of amity and frankness though she never claimed to be telling me all she knew. She would pass on tidbits like a dealer with a deck that may or may not be marked, handing out cards that were just good enough to keep me at the table and buying drinks.

One time, a few weeks after Army Day, I said, "Did you see Lai here regularly?"

"Every few months."

"Not so often then."

"He had other ways of entertaining himself."

"Yes?"

"He liked golf. He played a lot. Sometimes he even invited a few dancers to come along and watch him." She looked at the small notebook I was using. In a roomful of dancers, it made me look bookish. "You have played?" she said.

I had. Not that it had gone well. But I would try again if it might help me understand Lai. What was the attraction of the game to him? Chinese were rushing to adopt western ways, but I could not imagine Lai on a golf course. It seemed such a contrast to, say, karaoke. I could see him adopt a new voice — but not warm to parsed lawns and tidy score-keeping.

I asked Lili if she could introduce me to a golfing partner.

"I have never played myself," she said.

I thought of Fangmin. He might be able to help. I had not forgotten the business card ruse. I would forgive him for trying to pass me off as a U.S. diplomat on one condition. He would have to take me on a golf outing.

"You are familiar with the right people," I told him when we next met. "Your business friends."

Fangmin was still trying to set up a taxi company. He was struggling. His original idea had been to use foreign luxury sedans. Customers would pay extra for the prestige, he reasoned. But car prices were rising. Fangmin said Lai had been importing cars cheaply but now that he was gone the cost of a Mercedes was double. Fangmin tried switching to domestic cabs but there were new obstacles. He needed, among other things, a different license. For a while it looked like the officials we had entertained together at the seafood restaurant could help. They had arranged his old license. Yet perhaps expecting more than a dinner this time, they lost interest when none was forthcoming.

Fangmin was in a funk. For years he had been toiling and awaiting success. When he first arrived in Xiamen, he had run a vegetable stall that belonged to a military-run company. The company's director gave Fangmin a job because they once worked together in another military company in western China. Wedged in behind piles of peppers and onions, Fangmin was expected to take orders like a soldier and was paid like one.

He had come to Xiamen to escape orders and bad pay, about that he was clear. So as soon as he could afford to he quit and set up his own vegetable stall. It was a good business, he said. Migrants from the countryside needed vegetables. Yet the military tolerated no competition, even in matters such as peppers and onions. Fangmin had to close down again. He then pursued a variety of other ideas. A supermarket on wheels. A car repair shop. A long-distance bus company offering onboard gambling. None of them worked. There was always someone more powerful ahead in the queue. And now the taxi company was heading the same way.

Fangmin had employed an old man from the countryside to assist him. Employee Number One, his nametag said. The old man had no business experience. He couldn't even drive. But he offered to work for commission on revenue with no fixed salary. Only there was no revenue yet. The man could barely afford to clothe himself. His corrugated rib cage showed through thin cotton shirts. Then one day, Fangmin said the old man left. After that he rarely mentioned the taxi venture or any other.

Not everything had changed for him, though. When we dined together, Fangmin still did all the ordering. I might be paying the bill but I could not be trusted with the menu. Fangmin ruled the table. His appetite demanded it, matching his inquisitorial manner with waiters. Fangmin wasn't about to let anyone lower down get the better of him, even if he had been denied his share of boomtown riches by higher ups. He complained to waiters when dishes arrived late or differed from specific orders. It was all the fault of corruption, he said. People at other tables probably bribed the waiters to serve them first.

Ever since I first met him Fangmin had complained about corruption. He blamed his ills and those of the Chinese nation on it. There was too much money in everything, he said. Fangmin was by no means a purist. Entertaining officials was fine, no matter how lavish the meal. But real bribery, straight up, money on the table, or under, was not. So it was all the more surprising when Fangmin said in all seriousness one evening between the duck giblets and the winter melon soup in a by now rare flight of enthusiasm for a new and characteristically quixotic business idea, "I have made up my mind. Next time I will pay the necessary money. Everything will work out."

〜

I was lying in bed when Fangmin called to arrange our golf outing.

"The moment is here," he said. "Get ready."

"It's late. Are you sure?"

"The best time is now. Dinner has been great, the crab was fantastic, the lobster . . ."

"Okay, okay. Do I need to bring anything or wear anything?"

"Everyone is wearing black. You'll recognize us."

"Who are you with?"

"We will meet you at the Dong Fang club, as soon as you can," he said and hung up.

It was almost midnight. He wanted me to come out golfing now? I dressed and caught a cab to an industrial zone on the edge of Xiamen. I knew the Dong Fang club was set in the hills above a row of cement mills. A while ago I had been there with Andy in preparation for when Fangmin came good. The manager had told Andy and me the usual membership fee was $20,000, but only charged us $20 for a tryout. Our caddy said he had seen Lai on previous occasions. I asked if Lai tipped well. Yes, he did. Very well. Later, during the game, Andy reprimanded me for asking the question. Now we would have to tip well too, he said.

All that was during the day. I barely recognized the course when my taxi driver left the sulfur-lit industrial zone and started picking his way across the dark course. We were moving through a borderless pool of ink where tree trunks reaching out of the ground resembled the desperate arms of drowning men. At the top of the hilly course, a whitewashed, spotlit clubhouse towered like a shore beacon. We stopped at the half-full parking lot. I could see a few people stumbling around, but Fangmin was not among them.

For a while I stood by the clubhouse and peered into the lush shadows. Dew had settled on parked cars, and dots of errant light were caught in lazy drops. A stream gurgled somewhere. Or was it a pump? The trees loosely scattered across the course during the day had moved closer together, forming tropical clusters and patches of dense rainforest. I could still make out the industrial zone at the bottom of the hill, though. Factories puffed away, clouds of acrid steam drifting on to the course, mixed with the heavy night air that came off the ocean. I remembered Andy pointing out the view of the sea from up here, islands and boats dotted across the open water. But the sea, though certainly there now, had lost its sheen, threaded seamlessly into the wet earth, an extension of the golf course as it stretched into the dark.

I heard a car arriving in high gear. Three young women climbed out and walked off unsteadily. Since Fangmin had still not turned up, I followed them around the boxy building. On the other side I found a scene a world away from the parking lot. Lighting poles lined the fairways, illuminating them gaily. The entire hillside was dotted with poles and hundreds of golfers busied themselves as if it were the middle of the afternoon. They crawled along the narrow corridors created by the artificial glow, separated by stretches of wet, black forest.

"We light up the holes on this side, but not on the back. Those you can only play during the day," said a steward with baggy eyes.

"And many people come?"

"More than during the day."

"All night?"

"Yes."

"But why play golf at night?"

"Protection from the sun. Farmers have dark skin and none of our members want to look like farmers."

"Don't you lose a lot of balls?"

"We do. We pick them up again when it's light."

"And people's scores don't suffer?"

"Actually, it's easier to see the white ball against a black sky than against a blue sky."

He walked off to greet newly arrived golfers who were practicing their swing with one hand while holding a drink in the other. They appeared to think they were in a nightclub. And rightly so. Music came over loudspeakers embedded at the teeoff. Skirts were short and shirts stained from dinner. Waiters hovered at every hole in an atmosphere of amiable chaos.

～

A week earlier I had asked Fangmin why Lai might have been interested in golf. "The land," he said. "Imagine the amount of land you need for a golf course. It's a plot the size of a small city." The thought seemed to awe him. And I could see why. In the boomtowns, people lived more cramped than almost anywhere. But Fangmin's fascination with green open spaces was not aesthetic. "Think of how much money there is in golf," he said. "If land is valuable, golf is like pure gold."

By golfing Lai might have hoped to be close to future riches. Golf cemented business contacts in China just like anywhere else. But the game was more than that — a symbol for change. Until 1984, golf was strictly prohibited as a bourgeois nuisance. A decade later, China already had two hundred courses. Now there were another thousand under construction, most of them along the densely populated coast.

"Golf is very profitable. The rise in the number of courses shows our economic development is very fast," Fangmin said. There was a note of pride in his voice. "You foreigners took hundreds of years to turn your golf courses into big businesses. In China, it happened in less than a decade." I could ignore a nationalistic sleight of hand. Up to a point.

"Of course, it was Chinese people who originally invented golf," he said.

"I thought golf came from Scotland."

"No, it's a Chinese game."

Fangmin was right about one thing. Golf in China was profitable. Pedigree-hungry developers hired U.S. pro golfers at great expense to design their courses. The Dong Fang club was built by Greg Norman, a nearby course bore the imprint of Jack Nicklaus, and the main club in Shenzhen, the world's largest with 180 holes, or ten courses joined together, was in part created by Nick Faldo. The pros' work in China not only enriched them, but made them the country's top landscaping artists. Only the farmers who carved vast rice terraces in the mountainous interior could claim to have more land under "design."

⁊

When Fangmin arrived there were more people with him than I had expected. Three cars pulled up, spilling an untidy stream of passengers. Three more cars were on their way, he said after spotting me across the green. With a nodding of heads I was introduced to Bao Jianying, also known as Big Bao. He was the leader of the pack. In Mandarin, Big Bao's name sounded like Doggy Bag. Fangmin said so and laughed. Doggy Bag did not. He was of the terrier rather than the poodle variety. His hair was short and his nose flat. With him were underlings who wore short-sleeved black shirts, one of whom was a relative of Fangmin. They were accompanied by a group of women. One whispered with hands cupped over her mouth; another straightened out a frilly, low-cut top and adjusted the pleats in her skirt. They were no older than twenty and seemed to shiver in the night air.

Rocking back and forth on his heels, Doggy Bag berated his underlings. "We should never have taken them with us," he said, referring to the women. "I told you, you are not being serious. They can't even play golf."

"Should we teach them?"

"You didn't understand me."

"They can just follow us around."

"There is no room. Send them away."

"But we already paid for them."

Doggy Bag stopped questioning the men. His short, bobbing hair looked like a brush silently scrubbing out a stain.

Three cars were approaching. "Old Liu is here," Fangmin said. As soon as the cars had stopped, a combined mob of almost two dozen people set off for the course. At the first tee, a steward lined up forty female caddies dressed in gray uniforms, each with a bag of clubs. He made a practiced gesture of invitation with his open hand. Then the assistants haggled over who would get which caddy. They walked right up to one or another of them, staring them in the eye. "Surely there are enough caddies for everyone," I said to Fangmin.

"Yes, but they want the best. They are trying to see which caddy is the most honest, the least tired, and which has the best eyes to find a ball in the dark."

"But why so many?"

"Everyone needs two caddies. One to carry your clubs, the other to watch your opponent and make sure he doesn't cheat."

Fangmin said Doggy Bag and Old Liu had had dinner together, an elaborate affair, the point of which was to settle a business dispute. Several months ago, they had both been promised the same piece of land by a government official. The parcel was too small to be profitably split in two, so one of them would have to give up his claim. While the assistants got drunk together, the two men talked, but all they could agree on was a love of golf. To resolve the dispute, they settled on a winner-take-all, no-hard-feelings playoff.

Old Liu — Liu Shenghan — was first at the tee. Warming up, he swung his club round and round in big loops within an inch of our heads. In the harsh light that flooded the course his face seemed a mess. What looked like scars lined his cheeks. He was too young to have wrinkles. The lines bulged red as he grinned at the first stroke. It went straight into thick bushes not far from us but beyond the reach of the lights. He smacked two more balls into the dark. On the next few holes, his form improved. He still needed at least five shots each to finish but fewer balls disappeared. And when they soared within range of the floodlights they could easily be made out against the black sky. The steward was right.

With the addition of the caddies, our party had swollen to about three dozen people littered across a narrow stretch of green: black-shirted men, gray-suited women, and girls in pleated skirts and frilly tops. To make out who played with whom was difficult. A ball might as likely hit a player as the other way round.

Standing in the middle of this, I had an overwhelming sense of dread. As another of Old Liu's balls disappeared in the dark I thought if the need arose the bushes would not be a good place to hide. I saw a rabbit sprint from a bush, no, two rabbits. Doggy Bag was firing at them too. His form seemed little better than Old Liu's. He usually needed one or two fewer strokes than his rival though. His lead grew steadily. He pulled ahead by four strokes, and after initially walking from hole to hole together with Old Liu, he now raced ahead with the rest following at a distance.

I went after him. His short legs punched out surprisingly big strides. When I caught up he barely acknowledged me. We walked side by side for a minute. Then, without looking up he said, "I am sorry about earlier."

"Earlier?"

"The girls. You know, the prostitutes."

"Oh, them."

"I don't like it."

"It happens a lot?"

"All the time."

"Why don't you tell them to stop?"

"A lot of people bring girls. It's normal."

Doggy Bag sounded surprisingly helpless. His entourage was less pliable than one might have thought. Embarrassed by our conversation, he offered to help me improve my golf game. We started by balancing clubs in our hands to find the proper grip. "Hold the club as if it were made of peeled bananas," he said. "Squeeze gently with one hand in front of the other." We walked along in silence for a while, trying not to break the bananas.

"Did you ever see Lai Changxing on the course?" I said.

"No."

"Never?"

"Never."

"He could have built his own course, right?"

"He probably could."

I watched Doggy Bag's grip. It didn't change. The peeled banana was safe.

"Have you ever thought of building a course?" I said.

He made a whizzing sound that could have been a laugh. "You need very good government friends to get enough land."

What about the parcel that had been promised to both him and Old Liu? Might that be enough? Doggy Bag was a pensive man even when engaged in friendly conversation. At the mention of the dispute, his eyes fixed a point far beyond the green. I looked down at his grip on the club. It had tightened visibly. When he spoke, his voice was hushed. The land was important, he said. Then the glint in his eyes dropped down to the ground in front of him and he swung his club at a ball. It might have been his or might have been one of the many littering the course.

When we approached the putting green, Doggy Bag sent his caddy away. The other caddy, hired to keep watch on him, also withdrew some way. He didn't want to be disturbed, Doggy Bag said. I took this as my cue to leave. From a distance, I watched him putt. He raised his arms in triumph. It was an oddly effusive gesture.

When Old Liu walked past a few minutes later he put an arm around my shoulders and said, "You have watched the other guy. Tell me, will I win this game?" I could see the red lines on his face from up close. They made him look fireproof. "Who's the better player?" he said.

"I'm not an expert. How could I know?"

"No need to be modest. You think I still have a chance?"

"Very much so."

"You know what I want to hear." He squeezed my shoulders. I asked him why he liked golf. Was it the thrill of the competition, the business opportunities, the pretty companions, the revelry?

"You mustn't misunderstand the *renao* (heat and the noise)," he said. "I like golfing because it's the only thing I do where I have complete control. During the day in my office, it's so busy I never know what will happen next. But when I start playing golf I know I will be undisturbed for four, five hours."

Where I had seen chaos on the course, he had seen order. How peculiar.

"Do you always play at night then?" I said.

"More or less. There is a different type of people here during the day. Taiwanese and Singaporean investors. They look Chinese like us, but they think like foreigners."

"Like how?"

Old Liu pondered the question. "They don't like betting," he said.

"And you always bet?"

"Yes, but only here. Some of my friends like to gamble in casinos. But I don't. There are no limits to how much you can lose there. Of course, you won't lose everything in one hand. But you can in one evening. Golf is different. I can make my own special arrangement here. There is always an arrangement even if you can't see it. I don't like to lose control. You can easily be destroyed if you let things get too hot."

He released my shoulders and swung at his ball. It soared briefly, then dropped in about the right place. When we walked on I said: "You asked me if you will win this game. Well, how important is it to you to win?"

"Fangmin told you why we play, right?"

"Yes."

"Good, then you know."

I didn't reply. I was holding out for more. He laughed. "Okay. It's not a big secret. Big Bao and I are both close to someone who works in the city government. He is responsible for land allocation in the construction bureau. We both told him we wanted this one piece of land and he said we should work it out between us. That is the way modern government works in China. The citizens have to do all the work."

"Is it a big piece of land?"

"Not especially."

"So why do you both want it?"

"It's a good piece of land." That's all he was going to say. His caddy passed him a club for the next shot.

"So, my friend," he said after taking it, "why do *you* play golf? You want to go into the construction business?"

I told him I heard one of Xiamen's most famous sons regularly came to the club. That sparked my interest.

"Who?"

I said Lai's name. Old Liu let out a whistle. "You want to know about interesting people."

"Have you seen him here?"

"I used to."

"And you played together?"

"No, but I often saw him and his people. They were usually the biggest group on the course. It looked like they were having fun."

"Your golfing partner says he never saw him."

"Nobody wants to be Lai's friend now." Old Liu said Lai was reckless. Once he saw Lai drive his car onto the course. He parked it wherever he was playing. Perhaps it was for the air-conditioning. Such behavior won Lai a following. It seduced simple men. But Old Liu would not have played with him, he said. Then he stopped and frowned. The second caddy, the one hired to watch his rival, was coming back toward us from the hole ahead. Before she even had a chance to speak, Old Liu exploded. That cocksucker. That vile fuck. That turtle's egg.

There could only be one reason why the caddy would leave her post. She had come to report that Doggy Bag was cheating. Old Liu talked to her in a local dialect, pitching cascades of abuse at the distant green where his rival was stealing the disputed piece of land acre by acre.

～

I stepped back from the lawn. I had been searching for Lai for almost a year now and suddenly it seemed easy to imagine him — here. He would have enjoyed the thrill of going beyond the sensible. He could behave with impunity much as party bosses and government officials did. The golf course was a masquerade. It made reinvention exhilarating. Hidden by darkness, it removed the last constraints. And yet, it also showed up how unfinished new lives could be. The crude peasant ways of the past lived on. Lai might have worn a pressed shirt and creased trousers as he walked — or drove — from tee to tee. The parting in his hair might have been as carefully drawn as the rake strokes in the sand bunkers dotting the fairway. But he was still a farmer standing on a green field.

I walked over to the rest of our golfing party. Half were talking into their mobile phones now. The other half were either toasting each other with beer bottles or disappearing into the bushes, claiming to look for lost balls. The night hid them from prying eyes. Only the caddies were watching. They stood around unemployed, looking tired. I asked one to help me play a hole and we walked together to the next tee. Was there much cheating, I asked. She said it was common at night. The players were tired and couldn't drive the ball far enough. They expected caddies to drop another ball for them further down. Hence they were known as Three Hands, *sanzhishou*, a slang term for pickpockets.

"The dark makes it easy," she said. Some caddies swore that during the landscaping work on the course, criminal gangs buried a murder victim near the fifteenth hole. My caddy didn't know if that was true. "But I know who I'd like to bury there," she said with a tilt of the head toward the women in frilly tops. They were standing in a circle around Fangmin, who was showing them how to swing a club, hacking out successive pieces of turf. Behind them, the players' assistants were conducting relay races up and down the hills using a fleet of golf carts, cheering each near collision. They had become bored with trying to hit white balls into small holes after they were almost beaten up by another group of golfers for playing too slowly.

I never imagined I would understand the passions of the gentlemen of St. Andrews in Scotland — their pinched-mouthed, glacial-tempered delight at a shot well taken, but their etiquette certainly had appeal.

The main game was nearing its end and the two players were laying on expensive side bets, turning each hole into a separate competition. Various cars had already been won and lost on single strokes, including ones parked by the clubhouse. Then the players moved on to betting apartments they owned in new developments around Xiamen. Two-bedroom for two-bedroom, beachfront for penthouse.

Both men had hired a third caddy after the cheating furor earlier: the first to carry the clubs, the second to watch the other player, the third to watch the other player's caddy. Deprived of his advantage, Doggy Bag was steadily losing his lead and now trailed a few strokes behind. He had also lost most of the side bets, triggering a string of angry tirades directed at his caddies. Winding him up further, Old Liu walked down the course with an arm draped around one of the frilly, low-cut tops.

On the seventeenth hole, the two men got into an argument. The entire group, even the cart racers, was watching. Old Liu conferred with his caddies. Then he agreed to revise his score sheet up, mad-faced. The scene repeated itself at the next hole, the last. Both men alleged counting errors as soon as they arrived on the putting green, some going back to arguments at previous holes. Accusations flew between their assistants too. Swings were reenacted to prove contentious claims, or maybe the assistants were securing possession of the clubs as future weapons. The entire match, the question of who would get the disputed land, hung in the balance. Old Liu glowered at no one in particular, while another group of golfers was already lined up behind us.

I stood off to the side, inching toward the parking lot, when the focus of attention spun around like an executioner's blade, shifting away from the two players. A tight cluster of eyes peered at me, underlined by toothy smiles. "The foreigner will decide," someone said.

"Yes, the foreigner," said another. "The development of golf in his country is very advanced. Let him decide."

I had been in this situation before, a fact that meant I was even more anxious than I might otherwise have been. During a taxi ride once, my driver had got into a minor accident. Paint was scraped, little more. After an exhaustive argument between him and the other driver, they suggested I give my opinion, which I duly did. I sided with my driver. The other driver, far from settling the dispute, said foreigners always tried to sow dissent between Chinese, and that I probably expected to get a free ride for finding him at fault. The argument raged on for another hour.

"I wasn't watching," I said. It was not a credible answer. I could already see myself besieged by the losing party.

I was saved eventually when the two players wandered off together. They talked for a few minutes and when they came back a deal had been worked out. Old Liu won, but the side bets were off. Doggy Bag could keep the cars and apartments he had gambled away. That was it. There would be no fight and nobody had lost. As I understood it, nobody had staked out positions they could not row back from.

Without a grumble, the group drifted off to where the sharp line dividing the illuminated fairways and the dark shrub had begun to blur. The caddies went back to the clubhouse to sleep in bunk beds, evading a sprinkler system that suddenly crackled into life among the spindly trees. Above the course, larks made curious switchback turns, looking down at a small patch of green nestled among burly factories, just as a morning glimmer crept across the sky, mirrored in the ocean, where boats bobbed as they must have done all night.

I walked with Old Liu to the parking lot ahead of the others. He stepped cautiously down a slope, controlling his balance by stretching out his arms like an aerialist. "The grass is wet," he said. "Make sure you don't fall."

7

VILLAGERS

No. 5 Village Road, Shaocuo, Jinjiang County,
Fujian Province

LAI FLITTED BY me in ever-changing images. To get a better fix I would
seek him out on a journey away from Xiamen, I decided. My first destination was to be his hometown a few hours farther north, near the port city
of Quanzhou. The region had long been known for its lively commerce. In
the late thirteenth century, an earlier age of nascent openness, Marco Polo
had come here. He wrote:

> At the end of five days journey, lies the splendid city of Quanzhou at
> which is the port for all ships that arrive from India laden with costly
> wares and precious stones of great prize and big pearls of fine quality. I
> assure you that for one spice ship that goes to Alexandria or elsewhere
> to pick up pepper for export to Christendom, Quanzhou is visited by a
> hundred. For you must know that it is one of the two ports in the
> world with the biggest flow of merchandise.

Coming from a newspaper assignment, I got into the back of a red
Volkswagen taxi and gave the driver directions to a village near Quanzhou.
We fixed a price for the journey. After a series of shrugs and feints and the
refilling of his tea jar with hot water from a thermos, we set off. But after
less than an hour the driver stopped at a busy intersection, turned off the
engine, and climbed out of his seat. Without explanation, he walked over to
a group of men waiting in an industrial parking lot. From the back seat I
could see them stand among oil storage tanks linked to cold storage han-
gars connected to scrap yards.

The driver came back just as a fleet of eight-wheelers carrying coal passed by. Behind him stood one of the men from the parking lot. "This is Mr. Zhao," he said. "He has a good car and will charge you the same price we agreed."

"You think I should go with him?" I said.

"I have some business to do." I assumed that meant he had a problem, perhaps with the car, and he didn't want to say. I transferred my bag with the help of the haggard Mr. Zhao, who wore a calculator on a cord around his neck. "That's a factory making light bulbs for export," he said pointing out the window while driving. I nodded. "Do you think light bulbs are good business?" I said it probably was. "Do you trade in light bulbs?" I did not. "We could go into business together," he said. The taxi passed factories making commercial air conditioners, canning machinery, zippers, buttons, remote controls, and Christmas decorations. A roadside banner read, "Love laborers and employment." Mr. Zhao said he could help me set up a business relationship. He was a one-man trade show. I was grateful when after an hour he started making calls on his mobile phone. Soon he pulled over at a strip of tire shops and turned off the engine. He gave directions over the phone to someone and a few minutes later a minivan pulled up behind us. Mr. Zhao said sorry but could I go with his friend. No change in price. The two of them walked over to the van. I stayed behind for another minute, then decided I could live with not talking further with Mr. Zhao.

Lacking interest in more conversation, I sat in the back of the van. After driving for no more than a half-hour we came to a highway entry ramp and the driver pulled over behind a long line of cars parked on the curb. A group of men rushed up to us, crowding around the driver who was leaning on his door, shouting at them. They shouted back. The gaggle broke up as quickly as it had formed and the driver said I better move my bag. Before I could protest he had handed it to another driver and departed. I failed to understand why he did not want to take me to my destination.

"How far is it from here?" I asked my next driver.

"About two hundred kilometers."

"And how long will that take?"

"Don't know. I'm only going the next fifty."

"You'll pass me on to another driver?"

He nodded. It wouldn't cost me extra. I knew the drill.

"But why not take me all the way?"

"I'll never get a fare back from there. Too far. Few people can afford to go such a distance in a taxi, but from the next county border I can still get a return passenger."

I was traded twice more on the last stretch. At well-known road junctions arriving drivers shouted out final destinations, bids were made, money changed hands, then passengers were transferred. From the prices I was sold on for, I could tell I had not bargained hard enough with the first driver. My ride was trading at a generous discount.

⌇

Not far from where Marco Polo had landed we found the village where Lai grew up. Shaocuo consisted of little more than a cluster of houses along a country road. Most were set back, isolated among trees and divided by brick walls. The houses seemed to have been built in an atmosphere of suspicion. Each kept its distance from the next, but they unmistakably belonged together. They were larger than houses in other villages. Rather than just one floor they had three and four. Decoration also set them apart. I saw pagoda roofs and laughing porcelain Buddhas set in four-foot alcoves. The attempts at splendor seemed grotesquely out of place. This was the mud brick countryside. Quanzhou was an hour away. Rather than bring the city closer, the village's grandeur heightened the sense of isolation.

Some of Lai's family members were said to still live in Shaocuo, but would they speak to me? I felt I needed help. I called Kim, and she agreed to come up from Xiamen. We met at the village entrance the next morning. With her shorn head she stood out among the farmers' wives who wore their hair in trim buns. But not nearly as much as I did. The authorities were bound to be watching Lai's family. A woman with no hair would be less conspicuous than a foreigner, I hoped. Kim said I was being overly cautious and walked off while I waited by the side of the road.

The village was shielded from view by rows of devilwood trees, named so because the wood was "devilishly hard" to split. The short branches carried small green berries, and white blossoms gave off a sugary fragrance. The squat and gnarly trees looked like they had been planted along a stream or a swamp, but I couldn't tell from where I was standing.

When Kim came back she was flustered. Villagers had pointed her to a metal gate leading to a large house, but when she tried to enter a group of residents had driven her back out. "They accused me of wanting to repossess their home," she said. "They must have thought I was someone else. They wouldn't listen when I said I didn't want to take away anything." Rather than being frightened, Kim was angry. I asked what we should do now. "There is another place I was told about," she said. "And this time you will come with me. Nobody will think a foreigner is going to take away their house."

We walked along the village road past the devilwoods to an unmarked plot of land occupied by the hull of a building. Weeds were growing on the first floor and chickens fluttered higher up. Stacks of bathroom tiles — still in their original factory packing — rusted by the front steps. The half-finished building belonged to Lai but was abandoned when he disappeared, Kim said.

Walking toward the building, we heard the playground whispers of a child. A girl no taller than the concrete window ledges sat on a stool made from bricks, holding a mirror in one hand. Her hair was tied in the back with a white band. "Come in please," she said when she saw us. Liwei introduced herself as the sole resident of this mansion. She showed us her kitchen, a corridor filled with leaky buckets, and her dressing room, where she had hung up her coat on a steel wire sticking out of a bare wall. "Everything here is very luxurious and modern," she said.

"It's very nice . . . you have quite a lot of space."

"Everything is very luxurious and modern," she said and walked to a window. "Outside you can have many cars and inside is room for many guests."

"And you are completely alone here?"

"The others have all gone."

We told Liwei we were looking for family members of the man who built her mansion. He was called Lai. Could she help us? Turning on a heel, Liwei passed through a door frame and we followed her. "Almost everyone here is called Lai," she said. "It's a big family. But I know who you mean." She took us along the village road and the devilwoods back to the green metal gate that Kim had been to before. It was set in a marble arch and carried the inscription "The Morning Light Will Always Shine." Liwei yelled something and led us into a courtyard. It was bordered by brick buildings on all sides. Open drainage channels ran across the stone floor. A woman in her forties dressed in a buttoned jacket was peeling vegetables on a stool next to a younger man in a wheelchair who smoked in sunless torpor.

I couldn't resist the thought — where was all the money hidden? Or what had it been spent on? There was little evidence of ill-gotten gains. I saw a large television set through a window, but the shelves it rested on appeared to predate the television era, and leaning against the shelves was a hoe. It was a pitiful bandit lair.

Kim said she had been here earlier, trying to get in, and that we were not in the business of repossessing houses. The woman nodded and continued to peel. Kim told her we were eager to know more about Lai Changxing. Peel fell into the drain. The man in the wheelchair motioned clumsily for a new cigarette. The woman gave him one.

"Why would anyone want to repossess your home?" I said.

"His brother is Lai Changxing, that's why." She pointed at the man in the wheelchair. "His name is Lai Changbiao. In a fight in a nightclub in Xiamen someone hit him over the head. He almost died and now he is in a wheelchair. I guess he was never quite as smart as Changxing. But how smart was he really? He ran away from the government and as punishment they now want to take away his house. His own brother will have no place to live. But we're still here."

The woman had the confidence of someone who had known great wealth, which she matched with a sense of disbelief common to those who had lost it. She said we could stay for lunch. It would be ready soon, and in the meantime we could talk.

〜

In childhood, Lai Changxing had been nicknamed Fatty Lai. Given China's history of famines, that was not as bad as it sounded. Girth was something to be proud of — at least it was then. Fatty Lai was born at the start of the Great Leap Forward, Chairman Mao's attempt to implement socialism overnight. It caused the greatest famine anyone had known. More than thirty million Chinese had died (and left the rest with a lifelong hunger). Later, when Fatty Lai was a teenager, the threat of famine returned. In 1966, Chairman Mao launched the Cultural Revolution and denounced "rightist deviation." Private farming was severely restricted. All land was to be communal. But the father of the eight Lai children quietly converted a little-known swamp near Shaocuo into a personal vegetable plot. During the difficult years, it fed his family.

Education was more of a problem. The family could not afford school fees. The children all worked in the fields. Fatty Lai eventually went to school for a year, but then the Cultural Revolution shut down classes. He went back to fieldwork. Still, he got more education than his brother Changbiao. Until he landed in a wheelchair all he had was his talent as a joker.

When Fatty Lai turned eighteen, Chairman Mao died and his successor, Deng Xiaoping, began to change the political direction of the country. Small-scale enterprise was gently encouraged. Entrepreneurs were no longer called "tails of capitalism" that needed to be cut off. Now they were known as "running gangs of one" and everyone wanted to be one. But not yet Fatty Lai. He didn't feel ready to run on his own. He knew a group of businessmen who had set up a farming machinery factory and went to work for them as an apprentice blacksmith for two years.

Fatty Lai had no idea that the factory bosses had been importing odd-shaped bottles for another venture of theirs. Unbeknown to their employees, they were filling the bottles with alcohol and selling them privately, which was still against the rules then. The state had a monopoly on alcohol. Nonetheless, the manager of the farming machinery factory imported more and more wine bottles. Eventually, government officials found out and sent the manager and all the salespeople to be reeducated in long political study sessions. While they were away, the factory went bankrupt. Fatty Lai was out of a job and had no choice but to start his own "gang of one." He convinced four friends to lend him sixty dollars each and bought forging equipment to make car parts. Every week, he rode his bike a hundred miles to Xiamen to sell tire nuts and other products. Later, he set up a second forging business and then a shoe factory and several garment shops. He became a successful entrepreneur, but just as the manager of the farming machinery factory had got into trouble with government officials, so did Fatty Lai. And they didn't leave it at political study sessions.

᧐

The woman in the buttoned jacket peeled vegetables while we talked. Lai's brother smoked silently, never once looking up. His brain was damaged like a watermelon that had rolled off the back of a market cart, she said. The only thing he remembered from before his injury was smoking. All other tasks of daily life needed to be done for him. She was helping out as much as a hard-up cousin like her could, she said.

Having finished peeling the vegetables, she took them into a small kitchen on the side of the courtyard. She sliced them into a wok on an open gas flame. There were aubergines, onions, and garlic. Once fried, the aubergines turned a translucent brown. The first few batches cooked almost instantly. The oil in the wok became so hot it started to burn off in acrid clouds. Kim and I wandered back into the courtyard where we spotted Liwei, the girl who had brought us here. She was sitting on a doorstep leading into a darkened room. "I want to tell you a secret," she said and moved through the door. "My parents are dead. They killed themselves after someone cheated them." An entrepreneur from Guangzhou had apparently deceived them over a land purchase. Having lost their savings they committed suicide. I was at a loss what to make of the story — where did Liwei's fantasy world of private mansions end? There was no sorrow in her voice.

While she talked, Liwei led us beyond the darkened door into what turned out to be the Lai family shrine, an entire room devoted to ancestor worship. Incense sticks burned on an altar filled with dozens of wooden tablets the size of human hands and inscribed with the names of long-dead aunts and uncles. The tablets looked worn.

In the queasy silence of the shrine we could hear a couple bickering next door. I peered through a metal door off to the side and saw them. The woman was in her early twenties and the man no older. They both sat on a couch that appeared to be new yet already falling apart.

There was a third person in the room. An elderly woman was seated on a chair by the door. She smiled at me and I sat down next to her. Up close I saw that her smile was a permanent grimace of old age. Her skin was frozen into an unintended expression of cheerfulness. She was anything but.

"What are they fighting about?" Kim said.

"He says he should never have married into her family."

"Why?"

"Brought him nothing but shame."

"And she?"

"Says they will have to stay together because no one else will take him now."

"Is it her fault?"

The old woman shook her head. "It's her cousin's fault." Her cousin was Lai Changxing. "He pushed everyone into misery. We used to have a lot. There were always expensive cars outside, and feasts for a hundred in the courtyard. Important people came to visit. But no more."

After a few minutes, a boy of about six and wearing no clothes came running into the room to announce lunch was ready. We filed out into the courtyard where a table had been set. Fried aubergines served in a white dish were mixed with pickled chilies, ginger, garlic, and spring onions. The dish was called "fish-fragrant aubergines" although it contained no fish. During the meal, conversation revolved around the procurement and preparation of food and the earning of money, the base means of survival. While the Lais talked I looked over to the shrine where human spirits presumably loitered by the worn and splintered doorstep, and for a moment I felt closer to the Gothic churches of medieval Europe than to the successor of the world of refinement described by Marco Polo.

Throughout the meal, groups of local men kept coming into the courtyard, lingering for a few minutes and then leaving again. They didn't seem to care much for the food. Some whispered among themselves; others scolded the cousin looking after Lai's brother. "They want to know who you are," she said to me. "They always spy on us. I told them to go away." Who were they? Kim asked. "They are officials from the township government." And what did they want? "They say we shouldn't invite a foreigner for a meal here. They don't want us to tell you how badly they treat us. They have robbed us of our standing and most of our money. All is gone except the house. Police came and took everything. But there is no law against having guests. You will stay." And we did. Sitting together at the table in the afternoon, Lai's brother smoked and we talked.

꿍

The first import business that Lai ran was an operation selling foreign television sets in the mid-1980s. It was legal to sell the sets in China, and it was legal to bring them into the country. The problem was price. Import duties were high. To underbid rivals, Lai devised a clever ruse.

Foreign tourists coming to China at the time received vouchers to buy one color TV, duty-free. Most tourists of course had no interest in buying such a bulky keepsake, so Lai set out to collect their duty-free vouchers. He traveled to the border with then still British-controlled Hong Kong and asked visitors going across to bring him back a phone book (they were not available on the mainland at the time). When a traveller eventually did, Lai arranged his first international trade deal with a single call to a travel agent in Hong Kong. When the agent next brought a group to China, Lai collected the vouchers from the agent's clients. Soon he did so on a regular basis.

The business netted him tens of thousands of dollars, and his growing

riches were viewed with envy in Shaocuo, especially by the local government. Officials continually, and with growing urgency, demanded gratuities. For the most part, Lai refused them, which made him unpopular. Late
one evening in 1990, two officials came to this courtyard and asked to see
accounts for the television business. The only adult present was one of Lai's
sisters, who refused their request. The officials became angry and beat her
hard enough to send her to the hospital. The next day they started a tax
fraud case. But Lai fought the officials in court and eventually won. He also
started criminal proceedings over the abuse of his sister, to which the officials responded with a revenge campaign. All of Lai's businesses soon became tied up in spurious investigations.

Within a year his stores and factories were on the brink of bankruptcy.
He had little choice but to sell out and leave Shaocuo. He took his money
and moved to Xiamen to start again. But this time he would not be de-
feated by officials. This time he would play by their rules. After a decade of
market economics, everyone knew what that meant. Officials need to be
bribed. The end of the command economy has given them vast new powers. They levy obscure taxes on businesses dependent on them. Companies
are asked to pay instruction fees, assessment fees, and accident investigation fees. Officials will talk with a wink about their children's high university tuition fees or mention loans they are seeking to buy a home. Ordinary
Chinese have gained a measure of economic freedom from Beijing, but
they are increasingly enslaved by local stand-ins.

At least that was the view of Lai's family. The wording here is mine,
not theirs. But during hours of conversation, it was this sentiment they expressed. They spoke of Lai with pride. They said he had worked hard and
would not be caught. "The police tried to find him but they are not as
clever as he." The relatives kept returning to Lai's attempt to run an apparently honest business in Shaocuo. They described it as a formative experience. Greedy officials had bled him dry. He could not let that happen again.

Of course, every bandit myth started with accusations of an abuse of
power. It made the bandit cause a just one. The Sheriff of Nottingham was
an official in Shaocuo.

స్

The light in the courtyard was fading. Someone was pushing Lai's brother
around in idle circles. His teeth had recently started falling out, the family
said, and they feared further health problems. Long spells of immobility

were harmful, doctors had said, and suggested limiting his time in bed. Someone always pushed him around the courtyard in the evenings while he smoked. Finishing a cigarette he would stub it out on the same blackened spot on the chrome frame of the wheelchair.

As we watched him, Liwei appeared with a travel bag. She pulled out clothes she wanted us to see. Improvising a fashion show, she came strutting out of the house every few minutes wearing a green dress, a zippered sports suits, a pleated skirt, a woman's blouse. "Don't talk," she would say every time she emerged. "Look at me."

When the light was gone, Lai's brother was allowed to go to sleep. The family washed him with wet rags and applied cream to his back to prevent sores. Then they put a "massage machine" under his legs while he lay on his bed. The whirring machine produced regular left-right-left-right nudges. The massaged legs flopped back and forth without control.

It was time for us to leave, Kim thought. We said goodbye and walked back down the village road past the gnarled trees. Shaocuo was nothing like a normal Chinese village. Lai's riches had transformed it. He had paid for everything from paving the road to erecting a welcome arch at the village entrance (bearing his name). Nearby, he had founded a school for seven hundred students and a social club for the elderly. We could see them playing cards by dim light as we walked past the double-story club-house.

During the 1990s, the population of the village had grown from about four hundred to sixteen thousand. New residents were attracted by Lai's money and his financing of new houses. His relatives said Lai enjoyed being a benefactor. They described him as a dutiful and pious tycoon who obeyed Confucian precepts and became philanthropic after striking it rich. Ah, the misunderstood benefactor.

Down along the village road we saw a house set back even farther than the rest. The family had talked of it earlier. Shuiqiang, the eldest Lai brother, had built it. Its green glass roof was shaped like a thirty-foot pyramid and the front door opened onto a white stone bridge with intricate carvings. The house was extravagant even by local standards. In the dark, the pyramid roof gave off a green light from a distance. A radiant green light. That sounded familiar. "If it wasn't for the mist, we could see your home across the bay . . . You always have a green light that burns all night." Jay Gatsby said so to Daisy Buchanan in *The Great Gatsby*. Elsewhere in F.

Scott Fitzgerald's book Gatsby was staring at a "single green light, minute and far away."

To think of Lai as the Great Gatsby of China was filmy romanticism. But it wasn't such a bad fit. Both men believed in seizing the "green light," a dream worth any cost, and both their empires were built on crime, though not violence. It may be a stretch to equate their biographies, Gatsby's carnage-filled battlefields of Great War France and the starved countryside of Lai's youth. But they had both overcome darkness through the pursuit of wealth and ostentation, or perhaps they simply exchanged one darkness for another.

∽

Over the next few months I returned to Shaocuo several times. I wondered how other villagers had been shaped by conflicts with officials and built new identities around and away from them.

One evening I was sitting in a restaurant with neon strip-lighting by the highway to Quanzhou a few miles from the Lai home.

"A carton of cigarettes."

"No, a digital camera."

"A bottle of wine."

"No, no, too cheap. A Swiss watch."

"A real one? Too expensive. You're crazy."

Two men at a neighboring table were choosing a wedding gift. Wang Jin was the stingy one who wanted to give cigarettes or alcohol. His brother, Wang Huang, insisted on something more substantial, something appropriate for the owners of a small but profitable furniture factory. Across a simple plastic table heaped with shrimp tails they talked about the upcoming wedding of the local party secretary's daughter. "If we want to have a good relationship with him, we should give generously," said Wang Huang. "Or he will make problems for us."

"We will make problems for him if he asks for too many presents," said Wang Jin.

"You're bitter."

"You'll make us poor."

"If the gift is too small, you will regret it."

"Then let's give no gift at all."

"Perhaps a mobile phone for his daughter?"

"How about a bottle of poison for his wife?" Wang Jin held up an empty soup bowl. "Let's fill this with fertilizer. It will kill all of them with the first sip." He set down the bowl and turned to me. "Hey, foreigner, what do you think?"

Like everyone else in the roadside restaurant I had pretended to ignore their quarrel while waiting for my food. Wang Huang had tried to calm his brother and keep their talk private but had given up.

"In my country," I said, "we don't have a custom of giving poison at weddings."

"That's because your leaders don't demand presents," said Wang Jin. His brother handed the empty soup bowl to a waiter. "But what would you give?" he said. Both men were looking across the table, in agreement for the first time. An outsider would be their judge — whether to poison the local chief or bribe him. I could think of no compromise. "Why do you want to give a poisonous gift anyway?"

"Wang Jin has become very bitter," said his brother. "We have to be friendly with the party secretary and he doesn't like it." The Wang brothers, like everyone else, were having to pay gratuities to smooth their way through the bureaucracy.

"We shouldn't have to give big wedding gifts in addition to that," said Wang Huang. "It's not fair."

"That's what I've been telling you all along," his brother said. "We're already paying for the wedding. The limousines, the banquet, the flowers, the music — the families don't spend any of their own money on that. They will have a big party with eight hundred bottles of *baijiu* grain alcohol and they will use our tax money to pay for it."

Wang Huang said his brother was right. In two weeks, police would block the road running past the restaurant so the party secretary could hold a parade for his daughter's wedding. Hundreds of schoolchildren would be ordered to sing songs accompanied by professional entertainers hired by the local government, he said.

Both men wanted to give poison but knew it would have to be an electronic appliance.

8

BELIEVERS

Highway 15, Luozhuang Village, Zhejiang Province

WE WERE SITTING on a narrow concrete step. Behind us was a wooden cross by the side of a busy road. "I believe in Jesus," said Long Yaming. "I have been a believer for three years. I like it."

Long was breathing evenly. He was about a foot from my ear. His veined arms looked stiff but strong and the hairless folds of skin around his elbow wrinkled in evenly spaced troughs. His hands felt like they had been worn smooth in a thousand handshakes.

"To do this to another person you have to believe in something," Long said, "and to stand the pain, you also have to believe in something."

I was sitting next to Long, a repairman in a nearby garage. My back was turned toward him. Over my shoulder I could see him hold on to my arms. I could also see his legs on the step below, awkwardly angled into the concrete next to my feet. He said, "How does it feel?"

Long was forty-nine years old. As a teenager during the Cultural Revolution he had been a Red Guard. His main task was to run "denunciation sessions." Professors, doctors, healers — anyone representing the old order — was dragged in front of hysterical crowds by him. While the victim was showered with abuse, he held on to his or her arms and lifted them behind the back in what was called the "airplane position." If victims failed to agree with the shouted denunciations, their arms were forced upward. "Like this," Long said. He pulled very gently on my arms. "But normally the people were kneeling, not sitting down."

༄

Lai had at times been linked to religious groups. On one website I read that he had converted to Christianity; on another I read he had become a Muslim (and that he was running a restaurant in Beijing). One online report on religious conversions in China included an account of Lai's wife's newfound fervor for Jesus. The same report also mentioned Christians in the province of Zhejiang. It disappeared after a short while, removed by censors, perhaps due to the mention of Lai or because material on church activities was monitored as well. It was impossible to tell — but not without value. For my next trip outside Xiamen I decided to visit Zhejiang. The province was slung along the coast north of Xiamen and Shaocuo on the way to Shanghai. It was part of the boomtown belt. China's garment industry had its main base here. It had also long been known for its strong Christian sympathies. Proximity to Shanghai made the area a prime prowling ground for missionaries in the nineteenth century.

I flew to Ningbo, a port city like Xiamen, where I went to see a rebuilt Christian church in the colonial quarter. The rafters were freshly painted. The church stood at the confluence of two rivers, next to a modern convention center that had been built in the last year. From Ningbo I drove toward Wenzhou along the coast. Wenzhou was known as the most Christian city in China. In the 1980s, more than one thousand churches had been built here, though few survived. Bulldozers pulled them down, making room for more apartment blocks. Wenzhou had grown from a narrow warren of godowns and shop-houses to a city of seven million people, the biggest of the boomtowns.

At a highway exit north of Wenzhou, as a dim sun faded in late afternoon, I met up with a group of Christians. They were on their way to a carol service and already singing. They said I could come with them after checking with the organizers by phone. Their worship was wonderfully clandestine. It put the fun back into believing.

The group, four of them altogether, was traveling in a powerful silver limousine with blacked-out windows. When I climbed in I was greeted by a chorus of "Hallelujah." The driver, a young man with thin monkish hair and dressed in a business suit, introduced himself as Brother Dong. He handed me a tangerine and sped off into a valley flanked by fields. "The service will be nothing special," he said. "Don't expect too much."

I was sitting in the front seat next to him and while he steered the car I tried to concentrate on peeling my tangerine. So far none of them had asked me if I was a believer. I dreaded having to disappoint them. Coming from a country where worship was free, my agnosticism had to strike them as doubly errant. But eating their tangerine might at least convey sympathy for their cause.

The back seat of the car was filled with three stout women. Although they were not related the outing felt like a family event. Each of them had brought bags of food. After I had finished my tangerine, one of the women handed me a bag of nuts. I ate them too. I would eat whatever they passed me. "Our churches are nothing like those in your country," she said. "Not so old and not so big. We must be satisfied with less."

I assumed the women were organizers for an underground church. They mentioned "problems with the government" and "brothers in America" who had given them money and Bibles. Bible trafficking is a serious offense in China. Only state publishers are allowed to print religious texts, and they do so only in small numbers. Yet with every step toward economic openness the hunger for meaning and spirituality expands. Despite restrictions, Christianity is growing rapidly. To avoid the police, worshippers meet in private homes, called house churches. "If only they let us, we would build enormous churches," Brother Dong said. "Last year we built one with four rooms, but it was soon dynamited by the police. Our situation is terrible. We are counted with criminals and prostitutes."

I thought of Lai. Surely he wouldn't be aided by the faithful. But who knew? He would have been quite safe. The underground Christians operated an elaborate network of safe houses where they trained priests. One such house I had previously visited. It stood in a paddy field an hour outside Guangzhou, a structure a little bigger than the other farmhouses in the area, but otherwise unremarkable. A man calling himself Father John told me he wanted to keep it that way.

After an hour's drive, Brother Dong stopped on a road paved with loose stones among houses made of mud. His silver limousine looked very much out of place. Opening the doors we were enveloped by feverish excitement. Children with their parents thronged forward. At first I thought it was the limousine. But the crowds went straight past us and we followed them. We walked through a village that was shuttered and sleepy, which only heightened my surprise when we turned into a high-walled schoolyard and found a large stage in front of whitewashed classrooms. The yard was shielded from view on all sides and you could only get in through a narrow gate guarded by church organizers. A red banner above the stage said in Chinese, "Celebrate Christmas," with a large white cross between the words, and "Merry Christmas" written in English.

Brother Dong and the women seemed to be taken aback by the spectacle as well. There were at least five thousand people singing, many of whom had been here since lunchtime. A mobile generator powered spotlights and a public address system. A band of trumpet players, guitarists, and drummers accompanied hundreds of performers in extravagant costumes. Five-year-old angels in silver suits with wings and wire-rim haloes tripped around on the stage.

"What you see here may not look very risky," Brother Dong said, "but the girls and their parents and everyone in the audience could be detained by police." To be a Christian was not illegal in China, but the Communist Party required all churches and their members to register. Many refused to do so because Beijing demanded they acknowledge the General-Secretary, not God, as the highest authority. The few who did register were organized in so-called Patriotic Churches with close government supervision. This was definitely not a Patriotic Church event.

The congregation continued to cheer long after the sun had gone down and the temperature fell below freezing. From time to time worshippers would retreat to the backyard of a neighboring private home. There they were fed jellyfish, tofu in cabbage, boiled chicken on the bone, fatty pork, and rice. Each performer was also given a goody bag containing nuts, a pen, and a pair of socks. I had seen the bags earlier, but only found out what was inside when Brother Dong thrust me onto the stage. He wanted me to join a choir. He lined me up along with two dozen others and together we performed a jolly version of "Silent Night."

Then an evangelist read out testimonials. He was stout and wore a slick black suit, walking around the stage with a wireless microphone. "*Yesu ai ni*," he said. "Jesus loves you." Brother Dong said the man was a former gangster. During his long criminal career he was arrested only once. But following his recent conversion, he had already been taken in twice by the police.

When the music stopped at ten p.m., after nine hours of nonstop singing, dancing, and praying, the crowd dispersed so quickly and quietly that the schoolyard was deserted by the time the lights went out a few minutes later.

Before taking me back to the highway exit where we had met, Brother Dong invited me to dinner at a small noodle shop run by a fellow believer. The man was stooped and wrinkled like the broken spine of a well-thumbed book. He said he knew many of tonight's performers personally. They belonged to a regular dance troupe for children that was established a decade ago as a cover for a Christian youth group. It could book venues and gather at weekends, even operate a Sunday school in disguise. "We meet early, usually before eight a.m., when the police are not yet awake," he said. "We follow the civil war tactics of Chairman Mao. Retreat when the enemy advances and advance when he is asleep. Mostly now we use temporary venues, especially for large events."

The noodle shop owner seemed to enjoy the subterfuge. But after some prodding from Brother Don, he added, "Events like tonight's show are actually quite easy to organize. We get help from some of the local officials. They like what we do, for example, our work in education. They have no money for schools. They hope we can get donations from foreign countries to build some. They want us to do even more. Of course they can't say so in public. They have to tell us in private because the police don't like us."

∽

In many ways, Brother Dong and the noodle shop owner could not have been more different from people like Lai who worshipped money. But what struck me was how much they had in common. Entrepreneurs and Christians both exist in a gray area, a part of Chinese society where the government's writ is often ignored.

Probing continually (and carefully) they seek to find soft spots, and they often do so with the tacit consent of the government. Tolerating some gray areas is de facto policy. Many recent freedoms — like private employment — have arrived on the statute books after prolonged journeys through an official twilight zone. For instance, when the government decided to relax employment rules in 1981, it simply stopped enforcing a law limiting private companies to eight employees. The law continued to exist and enforcement could easily have been brought back. Then, in 1987, the rule change was deemed safe and useful. Only at that point was it made official, while entrepreneurs across the country were already employing workers by the thousand. They had taken all the risk as the government kept its options open.

Some officials would attempt to justify such muddling — Mao engineered social change overnight, they said. The result was famine and strife. By contrast, they were pursuing a slower pace of change. Flushing out the poisons of the past took time, they said, especially in a country the size of China. Neighboring South Korea and Taiwan might have been able to reform in just a few years, but China was no mere peninsula or island. The country's new infrastructure would span a continent, its civil society encompass a fifth of humanity. China needed a more organic approach. Rather than impose a new system from above, it was preferable for old ways to be corrupted in the margins. Where there were ports, the flow of trade would be allowed to wash in new ideas. Where there were strong desires, people would be given room to pursue them. And where there were proven leaders in enterprise, they would be given a free rein as long as they did not threaten Beijing.

This is a convenient stance. Officials avoid responsibility for difficult changes and keep a back door open. When their power comes under threat, they can still pull back. Religion is a good example. Churches were unofficially given greater leeway in the mid-1990s. But in April 1999, the well-organized Falun Gong cult challenged Beijing's ban on protests. Ten thousand followers surrounded the central government compound in a silent show of strength. Within months, religious freedoms — never codified — were rolled back.

Beijing is having it both ways. It encourages citizens to act ever more freely, but without guaranteeing the legality of their actions. Seen this way, the changes of the last two decades are not due to the efforts of political leaders. Sure, they set up stock markets and free-trade zones. But the real reformers are the private Chinese citizens who risked their skins barging through half-open doors. Their ambitions and desires shattered the old order, riding roughshod over dogma and bureaucracy to shape modern China. The country is not going through a top-down "reform process" as it is commonly described. There is no coherent, centrally managed plan. Instead China is experiencing a mix of retreat (on the part of the government) and revolt, with countless acts of private disobedience doing most of the transforming.

᠔

Before leaving I asked Brother Dong if there were any old churches in the region. I might like to visit one that predated the house church era. He told me to go to the town of Luozhuang, another hundred miles from the coast. Be prepared to "eat coarse tea and plain rice," he said.

A few weeks later I went to Luozhuang in a taxi. The road was narrow and climbed into dry hills, passing only single-story houses made from exposed brick. Arriving in Luozhuang I walked under leafless trees along a dirt path. How distant the boomtowns now seemed. Wenzhou was less than four hours away, and yet unimaginably far. Windows on many houses lacked glass. Where people had running water, piping was simply bolted onto outside walls.

The local church was looked after by a man called Brother Liang. "He chose the name himself. It means brightness," Brother Dong had said. "But he is not a priest." I found Brother Liang outside a large shed with cement walls and a red corrugated tin roof. He had a round face and a thin, long mustache that hung down the sides of his mouth. Wisps of it moved in wavy arcs when he spoke. His voice rose and fell in similar motions, and when he laughed, so did his shoulders.

"Are you busy?" I said. Brother Liang was sitting on a wooden stool, folding pieces of paper in his lap.

"I am busy. I'm preparing for the Sunday service."

"But it's only Tuesday."

"Exactly. We never have Sunday service on Sunday. We move it around the week to keep police guessing." He rose to his feet. "Come inside," he said and walked into the shed. He pulled on a cord coming down from the ceiling. A row of bare bulbs lit up a windowless room. Several dozen stools stood evenly spaced on the stone floor. A plain cross hung on a wall opposite. "Our church," Brother Liang said. When I didn't reply he said, "It was built one hundred fifty years ago. Of course it was rebuilt a few times. Only the stone floor is original." We were standing on tiles two feet in diameter. The surface felt porous as I ran my hands over it. "The whole church was originally made from this stone," said Brother Liang, "built in the 1850s when local people heard about a new prophet."

The prophet, it turned out, was Hong Xiuquan, a farmer's son from a hard-up village outside Guangzhou. On the streets of the old treaty port city the young Hong one day encountered western missionaries — it being an earlier age when old ways were also corrupted in the margins. They gave him religious tracts and soon he fell into a fevered dream. He became convinced he was the son of God and the younger brother of Jesus Christ, sent to the Middle Kingdom to save it from unjust rulers in Beijing. He reinvented himself as the leader of the "God-worshippers." During fierce sermons he rallied armed followers around him. They included bandits like "Big Head Yang," a pirate queen from Macao who was fleeing government forces. Hong named his troops — more than one hundred thousand of them — the Taiping Heavenly Army. He led them north and conquered territory with unexpected speed. In 1853, he controlled an area bigger than France. When he took the city of Nanjing, not far from Luozhuang, he set up a Christian capital, or "earthly paradise."

At the time, Brother Liang told me, a local merchant named Chang went to Nanjing. He was already a Christian, but what he saw in the city far exceeded his expectations. There were no angry voices and no long faces in Nanjing, and nobody wept. Hong had forbidden such behavior in a set of rules composed in verse and running to five hundred stanzas. In the evening all women at the palace played the *qin* string instrument — for Hong liked to hear its sound. When he bathed, separate groups of attendants looked after his upper and lower body, giving special attention to the area "near the navel." During public appearances he sat in a golden sedan chair followed around by some of his eighty-eight concubines carrying parasols. The silk robes and shoes he wore were yellow, the color of the emperor. The people of Nanjing prostrated themselves as he passed, as presumably did Merchant Chang. When he returned to Luozhuang he financed the building of a church to pray for the new prophet. But it wasn't enough. In 1864, after a failed alliance between the Taiping army and secret society gangs in Shanghai, Hong mysteriously died from poisoning. Beijing reasserted its authority. Nanjing was retaken, the church built in his honor in Luozhuang razed. In secret, the villagers later rebuilt it, and did so again after its destruction during the Cultural Revolution.

"You must understand," said Brother Liang when we walked out of the church. "We're Christians but we're also bandits." He shut the door and attached a chain with links as thick as fingers and padlocks at both ends.

I asked him about hotels in Luozhuang as it was getting dark and Wenzhou was far. He said there were none, only a massage parlor called the Dream of Old Er. After dinner I went there and sought out a masseuse in a private room. She seemed confused when, at the end of an hourlong massage, I told her I wanted to stay the night — but alone. She waited outside the room and came back in after a few minutes to check I wasn't just being shy. No, no, I said, I'm sleepy. Only then did she leave.

9

THE GOOSE LIVER KING

Beihai City, 1.7 million People, 3.3 million Geese,
Guangxi Province

OF THE MANY boomtowns along the coast only one had suffered a serious bust. Beihai, close to the Vietnamese border, was an urban morgue. It was littered with half-finished skyscrapers, stairwells that went nowhere, and brick walls failing to reach first-floor ceilings. Planks used as ramps for long-departed wheelbarrows sat around, pipes lay side by side rather than end to end, helmets taken off during the last lunch break gathered rainwater. Few lights adorned the concrete hulls — hunched along the main street at night they looked like a chorus line of dull eyes and broken teeth.

A century earlier, when opium was still traded, Beihai had been a colonial port, but a sleepy one since it was far from the main shipping lanes serving Hong Kong. When the Communists came to power it remained a backwater, marooned on the periphery. Propaganda tracts recorded only its beaches, praised as the best in the country. During the 1980s, the city missed the first wave of economic opening. Once again it was too far from shipping lanes. In the early 1990s, however, when the fruits of reform became evident, officials tried to make up for lost time — and personal fortunes. They decided to embrace the policy of allowing old ways to be corrupted in the margins. Beijing's reform plan would be their meal ticket. They would *chi huang liang*, or eat the emperor's grain. Local branches of state banks were encouraged to make loans to favored developers, who then channeled funds back to officials. Soon a stampede ensued. Beihai became one of the fastest-growing cities in China. Eight-lane avenues were built where only bullock carts had trundled before. Within a few years, the officials had their fill of kickbacks and admitted the obvious. There was no business to be conducted in all the new glass-walled corner suites. Construction work stopped. Office towers were left unfinished. All that remained now from the boom were the slogans. ("Protect the scenic environment: stop random construction" . . . I had come to think of China's ubiquitous signs and slogans as alternative guidebooks, indicating local anomalies, not merely inns and monuments.)

One of the few entrepreneurs to survive Beihai's bust was Chen Xiuhong, who ran a food business on the outskirts of the city. I had seen his name mentioned in reports on Lai. One said he had Lai's élan. Another suggested the two men had known each other, though none suggested criminal partnership. I went to see Chen, hoping for better luck than on my trip to Zhejiang. He agreed to meet me after several phone conversations with assistants. When I arrived at his office he was dressed in a shiny shirt and polyester trousers. Clipped to his belt were three mobile phones, one for creditors, one for debtors, and one for government contacts. From the ring tone he could tell whether to expect good news or bad, he said.

Chen's business aim was to popularize goose livers in China, served the French way, sliced and blanched. He told me he ate his first slice of foie gras at the Grand Hyatt Hotel in Hong Kong a few years earlier. What Chen remembered of that day wasn't the delicate flavor that turned a pound of butter into a moment of ecstasy, or the selfish glee in the eyes of his fellow diners as they reached for the last piece, or the sheer ease with which the brown slivers passed the tongue. No, he recalled being stunned that anyone would pay sixty dollars for a slice of liver. "Mine was this small," he gestured with his thumb and index finger. "An entire Chinese village could eat for less."

On return from Hong Kong, Chen built a farming complex capable of producing a thousand tons of foie gras a year, or three times France's total output. The margins were too good not to. There was plenty of fowl in Beihai — you couldn't lose. Chen was not worried by the fact that, apart from his malnourished upbringing in the countryside, he had no previous experience with animal husbandry. He found a French partner to train employees in the delicate art of force-feeding, and hired a French chef to teach local cooks the intricacies of poaching goose livers. (Much to the chefs' dismay most Chinese liked their foie gras crispy fried rather than runny inside.)

Sitting in his office at nine a.m., Chen asked the chef to serve us breakfast. Half an hour later, a silver platter laden with slabs of deep-fried liver was brought in. (Each one of them was so big — the size of a T-bone steak — and so thoroughly bronzed that I hesitate to call them foie gras.) Chen, a slight man with thin fingers, motioned for a handful of employees in the outer office to sit down with us at a conference table. They took the seats farthest away from us.

I could see no garnishes or accouterments on the table. To my left and right, chopsticks manhandled entire livers into mouths. I said a silent prayer that lunch be postponed indefinitely.

When Chen found our plates empty a few minutes later, he dished out a new round. The man next to me squirmed but wouldn't say no. Force-feeding was after all the company's business. "It's very good," Chen said, "isn't it?" His men nodded. They were rewarded with yet more liver. He prodded them to tell me their favorite ways of serving foie gras. Frying was very well, he said, but there was so much more you could do with it. The men said they liked liver soup and liver cooked in spicy sauce. They spoke reluctantly, as if they feared whichever dish they named would be served next.

After breakfast, Chen took me on a tour of the farming country outside Beihai. We drove in a Toyota sedan through land that was lush and flat to meet tenant farmers raising geese. When their animals were a few months old, they sold them to Chen who herded them into a central camp made of brick and corrugated iron. This was where more than one hundred thousand geese were fed before slaughter. Using a computerized machine with a pneumatic spout connected to a twelve-foot pipe, workers pumped cornmeal pellets into the geese four times a day. The machine made a sound like a tennis ball cannon: the pop of compressed air being released, followed by the whiz of an outgoing projectile.

"We feed them more than they do in France," Chen said. "It works very well. The livers grow to ten times their original size in just two weeks." To keep the geese calm during the ordeal known as *le gavage*, Chen had installed a PA system in all the huts. Loudspeakers above the feeding apparatuses played karaoke versions of popular Chinese songs. "This was my idea," Chen said. "It relaxes the geese and makes feeding easier."

"Karaoke?"

"Hah. You don't know what I did before going into the goose liver business."

Over pop music rhythms and the no less cadenced *pop-whiz-pop-whiz* of the feeding cannons, Chen claimed he was personally responsible for bringing karaoke to China. He had been the owner of the Pacific Ocean music company, when in 1987 a Taiwanese contact told him about a new video system that could display song lyrics while playing music. He ordered a few samples recorded by the Taiwanese singer Teresa Deng, who was then popular on the mainland at the time. "I realized Chinese people needed entertainment," he said. "We were working hard but we wanted to play too." Karaoke became a roaring success at a time when pleasure had only recently been deemed socially acceptable again. Karaoke was soon synonymous with the very notion of fun. Thousands of karaoke clubs sprang up across the country, many advertising with bombastic neon signs that shortened the name to three Roman letters, K-TV. Restaurants vied with bars and clubs for customers, inviting them to sing while they supped, doctors prescribed karaoke as a cure for chronic illnesses, and remote Tibetan villages set up communal karaoke machines in their temples. For years, Chen dominated the market for karaoke tapes and disks. When he eventually sold the company, he said, he made enough money to set up the foie gras farm.

From the force-feeding station we went on to the slaughterhouse. Chen strolled in with the swagger of a man entering his favorite bar, the place where everyone remembers the last time you fell off a stool. Some of the three hundred butchers he employed to kill geese were lined up to welcome him. Ignoring them, Chen raced to the far end of the large hall. This was where the geese met their mechanized end. Chen picked one off the ground and turned it upside down, hooking its feet into an overhead conveyor belt. The belt dragged the upended goose into a drum filled with water. The few seconds it spent submerged were meant to drown it, aided by an electric current in the water. But since this didn't always work, the geese had their throats cut as soon as they reemerged. Bleeding, lifeless, and wet, they journeyed on. In the next hall, men and women in white lab coats waited at different stations along the belt to remove one or another part of the birds.

Chen put on a lab coat and stepped up to the final station where the birds were already missing significant parts of their anatomy, looking like half-finished vehicles chugging through an automotive plant. He reached into a gaping goose cavity with both hands and pulled out the pièce de résistance, a liver the size of a bread loaf. It weighed two pounds.

At the end of the tour I asked, "Has the farm turned out to be as lucrative as you thought it would?" Chen said he had become the world's biggest producer of goose livers, dwarfing the family-run farms in the southwest of France that regard themselves as sole guardians of a national treasure. Once served only in western luxury hotels in China, foie gras was now being consumed at a rate of one ton per month in Shanghai alone. "I hope it will soon be served to China's leaders in the Great Hall of the People in Beijing," he said. "The Chinese president recently visited us here and really enjoyed our goose livers." Chen was lucky state security hadn't arrested him for staging a sneak attack on the president's coronary arteries.

〰

We missed lunch during our tour, which carried on all afternoon. Around seven, we sat down on the sundeck of a steel-hulled restaurant boat. It was moored in the Beihai harbor, surrounded by potbellied barges and reedy motor-powered junks. I was hungry again.

Chen said he preferred steamed rice and salted fish, the peasant food of southern China, to foie gras. It was what he had eaten growing up. His parents had been minor government officials. In the worst years, they bartered away food to give their son a decent education. He had read proper books instead of propaganda, which set him up for his business career.

I was reminded of how articulately Chen had spoken in the morning when recalling his days as a karaoke merchant. During the feeding frenzy at breakfast in his office I thought him boorish. I had underestimated him. Chen possessed an entrepreneur's brazen cleverness but he could be self-aware. That perhaps explained why he alone in China, where eight hundred million people still lived on the land, had been able to make a fortune out of something as common as goose livers. He said he estimated his personal wealth in the tens of millions of dollars, but few people knew that, including his family. To foster the ambitions of his teenage children, he never mentioned his millions to them. He told them he was a mere worker at the goose liver company, keeping his real identity a secret. "Otherwise they would become lazy and count on spending my money," he said. "My family is still renting a normal apartment."

I told Chen I too was renting an apartment — in Xiamen. I mentioned I had become interested in Lai while spending time there. "Oh, Bandit Lai," he said. We talked about the various homes Lai had kept in

Xiamen: a four-story townhouse at the top of the island and a glass-and-tile palace, known as the "Red Mansion." Chen had seen them both. I asked how he met Lai. Through the karaoke business more than a decade ago, he said. Were they still in touch? No. He didn't know what Lai was up to now or how he had got away from Xiamen. Nobody did. "If Lai doesn't want people to know then nobody will. He is too clever," Chen said, "and he has too many bandit brothers."

A waiter brought a tray with the rice and fish dishes we had ordered. During breakfast Chen had eaten very little. Now he devoured food. After a second helping, he stood up and walked across the deck to look over the steel railing. Night was falling on the harbor. Lights swayed on passing junks.

When he returned to the table, Chen asked me about being a foreign correspondent. Many Chinese viewed my occupation with unease, but not him. He was happy to be written about, steering conversation away from what he knew could hurt him toward what he didn't mind revealing. He knew the rules. Like Lai, he had shed old fears and inhibitions, hatching madcap get-rich schemes, riding speculative bubbles, and brokering and butchering goods newly available, whether wholesale, retail, or under the table. Men like him were successful because they understood the fundamentally haphazard nature of an economy perched in between total command and a free-for-all market, and they knew how to look out for themselves.

But Lai, Chen said, was still a special case. "As the son of a government official I had an easier start in my business career. Lai was a peasant with no contacts among officials."

"So?"

"He couldn't get loans."

"What about borrowing from friends?"

"Maybe," Chen said. "But you also need the government to get business licenses." To grow a company to the size of Lai's you really needed special relationships. Either you take over a state-owned enterprise or you have a relative in the government or some other backer. Chen listed bosses of large Chinese companies who owed their rise to more than their own wits. There was Yang Rong, China's manufacturing king, who worked at the central bank before he was handed control of Brilliance Automotive. Yang Bin, the ruler of the nation's flower markets, who previously worked in Holland

and was already a millionaire when he came back. And Zhang Yue, the air-con parvenu who built himself full-scale replicas of an Egyptian pyramid and a French chateau, and who had the backing of Chairman Mao's home province, Hunan. Many of China's new steel barons, sweatshop moguls, and property nabobs were in fact ex–Communist Party insiders who kept all but their membership cards.

"Lai was different," said Chen. "He only got official backers after he had already made his money. He didn't ride all the way up with the government." His company grew out of seeds he had planted, often based on little more than a hunch. There was the movie studio, the real estate business, and the shipping operation that I already knew about. In addition, Chen mentioned an electronics factory, a tobacco brand, a paper maker, and a hotel chain. "Lai was the undisputed master of these ventures," he said. Unlike state-owned enterprises, with all their bureaucracy, his companies were shells that existed only to support the head. You'd never find an organization chart in his office. No hierarchy existed other than the relationship every one of the hundreds or maybe thousands of employees had with Lai. And nobody knew how many people Lai employed. He probably didn't know himself. Instinct replaced statistics and market research, impulse became a substitute for strategy, business plans were unheard of, memos unknown.

I asked Chen to describe Lai's office. I suggested picturing him at his desk. What would one see? "Assembled in front of Lai were objects he expected to find on the desk of a powerful man," said Chen. He leaned back in his chair and looked across the harbor. By Lai's left hand, though rarely used, lay an oversized pocket calculator with large orange buttons given to him by a politburo member. Next to it were a crystal ball, an engraved clock, and some ballpoint pens in upright fluted stands. Over a desk of polished hardwood towered the kind of lampshade on a brass stand one usually found in hotel rooms. There were no Post-it notes, stray documents, or scribbled messages. Other than the objects Lai liked to display, the desk was empty.

Did he work alone or in an office with many people? "Usually just his secretary. Often she read to him aloud lists of the world's oceans and ports." These were the locations of his shipping containers. Lai sat in his leather armchair and just listened. He never read the lists himself — because he did not know how to. "Unlike me, he had little schooling," Chen said. Lai was barely able to decipher his own business card. To avoid embarrassment, he refused to engage in correspondence of any kind. In meetings, he stubbornly pretended to have already read the documents others were looking at, and on formal occasions when he was expected to put his signature on documents he made a habit of delegating the task to a minion. Only with great difficulty could he write the three characters of his own name.

Grinning, Chen dipped his index finger into leftover fish sauce on his plate and wrote Lai's name on the table cloth. "It's not difficult," he said.

"So how did Lai become so successful if he had no education and no official backing?"

"That's it," Chen said. "When he left home as a young man, his choice was between laying bricks, frying food, and manning market stalls. Eventually he managed to escape manual labor. Was it through hard work, cleverness, luck? A little bit of each, for sure. But most of all, what is needed is faith. We are still ruled by a Communist Party, as you know. A certain blindness to reality is a blessing if you want to make money completely on your own. You need to believe that you will not run foul of the party bosses."

When I suggested that Lai's faith seemed to have been misplaced, his disappearance proving the point, Chen grew uneasy. "Maybe, maybe," he said, his chattiness waning. We were bumping up against the safety limit of our conversation. From here on, he would not be drawn.

Having finished dinner, Chen suggested we go to a nearby beach. I assumed we would be strolling along it since the sun had long set. We arrived at a five-mile stretch of sandy shoreline filled with people in bathing suits. Swimming seemed to be as popular at night as golf. A number popped into my head. There are a hundred thousand people on this beach, I said to myself. The number wasn't far off. Sand and water were so densely populated that little more than a foot separated bathers visible in the moonlight. I thought back to the cramped force-feeding farm I had visited.

"*Xia hai*," said Chen and grinned. "*Xia hai*," I repeated. *Xia Hai* translated in Mandarin as "going into the sea." More commonly, though, people used it to mean going into private enterprise. Chen plunged in headfirst.

10

Bandits

Coxinga, AD 1603 to 1662, Xiamen Island

WHEN I SPOKE TO people about Lai they often called him a *tufei*, a classical term for a bandit. Chen did so during our dinner. He said Lai's criminal associates were *tufei gemen'r*, bandit brothers, a group from which he clearly excluded himself. Back in Xiamen now, I noticed others using the same term. Yet they did so in a tone of approval. They meant to elevate Lai above mere robbers and cheats. They implied he might be defying the authorities for just reasons. When I asked them to explain, they would name bandit figures from history (pre-Communist history, which was moderately safer) and liken them to Lai. The owner of a chain of restaurants said Lai had held cigarette prices down with his smuggling. Lai was like "Opportune Rain" Sung Chiang who "helped the needy and looked lightly upon silver." On another occasion, a university professor mentioned a bandit called "White Wolf," or Bai Lang, who pillaged villages on the North China Plain after the Qing Dynasty dissolved in 1911. Revolutionaries swelled his ranks and two hundred thousand government troops were sent in pursuit. In 1915 the White Wolf was trapped and killed. But a song survived him, the professor said, and if you changed the first line you might sing it today:

> Bai Lang, Bai Lang
> He robs the rich to aid the poor
> And carries out the Way on Heaven's behalf
> Everyone agrees that he is fine
> In two years rich and poor will be leveled.

Other Xiamen residents named fictional *tufei* as models for Lai. Many sprang from the pages of a single book, *The Water Margin*. Its characters were familiar even to illiterate Chinese from storytellers and itinerant drama groups. In the West the book was known as *All Men Are Brothers*, translated by Pearl Buck, the unlikely Nobel Prize winner and champion of the Chinese peasantry. In a bookstore in Xiamen I bought a copy — a counterfeit paperback with see-through pages. It told the stories of 108 bandits hiding out in swamps beyond government control, hence the name "water margin." Set in the twelfth century, when the late Song Dynasty was troubled by corruption, the stories describe the bandits outwitting greedy officials abusing positions of power. The merry band included Wu Sung, described as "tall, handsome, powerful, heroic, an expert in military." He was also a drunk. Another bandit was Chieh Chen, an orphan and hunter who was tall, tanned, slim, and hot-tempered. Both were frequently named as models for Lai. His most ardent defenders also put Ch'ao Kai on the list. Chao was known for his distaste of violence. After one raid he asked his followers, "Was no man killed?" They said nobody was. "Ch'ao Kai, hearing this, was mightily pleased and said, 'From this day on we are not to injure people.'"

A postscript in my paperback copy said — probably as a result of censorship in centuries past — there were two versions of *The Water Margin* with very different endings. In one, the bandits eventually joined forces with the emperor to root out corruption. In the other version they were executed.

∽

When I met Chinese who had been close to Lai I found they, too, used the *tufei* label. On my visit to Shaocuo, members of his family had said officials extorted money from him. Lai was forced into banditry like others before him. To back up their claim the family named another ancient bandit who had hid in swampy shallows. He was not from the water margins but from Xiamen. He was a figure of seventeenth-century history — his name was Coxinga. Apparently Lai himself had encouraged the comparison. Shortly before he went into hiding, he told his relatives to "believe in Coxinga's just cause."

I remembered that in Xiamen near my apartment there stood a hundred-foot stone statue of Coxinga gripping a sword. Coxinga was the city's patron saint, and had been even when the Communists forbade private commerce. From Xiamen, I read, he had run a trading network in the 1640s and 1650s, his vessels sailing across the strait to Taiwan where the Dutch East India Company had a base. They also went to Japan, the Philippines, and Java, usually carrying a cargo of silk. Unfortunately, trade was illegal. Just as Mao had walled off China from the world, the reigning Ming emperor decreed the Celestial Empire needed no offerings from the barbarians beyond the shores. To suggest otherwise was deemed heresy. But the emperor was unable to enforce the ban. An imperial report stated the coast around Xiamen was a place where "cunning bullies can carry out their crafty schemes." Coxinga had a fleet of hundreds of ships, the biggest in China. They anchored in coves and estuaries out of sight of inspectors. When they set sail they far exceeded the imperial limit of two days' water for the crew that would have forced them to hug the shoreline. The ships would make along the coast, then turn east when safely out of cannon range. Upon return they acted as if coming from nearby islands.

Coxinga gathered immense riches at his castle in Xiamen. Behind walls stretching three miles in circumference he kept exquisite gardens filled with fishponds, fountains, and pavilions. Private teahouses were decorated with calligraphic scrolls, golden artefacts, and hand-carved jade. As in Lai's age, trade brought not only great wealth but also new ideas and fashions. The previously unknown chili — soon to become a staple in Chinese cooking — was brought back from trade missions to the Philippines where the Spanish had introduced it from its native Latin America. Equally unknown at the time was tobacco. Word spread across China that sailors from Xiamen had obtained a breathable smoke that made one drunk. Tobacco was planted on nearby hillsides and a new industry was born, known as "dry alcohol." By 1650, it was said "everyone in the armies started smoking."

Eventually, Coxinga shed his outlaw status and found official favor — just as Lai had been made an honorary citizen, so his relatives might have pointed out. Coxinga was given the title Count of Loyalty, even while his smuggling continued (ditto Lai). Boats filled with silk still went up to Japan and returned with artifacts and silver. The Count of Loyalty was shameless. One smuggling vessel he named after himself, *Coxinga's Ship*. In the meantime, however, the country's leadership changed. New rulers were installed in Peking. The Qing court took over from the Ming. Coxinga's position was precarious once again and the new emperor sent troops to attack Xiamen. They took the city — raping women and taking bullion worth a million taels — but could not hold it. They retreated while continuing to harass Coxinga. He was able to hold out because the peasants along the coast supported him. They provisioned his ships and gave his sailors shelter.

Coxinga was the region's ruler in all but name. Realizing this, the Qing rulers opted for even more drastic measures. They evacuated the entire southern coast. Inhabitants were forced to retreat inland thirty miles, and their homes and fields were torched. Untold thousands died in famines. In the no man's land left behind Coxinga could find no shelter. One imperial report said, "The area is a wilderness inhabited by foxes and badgers, tigers and wolves." Coxinga was forced to flee Xiamen at last. He sailed his fleet across the strait to set up a new base on Taiwan. But the Dutch traders there were not especially welcoming. They fought him from the heavily armed Fort Zeelandia on the island's south coast. After a prolonged siege Coxinga ousted them in 1662, ending a thirty-eight-year colonial reign. Ensconced on Taiwan, he became stricken with disease, and possibly madness, dying in lonely exile a few months later.

On the mainland, however, his memory was kept alive. He remained a hero to coastal dwellers and even the Qing rulers eventually relented. To consolidate their reign and win over his followers, the "bearded sea-bandit" was posthumously given the title "Paragon of Loyalty." In later centuries, his reputation grew further. In 1875, he was elevated to divine status with temples dedicated to him. Chinese honored his ejection of the Dutch from Taiwan. The successful siege of Fort Zeelandia was portrayed as the Middle Kingdom's first major defeat of barbarian forces. Then, after the fall of the Qing Dynasty in 1911, Coxinga became an inspiration to republicans who admired his fierce independence. And when the Communists took over in 1949, they too claimed him, saluting his conquest of Dutch Taiwan, which bolstered their contention that the island was part of China. At the same time on Taiwan, Coxinga was hailed as a predecessor to the Nationalist leader Chiang Kai-shek, who had fled the mainland following his defeat by the Communists. Like Coxinga, he never made it back across the strait.

To this mess of historical claims and comparisons, the Lai family added their own. They speculated that Lai — and hence all of them — were descendants of Coxinga.

"Changxing's face looks almost like that of Coxinga," said an uncle during the lunch I had in Shaocuo.

"No beard though."

"No. But that doesn't matter. They have the same quality." He used the word *suzhi* for quality. It translated variously as culture or character or manners. It described a man's essence.

The idea of Lai and Coxinga being blood relatives was not as far-fetched as it sounded. After Coxinga's death, Taiwan was incorporated into the Celestial Empire and his relatives went back to the mainland. Some were resettled in the interior where they could no longer trade. Others remained close to the coast, perhaps not too far from Shaocuo. One descendant, Zheng Yi, and his wife, Xianggu Zheng Yisao, the "Pirate Queen," entered the history books in the early nineteenth century for much the same reason as Coxinga.

Yet even if Lai and Coxinga were related, this still left a crucial difference between them. In Conxinga's time the emperor had shunned contact with the outside world while modern China's rulers no longer did. They had under Mao, but he died years before Lai began to trade. Instead of closing off and burning down coastal areas, Beijing built new ports. When Lai told his relatives to "believe in Conxinga's just cause" before going into hiding, he must have hoped to add one more useful layer to his much transformed identity. He was trying to present himself as what Eric Hobsbawm, the British historian, called a "social bandit." These were "bringers of justice and social redistribution." They commanded public sympathy and only stole from the rich. They were brigands, desperadoes, highwaymen, freebooters, or Indian *dacoits*, Italian *banditi*, Balkan *haiduks*, Andalusian *bandoleros*, Russian *rasboiniki*, Hungarian *betyars*, and Mexican *vaqueros* (cowpunchers). Some were famous outside their home region. Dick Turpin and Robin Hood in England. Cartouche and Schinderhannes in continental Europe. Jesse James in the United States. Pancho Villa in Mexico. Ned Kelly in Australia. Many of them, of course, did not live up to the ideals associated with them. Little more than common thieves, their good deeds were often myths, much as one suspected in Lai's case. There was no evidence that he gave away more than a tiny part of his wealth or that he directly supported a political cause.

And yet the label seemed to stick.

Bai Lang, Bai Lang
He robs the rich to aid the poor . . .

Thinking it useful propaganda, the government in Beijing too indulged in games of historical parallelism. And the examples it borrowed from the past could be just as fraught as the ones chosen by Lai and his supporters.

Sometime after my return from Beihai, the *Xiamen Daily* warned readers to be vigilant against "bandit leaders" who brought misery to the city. The government paper did not mention Lai by name. But few readers would have missed the hint. The article recited the evil doings of Pock-marked Huang and Big-Eared Du, well-known gangsters from the early twentieth century. These "counterrevolutionaries" had run rackets in prostitution, gambling, and drugs in Shanghai before the Communists cleaned up. They were symbols of an era of rampant banditry. By some estimates, half a million Chinese had been members of criminal gangs in the 1920s. The country was gripped by postimperial chaos, or *luan,* one of the most feared as well as overused political terms in Mandarin.

After seeing the article I called a journalist at the *Xiamen Daily*. We had met a few times and she seemed to have a liberal bent. Unlike her boss, she never used slogans like "fulfilling our responsibility to the reader," code for giving them what's officially deemed good for them.

"I saw the story on the Shanghai bandits," I said.

"A real problem."

"I thought Huang and Du were dead."

There was a brief pause. "They may be dead but the problem hasn't gone away."

"You mean bandit leaders today?"

There was another pause. "It is terrible what bandits can do. You as a foreigner should understand," she said. "Did you not see the film about the prisoners on the train?" She was referring to *Shanghai Express* starring Marlene Dietrich, a pirated DVD version of which was available from street sellers. The film was based on an infamous raid on the *Blue Express* travelling between Tianjin and Pukou. In 1923, bandits led by Sun Meiyao kidnapped three hundred passengers including thirty foreigners. One of them was killed. The rest were released after payment of a ransom.

Fear of *Shanghai Express*–style banditry was not surprising. The government ensured memories of the 1920s were kept alive. It never tired of airing carefully chosen and manipulated snippets of history. Bandit dramas were a favorite, their crudeness a bonus, with some bandit patois surviving. To "hang up a sheep" was to capture a moderately wealthy man. To kidnap a rich man was to hang a "fat duck." To "release" a captive meant to kill him. To "burn the ticket" was to mutilate him with fire. To "clip the ticket" was to cut off ears or fingers. To "slap bean curd" was to hit someone on the behind. To capture a woman was to "get an earthy ticket." A virgin was a "two-five." Bullets were "white rice" and to eliminate a rival was to "wrap the tablet."

Some parallels between 1920s and 1990s China could legitimately be drawn. But these weren't always the ones the government liked to see. Sitting on the sofa in the apartment in Xiamen I began to read about the period that preceded the rise of the Communist Party. History books described it as a time of immense flux. Old allegiances were shattered. New opportunities beckoned. Railways allowed Chinese to travel longer distances. Migrants turned up in cities like Shanghai looking for work. In the absence of a decent government, gangs served to integrate and feed them, even if they scammed them at the same time. The descriptions sounded uncomfortably familiar.

Perhaps the most embarrassing part for today's government was this. One of the biggest beneficiaries of 1920s banditry had been the Communist Party. (So said foreign but not Chinese history books, which were still routinely censored.) During the first two decades after its founding the party repeatedly relied on bandits to survive. It sought allies in the underground and was never choosey about whom it dealt with or what their methods were. Mao himself started it in 1927. Hiding out in the Jing Gang Mountains and later in Ruijin, some one hundred miles inland from Xiamen, he joined forces with two local bandit chieftains. They added six hundred men to his troops. Surveying these "classless" members of society, Mao wrote, "They can be divided into soldiers, bandits, robbers, beggars, and prostitutes. They are all human beings and they all have five senses and four limbs, and are therefore one." He added, "These people are capable of fighting very bravely and, if properly led, can become a revolutionary force."

Where useful, the party's instinct to co-opt bandits survived Mao's death. In the run up to the contentious 1997 handover of Hong Kong by its British colonial masters, Beijing openly conspired with the city's "triad" gangsters. Deng Xiaoping, Mao's successor, said in an official speech at the Great Hall of the People that some of the triads were "good" and "patriotic." Soon afterward, a Chinese official met triad members to tell them Beijing "did not regard them the same as the Hong Kong police." He said the triads could continue their money-making activities as long as they didn't rob Chinese-owned enterprises. Tao Siju, China's police minister, even said in public, "As long as these people are patriotic, as long as they are concerned with Hong Kong's prosperity and stability, we should unite with them." In exchange for Beijing's benevolence, the triads acted as its eyes and ears in the city ahead of the handover. They infiltrated trade unions and reported back to a Beijing entirely comfortable with *tufei*.

✑

More than a year into my search for Lai, and with a growing collection of books surrounding me, I sat in the apartment. Andy was on the sofa next to me and a typhoon was blowing down the coast into Xiamen. The winds were strong enough to bend window glass. The two of us were watching from behind drawn curtains as the panes flexed. We had not been outside for two days and talked idly, waiting for the rains to end. I mentioned to Andy the government's cooperation with the triads in Hong Kong. He didn't believe me. At the time, there had been few reports in the media. But I was able to show him mentions in a book. He read them and when he was done he emphatically put the book down. "They are all bandits. Lai. The party. The leaders. A whole country full of bandits."

What he said resonated with me. "A whole country full of bandits." I was not concerned with how close he was to the truth. What fascinated me was the impact of so much banditry. What did it do to people, to society, I wondered? But then the moment passed and I forgot about it.

A while later, long after the typhoon was over, I saw a leaflet on a street corner in Xiamen. It was taped to an electricity pole and an ocean breeze rustled the grainy paper. A smudged strap-line across the top said, "Are you trying to be honest?" Below it was a phone number for a Mr. Li.

I called.

"This is Doctor Li," a male voice said.

"I saw your leaflet."

"Good. I am on Zhongshan Street. Where are you?"

"I am, hmm, near the bus station."

"Okay. You can come now." He suggested meeting outside a department store. When I got there Dr. Li apologized for the location. "I am waiting for my wife," he said. "She is inside." He preferred to stand on the street while she shopped. Until she came out we could talk.

Dr. Li was forty-five years old and wore his glasses close to his eyes as if facing into a storm. His hair was short without being harsh. He said his title reflected training in traditional healing. "What I do is closer to psychology, but it is difficult to get an education in that."

"What exactly is it you do?"

"I help people to be honest. Ten yuan per session."

"Is there a lot of demand?"

"It's okay. I am busy."

"And how do you . . .?"

"We talk. It doesn't matter what about. I tell them to just be honest with me. It's practice."

In advanced sessions, Dr. Li said, he might also discuss personal problems with patients. Occasionally he would give advice. But mostly he listened. It was important to talk to "someone who doesn't matter." It meant there was no reason to be dishonest, he said. Then his wife came out of the department store. She was about his age and had attractive strains of gray in her dark hair. Before they left I said I would call again.

The next day I arranged to meet Dr. Li at his clinic. He gave me specific directions. Arriving at Zhongshan Park I followed the prescribed path. From a distance I saw Doctor Li standing by a tree. He was in conversation, perhaps talking to a patient. I waved and he motioned for me to wait.

The park around us was busy. People pushed past each other between fenced-off lawns. Paths were lined with living room chairs. Next to the chairs were men and women in white coats. Some of them had hung small white flags with a red cross in trees behind them. Among the passing crowd they solicited for business. "Foot massage. Back massage," said one. Another offered "dental care, look after your teeth." When they found patients, they sat them down on their chair and treated them.

After a few minutes, Dr. Li finished his consultation. "This one over here is mine," he said when I approached. He pointed at a chair with thin metal legs and a beige seat cover. It had no armrests but stood in a nicely shaded spot. Dr. Li invited me to sit. He would stand, he said.

"How long have you been doing this?"

"Not quite three years."

"And before?"

"I was employed in a factory in North China making glass." Dr. Li said the factory's work had been leisurely. He had had time to talk to colleagues.

During intermittent breaks he would encourage them to consult him. He would listen. "The factory was owned by the local government. So there were always problems. Workers were cheated."

"Were you being paid?"

"Yes. But the weather."

"The weather?"

"It was very hot in the summer and the factory had no cooling system. There was a government rule that when it's forty degrees [105°F], they have to stop work. They also have to buy everyone ice-cream."

"They ignored the rules?"

"No. In the official weather report the temperature would rise and rise but never get above thirty-nine."

"You think the government fixed it?"

"Yes. When that happened a lot, workers started stealing from the factory. Eventually it closed. So my wife and I decided to come here. She found a job at an insurance company. She is an assistant and has a good salary. Twelve hundred yuan. I earn a little extra. But not much."

The chair next to us was only a few feet away. A man was having his ears cleaned. I could hear him cough. Presumably he could follow our conversation. Much as on a village square where itinerant blacksmiths and coffin makers offered their services, all treatment was public.

"You have patients come here and talk to you, right?"

"It's cheap. I pay no rent."

"And you treat them for dishonesty?"

"Yes."

"How come they need it?"

"A lot of things are changing in China so people change too. They act differently. They dress differently. It is a form of dishonesty. It starts with that."

"What do you advise them to do?"

"Sometimes it's easy. They might wear their old clothes again. Not all of the time, of course."

"And in more difficult cases?"

"I tell them to think of me as their spouse or boss. I ask them to talk honestly about their life."

"How long does it take to see an improvement?"

"I'm not sure. Some people come for ten sessions."

I asked Dr. Li if I could speak to one of his patients. I said I would like to see the results of his work. A few days later he called. A patient had agreed to meet me but preferred to do so outside the clinic. Public therapy was fine, but not an interview. Dr. Li suggested meeting at his apartment. When I arrived around noon I found the curtains drawn. His wife, whose gray hairs were less visible in the dark, said, "Before we came to Xiamen we lived in a traditional courtyard. It was enclosed and nobody could see in. To draw the curtains in an apartment is not the same. But it's close enough."

I took my shoes off and followed her to the living room where Dr. Li was seated on a plain sofa with his patient. He introduced him as Mr. He. Mr. He wore a gray suit and a tie. His face looked like something from the wilder reaches of the Chinese culinary universe — rabbit ears (steamed), an ox's flat forehead, and thin fish lips.

I asked about his case. "For a long time I would tell people that I earned a lot of money," he said. "But it wasn't true. I also lied about owning a car." Mr. He told his own mother he was the manager at the company where he worked, when he had been the assistant to the manager.

"Was Dr. Li able to help you?"

"I feel, yes," Mr. He said, then considered his answer for a moment. "You know, I try to be honest. I am not sure. Definitely a little bit."

⌇

I recalled once again what Andy had said during the typhoon. "They are all bandits. Lai. The party. The leaders. A whole country full of bandits." I wondered if correspondents should not be on her list too. Official reporting restrictions invited trickery. Almost daily I found myself concocting some ruse or feint worth confessing to Dr. Li. Though I never resorted to bribery I did on occasion use my wallet. The most helpful professional tool on reporting trips was neither a pen nor a notebook nor computer, let alone a mobile phone. Even my thickly embossed business cards showing the *Times* leader page crest with the clock face fixed at 4:30 came a distant second. Whenever I was stuck in a difficult interview or had to extricate myself from a small-town police station for overstepping reporting restrictions, I'd open my wallet as if looking for something, maybe a document or scribbled note usefully tucked in the back. I would not reach for the crisp bundle of red hundred-yuan notes, although I might be tempted. Instead I'd alight, as if surprising myself, on the laminated photograph visible behind my credit cards (which remained the least useful professional tool in China, where even cars were bought with cash; nothing else was trusted). The laminated card, no bigger than an American driver's license, was smudged and scratched from the countless times it had been passed around hallways filled with self-important officials, roadblocks staffed by soldiers younger than their AK-47s, and half-opened hotel room doors with me on one or the other side. It was this card I relied on to smooth my passage.

It showed a grainy photograph taken on one of the few occasions in China where I wore a suit. In October 1999, soon after my arrival, President Jiang Zemin, then seventy-three years old, had granted the *Times* an interview ahead of a state visit to Britain. Lord Rees-Mogg, the paper's former editor in chief, came to Beijing to beef up our side and at his suggestion I hired a photographer. His Lordship said he wanted the picture for the memoirs he was working on.

The president welcomed us in the Hubei Room of the Great Hall of the People, where the sepia carpet matched the faded upholstery, as I can tell from the laminated card. For me, the most memorable part of the interview came right at the beginning when Jiang glanced at the briefing papers placed by his seat, then looked up pointing one of his plump little fingers at me and guffawed in surprisingly fluent English: "Ha! You born in 1970s." The president wasn't going to let me forget that I had not even been born when he was already holding sway over the masses as a party functionary. The interview followed a similar pattern, though Rees-Mogg, who was Jiang's age, seemed remarkably pleased with the result. He later wrote that he learned Jiang "obviously has a very warm affection for his grandchildren." Before leaving the Hubei Room, we were invited to officially shake hands with the president, the moment for which we had brought our photographer. Smartly besuited, I can be seen giving Jiang a statesman-like grip as if we'd just agreed on a new division of colonial spoils or formalized an apology for the Opium Wars. The interview was a journalistic disappointment, except when I received the photograph a few days later Sophie, the *Times* assistant, suggested laminating a smaller print. She thought it valuable currency, and so it was.

Many of my colleagues have their own ploys and scams. They travel on unrecorded passports, set up shell companies to acquire pictures the state news agency sold only to domestic media, and befriend Chinese colleagues who have access to the propaganda ministry's weekly censorship list of banned stories — an ideal shorthand to what made news. When entertaining media-shy officials, one might take notes on scraps of paper hidden in a baseball cap, or as a text message on a mobile phone, or in extreme cases retreat to the lavatory at regular intervals to record as much as possible from memory.

Banditry is all around, one corruption begetting the next.

11

THE MADAM

No. 73 Quanzhou Street, Piano Island,
Gulangyu, Xiamen Municipality

FEW PEOPLE WERE more accomplished in concocting feints and disguises than Lili.

I was sitting on a doughy sofa in her nightclub, watching the spotlit stage. Around me, waiters sprinted and dancers cartwheeled, guests ordered flowers and drank XO cognac. On evenings like this, as the bounty-raided streets outside gentled down, I sometimes accompanied Lili on her rounds. She moved between tables, toasted regulars, and plucked stray sequins from her dancers' dresses. "Whoever they are," she said afterward, "in here the guests and the dancers are whoever they want to be. A street seller can pretend to be a company boss, a government official can be less formal or not formal at all. They can feel rich or free or beautiful. They can be whoever they want to be as long as the money is right. And I look out for that."

Done for the night, Lili was now sitting on the sofa next to me. We were watching the show, but my mind was elsewhere. I was thinking of something Chen, the goose liver king, had said. He mentioned a place in Xiamen owned by Lai and known as the Red Mansion. Others had talked of it too. They said Lai used the mansion as a bordello. Like Lili's club, it was filled with young women, except the clientele was limited to high government officials. Each had his own girlfriend, paid for by Lai, locked away, one per bedroom and exclusively theirs. The Red Mansion was what made Lai different from other corrupt businessmen. Many of them exploited lust as well as greed. But only Lai bribed in a currency issued by his own central bank. He hired the women and offered them to officials as exclusive consorts in return for their allegiance, removing some of the grubbiness of prostitution, and yet plunging all the deeper into it.

The Red Mansion was a potent symbol for China's current state: Small-time officials extorted village entrepreneurs. From there graft moved up the ladder with city and provincial officials joining in. Bribe begot bribe — until one arrived at the Red Mansion.

Lili, given her range of contacts, I hoped might know more. "The Red Mansion," I said during a break in the show, "you have heard of it?"

"Of course."

"You have?"

"Everyone has heard of it." She said rumors had been circulating for years. The mansion's outside walls were red but that wasn't why it was called *hong lou*, or Red Mansion. It got its name from the novel *Hong lou meng*, or *Dream of a Red Mansion*, a sprawling Qing Dynasty story about a wealthy Peking family. Five generations lived together with countless retainers, servants, courtesans, and relatives.

"What's inside the Red Mansion?" I said.

"There are rooms."

"And inside the rooms?"

"There are young women, quite a few of them."

"In Lai's mansion or in the book?"

"Both."

I asked Lili where in Xiamen the mansion was, not sure what I was hoping to find. She scribbled directions on a napkin. They were short, comprising only three characters. *Gu-lang-yu.* This was the name of a small island next to Xiamen, no more than a mile long. I took the napkin and left.

The next morning I walked from my apartment overlooking No.1 Wharf to a nearby quay. Sampans jostled in the breeze. Choppy water coursed through the narrow channel that divided Xiamen and Gulangyu, with churning eddies tugging at craft attempting to cross between the islands.

From a swaying pontoon I climbed onto a departing ferry. Its wooden deck — painted white and glistening with spray — had the air of a pleasure cruiser from a bygone age. And it might as well have been. For when the vessel docked on the other side, it appeared to have crossed to a place from a century or more ago. I knew Xiamen had once been a colonial outpost of the west. In 1842, after the First Opium War, foreign powers had established a trade mission here. In the main section of the city the legacy was buried alongside other more distant reminders of the past. But on Gulangyu the days of empire lived on, minus the gunboats. Standing on the spray-washed deck I could see grand residences left behind by the masters of the coolie and tea trade. Solemn steeples were dotted along green slopes — here a church spire, there a wayward gargoyle.

While I was gazing at the island, passengers clambered down from the deck past an idle turnstile and onto a small concourse. I was the last to disembark. Across the concourse I spotted an imposing red building with barred windows on the upper two floors. The Red Mansion? This was too easy. I walked up a few steps, shaded by gingko trees, and stopped at a plate glass window on the ground floor. Inside I could make out a self-service restaurant. Tofu strips in sesame seed oil were laid out on stainless steel trays. Around to the side I found a door opening onto a staircase. I was about to enter when a man in a Mao suit, possibly the first I had seen in Xiamen, came up from behind. He was not as old as the suit might have suggested. The darkness of his hair appeared to be natural and his legs robust. He had seen me peer inside, he said. "Are you looking for a room?" It sounded like an invitation and I said yes. Together we went up the stairs to a landing from where we could see into several rooms. They appeared to be for rent. Some were occupied — clothes draped over chairs and beds. Boys played cards in one, but there were no women. I turned to the man in the Mao suit and said this was not what I had come for. How to explain? I couldn't bring myself to say I was looking for the local bordello. I might be mistaken for a latter-day colonial — wifeless and weary after a sea voyage, arriving from London or Lisbon with an urgent wish to acquaint myself with womenfolk.

I said I wasn't so much looking for a room as a whole building, in fact, a well-known building that happened to be red on the outside. This was, admittedly, not the best way forward. Half the buildings on the island were red, some painted a traditional vermilion, others made from terra cotta bricks. I added that the red house I was looking for had a reputation for decadence and misery. That might do it. The man nodded. At the bottom of the stairs I asked him if he could point me in the right direction. He disappeared into a small room across an alley and came back with his slippers. "I know the way," he said. "It's not so far."

Zhu Yiling, or John, as he introduced himself, lived next door. He said he was called John in memory of a previous resident, a Christian. "I am not a Christian myself but most people on the island are. It's the result of foreign occupation. This building here used to be the consulate of Britain. Now there's a restaurant and some of the rooms upstairs are rented out. But once the whole port was controlled from here."

John moved briskly, his slippers clapping through cobblestone streets with not a car in sight. Behind wrought iron gates, bougainvillaea sprouted in hushed gardens. Xiamen was far away, except for a lone banner ("Rely on the working class wholeheartedly").

John said, "This wasn't such a happy place in the time of the British. Lots of decadence and misery." We passed a Victorian villa. Its second-floor balcony looked like a half-detached lifeboat — unable to float free and about to be pulled under by its tether. John said times here had been miserable for Chinese and foreigner alike. The first three British consul sent from London all died in their post in quick succession. Not one reached the age of forty-five, leaving behind pregnant wives and flocks of children. They had to contend with fevers, rebellions, and pirate attacks. Some called Xiamen the filthiest place in China. That's why the consulate was moved to Gulangyu from its original site on the main island, but it wasn't much better here.

We came to a large gate cut into a fence. The gate was locked but John neatly slipped through a gap in the wire mesh and I followed him. On the other side, we found ourselves a hundred feet above the water line on a grassy bluff that might once have been a gun emplacement. Below lay in pointillist detail the bay of Xiamen, dotted with boats and errant sparkles, while behind us stood the most imposing villa I had seen so far. The front door could only be reached via a flight of stone-carved stairs. The wooden floors inside, judging by the noises they made, were original. "This is your building," John said, "the residence of the British consuls." I had a quick look around and spotted a dodgy roof as well as weeds growing in some of the rooms. Neither Lai nor anyone else had spent the night here in a very long time.

"There is only one problem," I said. "The building is not red."

It wasn't, saving me further explanations. John pondered this for a moment and then led me to a cluster of smaller buildings. One was the house of the British customs director, another the one-time international club, apparently the site of the first bowling alley in southern China. One room contained a mini-museum made up of photocopies taped to the walls. They quoted an officer named C. Samuels on the lack of a sewage system and the frequency with which Indian manservants succumbed to fevers. Most photocopied passages on display had been chosen with obvious political intent. They made the colonial masters look despicable. Much attention was paid to British punishment expeditions to wipe out rebellious native villages. There were also repeated mentions of abominable jails, although wealthy prisoners appear to have been able to procure the services of prostitutes while inside. For the other prisoners, flogging was the most common form of physical interaction. Even though beatings were generally despised by colonial officers, they apparently prescribed them for "Asiatics" thought unresponsive to other forms of coercion. Worse still than the officers were the hundreds of foreign merchants who arrived in their wake. When not smoking opium, they colluded with local crimps to ship coolies to Latin America. Even women and children were forced aboard the slave ships. Colonial officers apparently attempted to at least regulate the trade, but with little success. They could hardly get enough women for themselves, although they were otherwise well provisioned. One scrap of paper reported: "There were over 80 bachelors and widowers as against just over 50 married men, but 13 spinsters and 2 widows were available. The *Amoy Gazette* appeared every day, European stores could be bought locally, Gulangyu produced its own ice and aerated water, and a supply of pure milk was planned."

When we left I said to John this wasn't what I was looking for. "The red building I meant is not a British colonial building. People still stay there today."

"Right," he said, "not a British building. I understand. I know. Follow me." We passed a row of stuccoed terraces shaded by cinnamon trees. Vines crept through arched windows with bits of washing strung up on a line. John was taking me to see the former American consulate. Apparently the building was known to have a secret level sandwiched in between the first and second floors. That sounded promising. But the building had been converted into a popular hotel more than ten years ago, and it wasn't red either.

Next, we went to the old Japanese consulate, which John referred to as the "Japanese imperialist consulate." The outside walls were covered in graffiti left over from the Cultural Revolution. "Long live Mao Zedong Thought!" It was currently used as a dormitory for teachers. John knew this was not the right building either.

As we went on we could hear piano music drifting down an alley. I had heard it earlier too. The *trill-trill* of Ravel and the *tap-the-tap* of Chopin. John said the nineteenth century colonials had brought missionaries with them, who in turn brought pianos, and more than five hundred of them still existed on the island. Residents called Gulangyu "piano island." As we walked on, airy tunes drifted down the alleys — music with perfect pitch for ruined art deco mansions.

"There is one more building I want to show you," John said. "It belonged to the owner of China's first toothpaste factory."

"Is it red?"

"No, but it has a very miserable story. The owner's son cut up a picture of Chairman Mao thirty years ago. Someone saw him do it and the child was sent to prison . . ."

"John," I said, "no more please."

"But why? It's my job."

"Your job?"

John worked as a guide, walking guests around the island. It dawned on me he had just given me what must be his regular tour. So much for getting an inside track, and I would have to pay him as well.

৩

I went back to Lili's club. By the bar, I told her I failed to find the Red Mansion. A glass of XO cognac would take the edge off my disappointment, she said. "Why are you so keen to find that place anyhow?" Lili rolled a glass in the palm of her hand, a soft drink. "You don't need to go there to see how it works. This place is just the same," she said.

"How do you mean?"

"You know what I mean."

And, of course, I did. Businessmen hosted government officials here every night of the week. When they sent flowers to the stage dancers with three-digit number tags clipped to their waists they expected more than just a smile and a thank-you.

"But," I said, "I would still like to find Lai's mansion." Obsessions were common enough in Xiamen. What else did one have to hold on to in a place filled with quicksand? Lili, surely, would understand.

She ordered me another cognac. "I'm not busy during the day tomorrow," she said. "You want me to come with you to look for the mansion?"

I accepted her offer gratefully, and that's how I found myself back on the piano island. I wasn't feeling entirely well when I got there, having left the club only a few hours earlier. Lili was already waiting for me, sparkling like an ice cube. Rather than wearing her sober leather shoes from the club, she was teetering on high heels. With an unblinking grin on her face, she watched me step off the ferry — even more gingerly than she must have done.

For an hour we trawled a faux-Victorian development that disgraced the edge of the island. All around us were semidetached villas, recently built and looking more suburban than colonial. Some were painted a bright acetylene red, others pink, orange, and lavender. New Xiamen had gained a foothold. But rather than being outraged, residents wanted more such construction. When Lili struck up conversations with local residents they told her, "Most people have to go over to Xiamen. The old houses are in such bad shape. They are protected by the government."

The residents complained about falling plaster, rotting bathrooms, and sagging roofs. They all wanted to live in a new development. Eventually, having gained token trust, Lili would ask about Lai's Red Mansion. When she did, she was straight up. "Say, is the Red Mansion of Lai Changxing anywhere near here?" The residents shook their heads. No, it wasn't around here.

We climbed up into the hills behind the villas and passed an old cemetery with Christian crosses hidden behind moss-grown walls. The conical hats of gardeners bobbed up and down but there was no Red Mansion, and no boaters or bowlers hats either. I would have been thankful for any kind of miracle, however small or useless. The weather seemed right for it. Heat had invaded the shady spots. I was ready to see things.

From the highest point on the island we went down a narrow alley filled with peanut fryers, fish mongers, and hawkers offering lukewarm beer in glasses gone opaque from a thousand uses. Further along, a group of women was making a local dessert. They molded cooked rice in their palms, then cut the grainy dough open with a knife, filled it with sugared peanut flakes, and dropped it on a tray with sesame seeds.

Customers buying the sticky balls had their money taken with chopsticks. The women never touched the notes with their hands. Lili, impressed by this, asked them about the Red Mansion. After a lengthy discussion among themselves, they said there was only one building connected to Lai on the island. We should try No. 73 on Quanzhou Street. Cai Haipeng, a senior member of the customs bureau, lived there. He had been a close friend of Lai and when Lai disappeared, so did he.

Interesting, but no, that wasn't it either.

⟋⟍

On the ferry back to the main island Lili told me she left her parents' home in the countryside a few hundred miles northwest of Xiamen when she was twenty-six. That was ten years ago. "Xiamen was still a backward place," she said. "People didn't have shampoo to wash, only soap. You couldn't buy shampoo anywhere." She came to Xiamen after losing a job at a local factory. It had closed during one of the frequent downturns in China's early boom. Lili saw a recruitment poster for a Xiamen nightclub soon after. Her mother was against her going but Lili insisted. She started work as a waitress and instantly increased her factory salary tenfold. Every month she sent money to her parents. Still they disapproved. After a year, they came to Xiamen and pressured her to return home. Within a few weeks Lili had left once again. She didn't see her parents for five years — out of defiance, she said, but probably also out of shame. Even now her parents were uneasy about her job. "I told them I was never a dancer at the club but they don't believe me." Lili had been so successful as a waitress that she was promoted straight to her current position. She said this with a tinge of defensiveness. It was the first time. I had not heard so much as a whisper of unease before.

I found it hard to know Lili. She was more generous with her time than anyone else in Xiamen. She spoke with great clarity and had no obvious inhibitions. And yet, until today I had rarely heard her talk about her past. Conversations had always led us back to the club, her work, her guests, her dancers. Even now she was headed that way. She told me how she and some of the dancers would fly to Guangzhou for the day just to get their hair done. They went in the morning and returned in time for the evening show. "Once I had a heavy perm put in," she said. "The style was called Old Shanghai. But it made the hair very thick and I got hot under it. In the club with all the spotlights it was unbearable. The next day I flew to Guangzhou once more to have it taken out."

I suspected Lili felt uneasy talking about her past because the values of her parents still exerted a pull, exposing her new identity as skin deep. She came close to saying as much herself. She disagreed with me when I said the dancers in the club had reinvented themselves, new hair and all. She thought they had moved up, but no more. Behind their new lives in Xiamen were still old selves. Their new identities were little more than pretensions of modernity — underneath one found peasant crudeness. In their language it was all too obvious. Lili tried to teach them how to drop their regional accents but it rarely worked.

But why did Lili tell me about her past today? What was different? Perhaps she felt embarrassed having sent us on a fool's errand. There was no Red Mansion on Gulangyu, that much was clear. Sitting on the ferry deck now, she smoked a cigarette. She did so with a worldly ignorance wholly at odds with her club persona. I knew her as shrewd and judicious, yet her smoking — big blowy puffs — had an unfamiliar abandon. I had never even seen her smoke. At the club none of the women did. It was viewed as mannish, and only male guests did. A third of the world's smokers were Chinese men (my favorite Sino-fact, along with Chinese consuming half the world's pork and cement). For a Chinese woman to smoke in public was a sign of rebellion.

Until today, I had only ever seen Lili in the plain gray trouser suits she wore at the club. In them she was no competition to the peacocks on the stage, and that was the point. Guests were to focus on buying flowers for dancers. But now Lili was wearing denim shorts and a matching T-shirt with sequins stitched to the front. When she looked at the tracksuit I had thrown on in the morning, she said, "You should dress better." The comment was like a fragment from an otherwise unremembered dream. She had not once remarked on my wardrobe before.

When we disembarked Lili casually admitted she didn't know the location of the Red Mansion. "It's named after on old book," she said, "so I thought it would be in an old part of the city." Across from the quay where we stood was a small section of colonial dwellings, similar to those in Gulangyu. This last bit of Old Xiamen stretched for a third of a mile along the waterfront. Lili suggested looking there for the mansion. It was our best option, but first we'd flush out XO leftovers.

We stopped at a self-service restaurant on the quay. I piled cooked cabbage and plain rice on a tin tray. Lili, having raced to the cashier ahead of me, paid for both of us and sat down at a table. When I got there she said, "I know this outing is part of your work as a reporter, but normally when you take out a girl you should pay for her meal."

Lili knew all about paying for people. I sat down and resolved to ask her about the darker parts of her club, the parts she had hinted at in reference to the Red Mansion. "The dancers," I said seated on a bench next to her, "how does it work with them and the male guests?"

"You mean the girls who go home with guests?"

"I guess so, yes."

"The guest has to order at least fifteen flower rings. They cost one hundred yuan each, so altogether it's fifteen hundred."

"And who gets the money?"

"The guests pay the club and the club pays the girls. It varies how much each girl gets."

"It seems a rather complicated system."

"It's not complicated at all. It's easy. The girls are guaranteed their money and the club gets its cut. And if anyone claims there is illegal activity at the club, well, let them prove it."

"But don't you still get raided by the police?"

"Of course. They know what goes on, but they tell their bosses they couldn't find any illegal activity."

"And all the girls in the club participate in this activity?"

"Not at all. Less than half. The majority only *zuo tai* (they sit and drink with guests during or after stage shows). But in every club there are some girls who *chu tai*. Otherwise certain guests wouldn't come. On a normal night, about fifteen dancers go home with a guest."

"And what role do you play in all this?"

"The guests want to know which girls *zuo tai* and which *chu tai*. I tell them."

"That's it?"

"Actually, it's quite a lot of work." Lili had finished her lunch and leaned back on the narrow bench next to me. She appeared very much at ease with her chosen profession. She was almost flaunting how comfortable she was with it. "Guests like you," she said, "have a lot of choice now in Xiamen, isn't that true?"

"I guess so."

"There are many clubs. We can't just wait for guests to turn up and hope they will spend a lot of money. We have to give them a good service — make sure they come back. That's my job. I have dinner with them beforehand, tell them about the club, which dancers will be performing, see if they are interested in meeting any of them, find out what their tastes are, tell them which dancer might be interested in them. I have dinners like this most nights before I go to the club. Often more than one."

"And it works?"

"I think so. I see the same customers at the club all the time and keep a good relationship with them. Sometimes when I know them well and they want to spend more money than they have with them, I give them credit. The next day I turn up in their office to ask for the money. For that, I always wear the gray suit I use in the club, not clothes like these." She plucked at her denim shorts. "When I am at their office they pretend not to know me. They are very reserved, especially in front of their staff. It's funny how different they are compared to the evenings. They talk so loudly then. But I don't say anything. At least not until they return to the club."

"And then you say what?"

"One guy came back and wanted to impress some friends. I said to him plenty of people here have more money than you. He pretended to be hurt and to prove he had a lot he asked to buy our most expensive cigar. But instead of asking for a cigar (*xue jia*) he asked for something that sounded like eggplant (*xue qie*)."

A waitress came to our table and took away our plates without saying a word. Lili watched her silently. When she was gone, Lili said, "I would never have her at the club. She has a bad attitude. She is pretty but so are many others."

"How many women do you have at the club?"

"Usually between four and five hundred. It varies. They come and go. There are ten of us who work in my position and we handle about fifty dancers each. At the moment I have forty-four. Six left recently to become permanent girlfriends of customers. That happens all the time."

We got up and walked out of the restaurant. The heat was intense. Xiamen's last few blocks of colonial dwellings stood close together and blocked the breeze coming off the ocean.

Shopkeepers piled up their wares in shaded colonnades. A man squatted by a red canvas bag that bounced around unaided. He said he was selling live frogs. Further along, a woman was watching shrimp fling themselves out of a wicker basket in a futile bid for freedom. An array of professions was on display here that had already died out elsewhere in the city: bamboo steamer makers, streetside seamstresses, coal sellers with blackened faces riding tricycles, bare-chested "stick soldiers" carrying loads slung to poles resting on their shoulders, bearded elders mixing potions from roots and weeds stored in glass jars.

We walked aimlessly. Lili stopped every few minutes to ask about the Red Mansion, but with scant success. After a while we drifted back to our conversation from the restaurant. She said, comparing herself favorably to the shopkeepers around us, that she earned thirty thousand dollars a year at the club. The dancers could make as much or more, but most didn't. Some of them made almost no money at all. It depended on the flowers.

"So if girls go home with guests," I said, "they make more money?"

"Of course!"

"And are any of them forced to do it?"

"That's not how it works."

"No pressure at all?"

"There is pressure, but not to go home with guests. The girls have to earn fees of four thousand yuan [five hundred dollars] per month."

"Pretty harsh."

"Oh, they only need to get one or two flower orders per night to make their quota."

"And if they don't?"

"If they fail to make the four thousand they get fired."

"I see."

"We also do a lot of good things for them. It's my job to help them wherever I can. One girl got into trouble with a Taiwanese gang. Their leader was obsessed with her. I told him again and again she doesn't go home with guests, but he wouldn't listen. Every night he came and sent her flowers. The girl didn't even go out to dinner with him. He got very upset, but still he sent flowers. For a while she was making fifteen thousand yuan a month. The tension was unbearable. In the end, I told her she should take a rest. She dropped out for a while and went home to her family. The Taiwanese gangster never saw her again."

"Okay."

"Another time I got a call early in the morning from one girl. She said she had been drunk the night before and had gone home with a guest. She wasn't sure what happened. But now she was in a mental hospital. She had no idea how she got there. She had already called some of the other girls to get her out but they were too scared. So eventually she called me. I put on my gray suit and wrote a letter pretending to be from a big company. With that I went to the hospital. The letter said the girl was a sane employee of my company and that the company would take full responsibility for her mental state. So the guards let her go."

We were still walking. The shade of the colonnades made the heat bearable. Coming toward us was a man with a leather satchel. In his hands he held two large blades. Lili said he was a knife-sharpener. Men like him went from house to house, announcing their presence with a metallic clanging of their blades. They knew the neighborhood better than anyone. Lili asked him about the Red Mansion. He shook his head without breaking his stride.

Further on, Lili turned into a covered passage used as a wet market. Over several hundred meters, stalls offered live fish, betel nuts, lotus leaves, seaweed, melon seeds, ginger roots, sweetbreads, cuts of pork belly, and much more. While Lili bought freshly ground beef, I watched an ice merchant at work. He supplied sellers with slush to preserve their wares and to cool the water in fish tanks. The merchant would grip three-foot-long blocks of solid ice with black metal tongs, drag them off a small van in which they had been delivered, bounce them on an old car tire, and feed them into a shredder. Around him the air had a pleasant chill.

The market ended in an alley near Zhongshan Street, where spaces between buildings widened. New structures crept in, and so did official banners ("Rally closely around the Party Central Committee"). Lili said she had one more idea how to find the Red Mansion. She would talk to a colleague at the club who had known Lai better — maybe she would know.

Once Lili left I went into a bookshop on Zhongshan Street. The shelves were filled with business bibles and the autobiographies of well-known entrepreneurs. I saw six different versions of the memoirs of Jack Welch, the former head of General Electric. One was an authorized translation, the others were pirate editions printed on thinner paper. A sign on the door in English and Chinese said Xiamen had the highest per capita expenditure on books in the country, about twelve dollars per month. In the back I found a translation of *Dream of a Red Mansion* by Tsao Hsueh-Chin, the fictional model for Lai's mansion.

⁌

The next afternoon I met Lili where we had parted. She said her colleague had been very helpful. She now had directions to the Red Mansion: we would go to a district called Huli — people there could tell us more. We got into a cab on Zhongshan Street and the driver made a wide turn on to Lakeside Drive and sped up away from the colonial quarter. Outside, a very different Xiamen came into view. On our right were concrete office blocks and residential towers. On our left was a newly dug tidal pool. It stretched most of the way to the center of the island and everyone referred to it as the "lake." Why a city by the sea needed a lake nobody could say, but at high tide water rushed in from the ocean through a system of sluice gates and canals. Palm trees and lawns lined the lake's fringes.

Lakeside Drive was the main artery of the New Xiamen. High-rises shot up here in a matter of months. Time was always tight. Investors expected to make back their money in no more than half a year. Anything longer than that and the risks became too great. Who knew what would happen in six months? The bubble might burst. Speed was everyone's paramount concern. Builders mixed ammoniac into the cement to make it set faster — which unfortunately also made it crumble faster. An earthquake in Xiamen would be devastating. But even without one, construction was known for its thunderbolt deadliness: builders died in accidents, slipshod practices killed passersby, rival developers disappeared in the course of vicious turf battles.

And yet the look of most building sites was quaintly elegant. Construction companies used bamboo poles tied together with twine for scaffolding. Rattan and wicker rose up on the outsides of concrete shells. Bamboo was cheaper than metal and some said it was more flexible and thus safer. Unlike metal, it bent with the wind. From our cab window, Lili and I saw workers limbering up thirty floors on spindly poles, past the usual banners ("Make a civilized citizenry") and a new one ("Shout fewer slogans and do more practical things").

Halfway up Lakeside Drive our cab overtook a small van that I recognized. It was the ice merchant's from the wet market. He was probably off to fetch new blocks of ice. The discovery strangely cheered me. I pointed out the van to Lili and said, "You must be at home somewhere if you recognize the cars on the street."

"You at home here?"

"Yes."

"If that's so you should come and work for me."

"And drink with clients?"

"Of course. We sometimes have female guests coming in alone."

We got out of the taxi on a street corner in Huli and started walking. Around us towered the high-rise city Lai had built. One part of Huli was called Yuanhua City after one of Lai's companies. This was his domain, his fief. For years, nothing had happened here without him knowing — his government contacts saw to it. He was master over Huli residents as much as anyone could be said to rule such a driven and independent bunch. He created jobs and provided places for them to live and to bring up children who might one day be genuinely free. A little more than a decade ago, there had been nothing here but farmland. Now we were walking through a little New York City. Huli followed the same commercial laws of hazard, chance, and hope. On one building I saw a sign advertising the Xiamen Charming Industrial Company. That was the spirit. The city housed many a monstrosity, but as a whole — soaring and raptor-eyed — Xiamen was a marvel.

We passed the Golden Egret Special Alloy Company, then the Xueliang eyeglass store, which got its name from a Mao saying, "The people's eyes are as bright as snow [*xueliang*]." The eyeglass store was one of many to borrow from the Communist canon. "Away with all pests," an insecticide maker crowed, quoting a Mao poem; meanwhile, a maker of vacuum cleaners advised customers that "dust won't disappear of its own accord," parroting the chairman, who had once said, "Reactionaries, like dust, won't disappear on their own".

We were lost walking through Huli and no longer paying attention, entranced by its scale. Then suddenly, following a few more hapless enquiries along the way, we found ourselves right in front of the Red Mansion. There we were, to my surprise, facing an unremarkable building on Huaguang Road. On the roof was a sign proclaiming in large letters, "To Pay Taxes Is Glorious." So Lai had a sense of humor. "To Get Rich Is Glorious" was a slogan — attributed to Deng Xiaoping — that propelled the reform era.

I squinted. The seven-story building had red walls and blue-glass windows. It was set back from the street. The windows were shuttered, the front gate locked. There was no obvious way in and nobody inside. If there had once been modern-day concubines locked away here, they were long gone.

We had found the mansion . . . Lili gave me an aren't-we-good-together wink. No doubt our success bode well for my future career at her club. But now what?

For a few minutes we stood at the gate and peered in silently. The mansion looked diminutive. It wasn't much different from the surrounding apartment buildings. It was blocky and made no extravagant claims or gestures, devoid of sweeping lawns or imposing spires. The red tiling on the exterior walls recalled a bathroom and the paved driveway leading up to the front door was too cracked for even a two-star hotel. I had expected something in line with Lai's Forbidden City — a stately pleasure dome, a redoubt worthy of a bandit king. But, as in most things, Lai had been careful to exhibit conformity. He drove sedans, not sports cars, and he hid his personal bordello behind a façade more suburban than sumptuous. There was not a hint of Lai's legendary relationship-building skills here, described in local slang as *pangaozhi*, to ingratiate oneself with the powerful, and *taoci*, to act as if you already knew someone, and *ceng*, to benefit from association with higher-ups.

Lili must have sensed our discovery wasn't quite what I had hoped it would be. We walked back down Huaguang Road and she said it was time for her to cook dinner. Did I want to come with her, see her apartment? I said yes.

Her place was a short cab ride away in a newish development just off Lakeside Drive. She unlocked her front door and very quickly it became clear the dinner she would be cooking was not for the two of us. It was for her dog. Lili did not currently have a boyfriend but lived with a two-year-old, twenty-pound terrier. Every week, she made fresh sausages for him. "I eat them as well," she said. "They're good. But mainly they are for him. He doesn't eat anything else. He refuses dog food. I have to cut the sausages into little pieces for him. I always give him exactly one and a half sausages every day. One day I was careless and gave him only one sausage. He wouldn't touch it. First I couldn't figure out why. I thought he might be sick. But then I added another half and he ate it. I really spoil him. He also gets coconut milk and Coca-Cola to drink."

Lili opened her fridge and got out the ground beef she had bought in the wet market. "I saw him in the street two years ago," she said. "Somebody was selling puppies. But when I bought him and I went out to work every day he was very lonely, so I brought my mother in from the countryside to live with me for a while. Now he is older and quite lazy and doesn't care anymore who is around. When I let him out to pee he is usually back at the door within a minute."

Lili saw me laughing. I was standing off to the side, hoping to escape her notice. "I know what you are thinking," she said. "There is a certain type of woman who has a dog. You're right. Dogs are much more friendly to us than men. Some of the dancers at the club have one, too." Lili had started to knead and spice the ground beef. "It's quite expensive to have a dog. In the first year, the dog tax is thirty-six hundred yuan [four hundred fifty dollars]. After that it goes down to six hundred yuan. But that's still six flower orders." She said she didn't pay the tax. Since her dog never went outside for long there was little chance she would be caught. The only real danger were the dogcatchers. Sometimes they came and surrounded a whole neighborhood. "If you can't show a tax receipt or if a dog is too big, they take it away."

"And eat it?"

"Maybe."

In the poorer parts of Xiamen, where the most recent arrivals from the countryside lived, I had seen dog on restaurant menus. Nowhere was the unfinished transformation of the city and its residents more obvious. Perched between modern and ancient, there were those who groomed dogs and those who ate them.

While Lili fed her dog I wandered around the apartment. I tried to imagine what her mother might have made of the place when she came. She probably approved of the metal-sheathed front door and the wire cages covering the windows to ward off burglars. But what about the vanilla baseboards and mock rococo moldings? And the manless double bed? Not just the design of the place but the lifestyle it hinted at must have been suspect.

I sat down on the sofa in Lili's living room. In front of me on a glass table lay a photo album. It had been shot and printed in a professional studio. Page after page showed Lili in various poses and dresses. As a vampy temptress in black, a *qipao*-wearing maiden, an all-in-white bride, a jeans-and-blouse cowgirl. This was a common vanity project. Make-believe albums such as this one were popular among young Chinese — glossy pictures embroidered with mangled lines from western pop songs, like "always lover you" and "rainbow sets over sun."

While I was looking through the album, Lili clipped her mobile phone to a cord around her neck. It was within easy reach now and soon rang. Clients were calling. This was their time. They wanted to know about the evening's show and whom they might see onstage. Lili's manner changed with every call. She had a distinct voice for each of them. It was as if different selves came alive from the pages of her photo album, from blousy parry to whispered confidence. Then, around seven, she changed into her gray trouser suit and a pair of flat leather shoes and said she was going to work. "You want to come with me?" she said. I pleaded lack of sleep from the night before. On my way home I thought, Who was I to turn down the invitation of an honest woman? Well, maybe honest woman wasn't the best way to describe Lili. But I liked her.

12

FUGITIVES

No. 22 Huaguang Road, Huli District, Xiamen

LAI WAS STILL a fugitive. And then one day he wasn't. Rather oddly, the news came from the Canadian embassy in Beijing. It issued a statement saying Lai was in Canada. Another red herring? I called the embassy and a spokeswoman confirmed Lai was detained in Vancouver for overstaying his visa. That was it? After almost two years on the run Lai was held on a technicality by the Royal Canadian Mounted Police with their red frocks and flaxen mares? What else could she tell me? I asked. Very little. A woman presumed to be Lai's wife was with him. There may be young children, too. All of them were held until their status could be determined.

Beijing responded to the news the next day. A story in the official *China Daily* newspaper demanded Lai's extradition. A jubilant foreign ministry spokesman was quoted as saying, "The net of Heaven has large meshes, but it lets through nothing." A few hours later the prime minister gave a rare televised interview. "I have read the reports," he said. "We will contact and consult the Canadian side." Asked if he was confident Lai would return, he said, in English, "I will try my best." That was different from what he had said about Lai not long before. "He should be killed three times over, and even that wouldn't be enough," he told reporters on a trip to Southeast Asia.

Four days later, Lai was brought in front of an immigration panel in Vancouver. He was dressed in a green prison overall wearing handcuffs. He looked a shadow of the man I had seen in photographs. The sheen was gone. Lai had reverted to being the nameless peasant he once was — no different from thousands of other migrants seeking jobs as dishwashers and waiters, as powerless abroad as they were at home. His stare was empty and he showed little interest in the proceedings. Zeng Mingna, his wife, sat next to him, her face buried in her hands, wearing a suede jacket, flowery pants, and spangled high heels.

An immigration official, acting for the Canadian government, opened the hearing by telling the panel Lai was a fugitive. "Canada may not be a safe haven from China," he said. The Lai family ought to be sent back, and until then they should remain in detention. There was a risk they might abscond. "The last time the stove got hot, they fled immediately," he said.

A lawyer acting for Lai responded by making an application for political asylum on the grounds that he faced persecution at home. None other than the Chinese prime minister had publicly called for his execution, he said. Canada was constitutionally committed to sheltering anyone facing the death penalty. Furthermore, there was no formal extradition treaty between Canada and China.

The prosecution acknowledged this last point but said, "Mr. Lai and Mrs. Zeng are excluded from claiming refugee status because they have committed nonpolitical crimes in China punishable by sentences of more than ten years."

I followed all this on the Internet. Chinese websites were competing furiously in their reporting of the case. Many felt emboldened by the Beijing government's demand for Lai's extradition. It cleared up the rules a little. Sites could write about Lai as long as he was depicted as evil. They could not question the government's position, but such restrictions hardly mattered at the moment. The story was compelling enough. Readers flocked to the sites. Spurred on by so much interest, some sites hired local correspondents in Vancouver or dispatched their own. Meanwhile, the official media behaved very differently. After an initial flurry of reports and high-level television interviews following Lai's detention, it fell silent. A door had opened briefly and then shut again.

Following a review of Lai's tourist visa — it had long run out — the Vancouver immigration panel moved on to his alleged crimes. The prosecution, using information supplied by Beijing, said Lai had led a smuggling ring based in Xiamen that illegally imported cars, oil, and cigarettes, fraudulently avoiding $3.6 billion in taxes and fees. Lai's lawyer responded by calling the allegations themselves "an enormous fraud." Pointing at Lai and his wife, he said, "The prosecution they face in China is politically inspired." Chinese leaders were waging factional battles in the politburo, he said. Some of them happened to be friends of Lai and, to smear them, rivals invented the smuggling and corruption charges.

The panel took note and moved on. Over the next week, it heard accounts of how Lai had spent his time in Canada prior to his detention. Following his arrival more than a year earlier he had paid $1 million in cash for a house in Vancouver's exclusive South Granville district. His children went to private school at a cost of $4,000 a year each and his wife had opened a bank account with an initial deposit of $1.5 million. Lai himself moved around in a chauffeur-driven $90,000 sports-utility vehicle. The Chinese websites loved these details and repeated them in full.

When Lai was detained, he was apparently on the twenty-eighth day of a gambling spree in Canada's honeymoon capital, Niagara Falls. Officers approached him after he had spent more than seven hours in one casino during which he lost $12,000. Three days earlier, he had lost $55,000. Lai was a regular and the casino kept very good records. Over the previous year he had gambled on eighty-four days, buying $3 million worth of chips. On his best day, he had been up $160,000, but overall he lost $300,000. That's how Canadian police apparently noticed him. They suspected he might be involved in money-laundering or loan-sharking.

What interested me most was how Lai had managed to escape from China and make his way across the Pacific. Here, too, the hearing offered clues. Lai said he had been in Hong Kong when the Chinese government moved against him. An official in the immigration department there notified him of an arrest warrant from Beijing. "He told me about the warrant and advised me to leave Hong Kong immediately," Lai said. "He warned me against going to a Southeast Asian country and urged me instead to go to Canada from where perhaps I could work something out." The officer was "a friend of mine," Lai said. He was also dead now. Leung Kam-kwong had died a few months earlier during an arson attack at a Hong Kong immigration center. He was posthumously given a bravery award for trying to save others during the resulting fire. The Hong Kong government responded to Lai's testimony by saying, "These claims are totally baseless. We regret that such an allegation has been made against a deceased officer who can no longer defend himself. This is grossly unkind, unfair, and one may consider it an act of malice."

At the end of the last day of the hearing, a Chinese reporter at the back of the room shouted in Mandarin: "Are you or are you not the boss of the smuggling ring?" Lai swung around. "It's not true," he said, "it's not fair. Nothing like that happened." Then guards bundled the handcuffed migrant out of the room to await sentencing.

৩

When I spoke to people in Xiamen they were no longer so reticent to discuss Lai now. They all knew of his hearing in Canada and felt emboldened by the coverage it received on the Internet. But their reactions differed greatly. A doctor at a local hospital who had been trained in Texas told me, "The death penalty is legal in America, so why not here?"

My apartment neighbor, standing in his newly decorated living room, said, "Lai has given Xiamen a reputation for crime. He should be punished for that."

"What if he had been from Beijing?" I asked.

"Everyone is corrupt there. Nothing you can do about that."

There were plenty of critical voices. But on the whole, sympathy for Lai outweighed support for the government's extradition request. The attendant at my apartment building, an elderly man who rushed over to open the front door, said, "I don't understand these things. Maybe he was a bad man, but many innocent people profited."

"Lai is a hero," said a taxi driver parked by the building entrance. "Petrol was cheap when he imported it. Now it costs me double to fill up. And cigarettes are more expensive than ever."

Once again, stories about Lai's legendary largesse circulated. He had given money to the poor, websites reported, even the deeds to his homes and the keys to his cars. Everyone whom he met in the days before he fled was given something.

The majority of Chinese lived on less than a dollar a day — many were ready to believe the reports. Chinese at the other end of the wealth spectrum also found reason to side with Lai. They quoted his example to justify their own rule-breaking. "It's the only way to get things done," said a friend who owned a software company. His business partner added, "He imported goods. He didn't rob banks. He was doing something useful. That's more than you can say about most officials."

Sympathetic opinions were lent strength by the fact that official China lacked its own heroes. The greats of the civil war and the Communist revolution were long dead. In desperation, Beijing tried to manufacture successors. Every year it anointed a batch of "model workers." They were hailed in bombastic language ("Be disciplined, honest, and upright"). State media compared them to Lei Feng, the original model worker who had been honored for working himself to death in the early days of revolution. But most Chinese now thought Lei Feng a joke. By using his black-and-white picture the government only confirmed its lack of credibility and legitimacy.

Images of Lai as a fugitive in Canadian custody, on the other hand, struck a chord with many Chinese. Lai appeared helpless. This was a position they could identify with. In pictures reproduced on the Internet they saw a man who had tried and failed to remake his life. He was lost in an unfamiliar environment, unable to communicate in a foreign language. No website said so but people in private did. Kim, not given to sentimentality, told me, "He looks like just another illegal immigrant." Alongside the pictures of Lai, websites reported comments by Chinese officials. That was safe to do. The officials denounced Lai, but most readers knew to believe the opposite of what they read. The more often the government said Lai was a counterrevolutionary, the more people were prepared to think — rightly or wrongly — that he was a gentleman thief. Their sympathy went beyond sentiments of wanting to be "rich like Lai." The Texas-trained doctor told me a few days after he had endorsed the death penalty, "I always thought Lai was greedy and absurd. Now I am waiting with interest. He is standing alone against two governments."

A few days later, news came from Canada. The immigration panel announced its decision in a written statement that appeared almost instantly on Chinese websites. It said Lai and his wife had to remain in detention until their claim for political asylum could be heard. Daphne Shaw Dyke, an immigration adjudicator, wrote: "After considering the evidence and submissions presented to me, it is my decision that Mr. Lai and Mrs. Zeng are unlikely to appear for removal from Canada. Their detention is ordered to continue." She rejected a request by Lai's lawyer to free them once a bond had been posted. "A huge bond would be unlikely to tether them to Canada as they have a great deal of money, which judging from Mr. Lai's gambling activities in Canada they are quite prepared to lose. I have already stated they have the history, financial means, and contacts that easily would enable them to disappear very quickly." She also turned down a separate request for the release of Mrs. Zeng on the grounds that she needed to look after their children. "I realize that detention is a difficult experience but Mrs. Zeng's situation is inextricably connected to that of her husband. She is in just as desperate a situation as he is."

So much for my chance to finally meet Lai. First, he was on the run. Now, he was in prison. If he had been freed I would have flown to Canada, but more likely he would soon be flying in the other direction.

⌇

Fangmin and I were riding in his car, a domestic manufacture.

"You heard? They got him," he said.

"Got who?"

"Your friend, Lai Changxing."

"Yes. I know. But I thought we don't talk about him." At Fangmin's request, I rarely mentioned Lai.

"That was then," he said.

"And now it's okay?"

"Sure. He's been caught."

"Yes, but by the Canadians."

"Soon he'll be back in China. I read the Canadian government is cooperating."

We were driving down Lakeside Drive. It was late evening. Lights on the other side of the tidal lake were bent out of shape in swampy reflections.

"If Lai is sent back to China, does that change anything?" I said.

"Of course. The police were looking for people who knew Lai, thinking it would lead them to him. Soon that'll be over."

A few blocks further on Fangmin said, naturally, he didn't care about Lai. Why should he? But one of his cousins had known Lai. The cousin was definitely not a criminal. Like hundreds of others, he had worked as a driver for Lai a few times. Perhaps not Lai himself but his guests coming down from Beijing. The cousin did claim to know Lai personally, but lots of people in Xiamen said so. It was considered an honor, even if risky, because police were seeking absolutely anyone who had cooperated with Lai; hence his cousin was lying low at the moment. He wasn't exactly in hiding but he avoided meeting people he hadn't known for a long time. This last bit I took to mean he wouldn't talk to me, an outsider, a foreigner, a reporter. I assumed Fangmin knew I would want to talk to his cousin.

"He is just sitting at home, is he?" I said.

"Yes."

"He must be bored."

"I guess so. I wouldn't know."

"But you do occasionally see him?"

"Occasionally."

We stopped in front of a traffic light. Next to us stood a half-finished building belonging to Lai, abandoned when he left. Weeds were growing out of the concrete floors.

"Now that Lai has been caught, your cousin will be coming out of hiding, right?"

"Forget it. He will not talk to you."

Over the next few weeks, we had several more conversations about his cousin. It was me who started them. Was the cousin well? Did he need anything? The Chinese practice of talking around a subject gave me plenty of opportunities to make my case. But in vain. The cousin was as well as he was going to be, and if there was one thing he did not need it was the company of a reporter. Eventually, however, he made one concession. He told Fangmin he could put him in touch with people I might want to meet. First, though, he would need to know what specifically I was interested in. Without thinking much I said, "To visit the Red Mansion," expecting little more than a face-saving shrug.

But Fangmin soon came back with a list of contacts. Over the next few days we visited them one by one. In some distant way they had all been connected to businesses Lai operated. Yet unlike the cousin, most of them were not worried about our meeting. They were in good cheer. They had all done well in the last few years. The women wore jewelry; the men talked of expensive meals. Unfortunately, none of them could help. They were chatty and loose-limbed but had no suggestions for how to visit the Red Mansion. The building had been confiscated and was supposed to be renovated, one said. That was all we got.

Then, several months later, Fangmin met an interior decorator who was involved in surveying the mansion and working on plans for future use. He was the friend of a friend, and so it happened that one Sunday afternoon the decorator unlocked the main gate, where I had stood forlornly with Lili, and led us to the front door. He wore a meticulously assembled combination of pleated and checkered leisure wear. He was only slightly older than Lai but had none of his verve. Once we were in, he said he would give us fifteen minutes to look around, no more. The building was officially still closed.

We told him we were grateful and raced into the lobby. The curtains were drawn and the air stale. Straight ahead was a ten-foot scroll inscribed with "Good luck is on your side." It was framed in a gilded case and mounted on wood paneling as if painted by an old master. Off to the side were white leather sofas standing on a tan marble floor inlayed with an eight-sided black star, "like a funeral parlor," Fangmin said.

The elevator didn't work since the power had been shut off, so we took the dank cement stairs. Along the corridors on the lower floors we passed massage rooms and movie theaters. Chairs were upholstered with faux brocade and drapes threaded with fading gilt. I ran my hand over some of them — they were as dusty as an old library. Higher up we saw rooms fitted with marble Jacuzzis and long, thin red carpets leading to extra-wide double beds.

This had to be where Lai's stable of courtesans once resided, women occupying the pinnacle of a thriving industry. (Even with the world's largest standing army, China still had more prostitutes than soldiers.) At the bottom rung of the industry were the "tents of the migrant worker," who frequented construction sites and the "doorknob girls" who paced hotel corridors (a female friend answering her door was once asked by a doorknob girl, "Is your husband in?"). Then there were the "hairdressers" who sat in the windows of barbershops, and the "three entertainments girls" (singing and dancing and one more — Lili's dancers fell into this category). Still further up the ladder were the *er nai*, the second wives, or literally second set of breasts. They addressed their clients as "husband," of whom they rarely had more than one. They were paid by the month rather than the trick, and expected to receive additional gifts and favors. Men sometimes bought fashion boutiques for them to run, giving them status and to ensure they were too busy for other entanglements. On Xiamen's *Nü Ren Jie*, or Women's Street, two thirds of the shops belonged to *er nai*. Eventually, the women expected to be given an apartment, their "family home." Often they chose one in a so-called concubine village, a place where many of their *er nai* girlfriends lived. The most popular one in Xiamen was the Taiwan Mountain Village (near Wal-Mart). The lawns between the highrises were populated almost exclusively by women.

How their relationships worked was not entirely unfamiliar. I remembered reading about Regency England and prerevolutionary France, where bored aristocrats, pursuing the ultimate luxury, would attempt to win the favors of a resourceful and witty courtesan, a Fashionable Impure, a *Grande Horizontale* (did Harriette Wilson not tell the Duke of Wellington, on hearing he thought of her when going to bed, "How polite to the Duchess"?). The women were promised horses and an address near Hyde Park or the Bois de Boulogne. In modern China, the accouterments were different, but not the methods. It all became clear to me one day when my girlfriend in Beijing was propositioned in a hotel lobby by Qiu Jibao, China's sewing-machine king, apparently a man who grasped opportunities wherever they presented themselves. Following a brief conversation he invited her for a drink. After his first Melonball cocktail, he attempted to present her with a half-ounce twenty-four-karat gold coin and made her a very straightforward offer. He would pay for an apartment if she agreed to be his *er nai*. She would have use of a car and all bills would be taken care of. "I'm tired," he then said. "I will stay the night in this hotel." He stood up. "I will go to the front desk now and get a room. You can stay too, if you are tired." She was not.

While searching for a way into Lai's Red Mansion I had come to read the book after which it was named. *Dream of a Red Mansion* was regarded as China's finest novel. Bookshops had entire shelves filled with criticism devoted to this urtext of Chinese literature, an equal to the *Iliad* or *Faust* or *Ulysses*. Successive generations had come up with new interpretations, seeking their own reflection in it. Under Mao's rule the book briefly fell into disregard — in line with the Chairman's public distaste for the past, though he himself continued to read it (just as he continued to read history books). Today every schoolchild reads at least a few of its one hundred twenty chapters, peopled by fifty-six main characters as well as about four hundred minor ones. The author, Tsao Hsueh-Chin, had died in 1764 at the age of forty-nine after exhausting himself in the writing of the first eighty chapters. The rest was composed by Kao Ngo in around 1791.

During the 1980s *Dream of a Red Mansion* was made into television miniseries. It showed concubines in alluring costumes and became an instant hit. I assumed this was where Lai, who could not read, had found his inspiration. The series showed concubines as an established part of life in the vast mansion of the Chia family. Children of concubines mingled with those of the wives, and when a daughter was invited to join the imperial household as a concubine, all rejoiced for it meant the family would grow in both affluence and power.

As I walked through the real-life mansion built by Lai, I tried to spot the book's influence. On the upper floors, Fangmin and I saw rooms with karaoke machines and microphones. The décor was similar to Lili's club — deep sofas and chintzy borders tracing the doors. It was easy to imagine Lili and her dancers here. Higher up the stairs we came across a kitchen and an adjacent dining hall filled with banquet tables. Place settings were seemingly undisturbed since Lai's departure. White ceramic dishes were decorated with blue animal imagery, chopsticks were carved from ivory, and a cabinet was full of XO cognac. In the kitchen, the cupboards were stacked with cleavers, whetstones, steamers, and steel blades. Other cooking implements hinted at the preparation of intricate wraplings and the extraction of seafood from shells.

Was it too fanciful to see Lai as trying to associate himself with refinement depicted in *Dream of the Red Mansion*? Its fictional residents ate goose foot preserve and cypress-smoked Siamese suckling pig, and they drank a particularly fragrant kumiss. They could distinguish between pure rainwater and melted snow taken from the branches of a flowering *mei* tree (critics pointed out this was easier than it sounded — *mei* flowers have an intense fragrance that flavors the snow lying on them). One main character in the book rejected as inadequate not only noodles but "shrimp balls in a chicken skin soup, a bowl of duck steamed in wine, a plate of red salted goose slices, another plate on which were four cream rolls stuffed with pine kernels, and a large bowl of delicious, steaming-hot, fragrant green rice."

The men who owned the fictional mansion were merchants who had grown rich from trade along the coastal routes. Their wealth and exalted rank were reflected in what they ate. In one chapter a merchant's son visited his maidservant at her home. "After surveying the carefully arrayed dishes of cakes, dried fruits, and nuts, the best that [she and her family] could offer to their young master, Pao-yü's maid realized sadly that there was nothing there that Pao-yü could possibly be expected to eat."

When Lai's guests sat down at his banquet tables to be served expensive delicacies, they crossed a class barrier, or at least they were given the illusion that they had. Most of them would have been familiar with the *Dream of the Red Mansion* and would have known what a symbolic place food occupied in the book. Some may even have appreciated how food imagery, in the prudish eighteenth century, hinted at sex. The shaded bedchambers in the fictional mansion were described as having "blinds looped and fringed like a prawn's belly." The young women inside had "cheeks as white and fresh as a fresh lychee and a nose as white and shiny as soap made from the whitest goose fat." Lovers got to know each other while eating, and one scene of sexual initiation was set in the White Bread Priory, "so called because of the excellent steaming white bread made in its kitchen."

By adopting the book's name Lai must have hoped to lead his guests further into temptation. He had created, in analogy to the famous text, a private world dedicated to sensuality, a rare quality in modern China where until recently everyone wore the same coarse, buttoned jackets. Lai offered his guests seduction, not only by a woman but by a dream, the dream of the Red Mansion, a dream promising fulfillment and prosperity. As long as they were his guests — he seemed to say — they would be given access to a fantasy world where their personal consorts awaited them, as well as envelopes filled with cash. Lai offered them what they had come to Xiamen for, and may not have been able to get elsewhere. Lai promised them the essence of the boomtown. In the hours — or days — they spent in his private chambers they could become part of the fictional world of the Red Mansion. This was perhaps the true genius of Lai. Not only had the former farmer managed to reinvent himself, but he had found a way to exploit the desire of others to do the same.

There was only one problem. Lai didn't seem to know the story of *Dream of a Red Mansion* all that well. Or maybe he did but assumed his guests didn't. A much better model for his bordello would have been *The Sing-Song Girls of Shanghai* by Han Bangqing, another classic I found in a local bookshop. First published in 1894, it described the fin-de-siècle decadence of the treaty ports. One reviewer described it as "a never-ending round of parties where men grown rich on foreign trade play drinking games all night and courtesans stroke their opium pipes."

Dream of a Red Mansion knew no such acts of vulgarity. Or if it did, it implicitly condemned them. On closer reading, the book revealed itself as being opposed to everything Lai stood for. The dream cited in the title was not one promising sensual fulfillment. It was full of rottenness and corruption. Pao-yü, the young Chia merchant's son and one of the main characters in the book, dreamed that:

The high official's fortunes will decline
The rich man's gold and silver melt away
The kind of heart will escape death
The heartless will receive their just desserts
He who takes life will pay with his own
He who causes tears will weep 'til his eyes are dry
One who sees through this world will enter holy orders
One enslaved by love will die a fruitless death
When all food is gone, birds will fly to the woods
Leaving nothing but bare naked earth.

Tsao Hsueh-Chin had written a deeply moral and pessimistic book. His characters' lecherous lifestyles led to bickering and suicide. One by one they hung themselves, plunged into wells, and swallowed golden thread. Having been warned in his dream, Pao-yü wanted nothing except to marry his childhood friend, Tai-yu. But his family chose another bride for him and tricked him into marrying her with the help of a wedding veil. When he found out he descended into madness.

Pao-yü's life and those of the other Chia were a metaphor. Tsao's novel meant to portray the extraordinary corruptness of the Qing Dynasty. In the eighteenth century when the book was composed, officials routinely extorted money from landlords and merchants, like the Chias. They in turn squeezed the peasantry to raise the necessary funds. There were plenty of examples in the book. Some critics even thought it a coded call for rebellion. The Qing court was weak at the time. It had managed to defeat Coxinga, the bearded sea bandit (whom Lai had also adopted as a historical model), but unrest was still building. The court almost fell under the assault of the Taiping led by God's self-proclaimed Chinese son. Saved from the Taipings by millenarian self-destruction, the court was finally knocked down by republicans and their often unwitting bandit collaborators in 1912, paving the way for civil war and eventual rule by the Communists — who then in turn became as corrupt as the Qing had been.

None of this, of course, needed to worry Lai. He was a bandit, not a cultural critic. He was free to pilfer the history books, stuffing his evolving identity with ever more trophies. It was one of the liberties Chinese had gained. Since Mao's death, the imperial past was more accessible, even if still partly mined. Lai had spotted an opportunity. After robbing state coffers, why not the libraries too? And he behaved like a true gentleman thief, with humor, even if unintentional. For him to appropriate *Dream of a Red Mansion* was like changing the name of Colosimo's Café in Chicago — where Al Capone began his career — to Great Expectations, after Charles Dickens.

Seeing Lai's mansion from the inside made the hilarious perfidy of its name more glaring with every step. Fangmin and I were still climbing higher, onward to the top floor, the seventh. Just off the main corridor we saw the outlines of a large animal pelt — a spread-eagled lion or tiger. It had been sketched on the floor in chalk as if this were a zooicidal crime scene. The glum and silent beast, or at least its ghost, peered at us. I let out a shriek. It echoed down the staircase. A moment later, we heard someone answer back. "What happened?" The interior decorator was following us at a distance. He wanted to know what we thought of the mansion. Earlier he had told us the design rated among the finest he had seen. Lai was a criminal but he had remarkable taste. When our time was up, he called for us to leave. We came down and he locked up.

"A terrific building, isn't it?" he said.

"Oh, quite beautiful."

"Very impressive."

"Stunning, really."

"Exceedingly gorgeous."

〰

The Red Mansion was grotesque. It was a sign of remarkable self-confidence on Lai's part. It was also a gift to a prosecutor. It smacked of criminality. A Bond villain would have felt at home.

So what now? I had seen the Red Mansion but still didn't know much about how it worked.

I decided to reinterview, by myself, the people Fangmin's cousin had originally listed for us. They were no help getting into the mansion. But there must have been a reason why he suggested approaching them. I hoped they would at least have some familiarity with the mansion in its previous, less lugubrious incarnation. Perhaps someone would know the origin of the spread-eagled pelt.

On these visits, most told me they had nothing more to say. They knew no more than I did. The mansion was closed, thankfully. The pelt likely be in police custody. The only exception was an elderly woman, Mrs.

Zhuang. She wore a floral print dress and sock-length stockings on hock-like calves. Untidy white roots were showing in her black hair. She said her family had come to money over the years. Her children and grandchildren were involved in the import and real estate business. They had bought six apartments all together. Some were rented out, others stood empty awaiting offspring.

We were talking in a park outside her apartment. She was sitting on a stubby plastic stool she carried around with her on walks, and I sat on a low wall under a banner ("Unite as one, fear no difficulties"). Neighbors came past and she greeted them in a firm voice. It cut through the jackhammer symphony coming from building sites nearby where scaffolding rose above a dusty pawnshop filled with stereos and computers that Mrs. Zhuang still couldn't work but others had already discarded.

I reminded her of our earlier conversation about the Red Mansion. She had said at the time she'd never been inside. Well, since then I had, I said, and recounted details for her. She seemed quite taken with the interior decoration. I asked if she knew anyone who had been to the mansion before it closed. Not personally, she said, but she knew enough about the goings-on from her sons. They had said Lai was his own best customer. He enjoyed the company of many women. But he was not greedy. He always had a lot of guests. Mainly they were older apparatchiks. "When they were young, relations with women were very different from what they are now," she said. "Most of the old men had arranged marriages and never interacted with modern women until they were introduced to one by Lai. You can imagine their reaction. They became great wine-and-meat friends with Lai." Wine-and-meat friends? "Yes, they always drank together and enjoyed their Miss Temporary." Miss Temporary? "That's what they were called. They came from other cities to Xiamen for a while to work at the Red Mansion. Lai paid them more than a thousand dollars just for being there. He had special recruiters who traveled around China to find them. The women had to be at least one meter sixty-five tall and have a high school diploma."

"How many Miss Temporarys were there?"

"Hundreds."

"And they were paid a thousand dollars just to be there? Seems a lot."

"To be there with Lai's clients, of course," Mrs. Zhuang said — unembarrassed. "The clients could have any wish. It would be fulfilled. There was one who didn't like pop music. So they hired a live musician every time he came, an old *erhu* player. The musician was blind so he couldn't watch the couple. He would sit in the bedroom with his instrument, waiting for them to arrive and then play without saying a word."

∽

It was no coincidence I approached Mrs. Zhuang and the others on the list on my own. Having Fangmin there, I feared, would make things more difficult. On our first round of interviews he had picked a few fights, the worst one with a car salesman called Mr. Wang. Fangmin had met him before. They were old friends, he said, but rarely saw each other now. Fangmin accused Mr. Wang of avoiding him. "But I am here standing in front of you," Mr. Wang said. Fangmin called him a snob. "Now that you're rich," he said, "you don't want to see me anymore. You refused to introduce me to your business partner. Old friends should help out each other." We soon left.

Fangmin's belligerence wasn't a surprise. His career was failing. He was increasingly short of money and at one point stopped paying his phone bill. For a while he was unreachable. It seemed he had given up on his hopes. "I am stuck halfway," he said in a rare moment of introspection. "In the small town where I grew up, people are poor but life is simple and easy. When I left I wanted to become rich. If you are rich, China is the best country in the world. You can have anything you want. But if you get stuck in the middle, your life is very complicated and bitter. All you can think of are the things you cannot afford."

In the past, Fangmin had spent hours observing other people's possessions. On the street, he would delight in spotting unusual cars. "That's the limousine Buick just started making in Shanghai," he once said. "Its engine is ten percent bigger than the two-liter limit set by the government for officials. So Buick asked the government to lift the limit and it soon became the top choice among certain officials. In black, with tinted windows."

When Fangmin saw expensive cars now, he cursed them, and when he heard of misfortune befalling their owners he pronounced it just. Fangmin had turned against his own class, or rather the class he had longed to join. After visiting the Red Mansion, he told me Lai should be returned to China and put to death. "He enjoyed luxury without deserving it. I have finished high school. I read books. Lai couldn't even read his own business card." We were standing on Huaguang Road near the mansion. People were pushing past us on the sidewalk. Fangmin suggested I take him to a restaurant and spit blood, *tuxie,* meaning foot the bill. I declined at first. He complained he had not eaten out in days. It was hard to tell sometimes what upset him more, modern-day mansion owners or the fact that he wasn't one of them.

I bought Fangmin a meal and watched him eat. In front of him were spare ribs with water chestnuts, lotus leaves, shelled peas, pig's trotter, and wood ear mushrooms. He ran his chopsticks through them. He parsed the peas and shuffled the chestnuts. He peeled one lotus leaf from another, then put them both back. He moved the spare ribs around in their steamer — the meat, hanging off the bone in loose strips, went cold. Eventually, Fangmin ordered a bowl of plain rice and picked it clean.

When he was done he said he missed restaurants, mostly for the cool air. "At home, my power is off," he said. "I don't have air conditioning anymore." Fangmin wielded an imaginary remote control, his outstretched arm pointing at the ceiling. He was spending a lot of time at home nowadays. He had little else to do. When his small high-rise apartment got too hot he went down the stairs to the underground parking garage. It was always cool there, he said, and unlike other public spots it was empty. "Xiamen is so crowded. *Zhu jiaozi* — like boiling dumplings in a pot. Everywhere is full. You cannot be alone. Too many of us." Having tried in vain to find what satisfied him, Fangmin now wanted to escape those who had. He desired seclusion, but of all the goals to pursue in Xiamen, that was perhaps the most ambitious.

13
NIGHT TRADERS

ISBN 7-80647-308-4/1-215, Hubei Provincial
Publishing House, 32 yuan

THE STREET MARKET near Xiamen's train station was the sort of place that Fangmin avoided. It was densely packed and people constantly pushed past one another. But I liked it. A tense underground trade took place here. The wily sold to the sly, the cunning cheated the merely astute. You could buy bona fide receipts, serial number and all. Just say how much to make it out for, pay one thousandth of the face value, and an elderly woman will hand it to you. The sellers were all elderly women and they all held young children in their arms. It made arrest less likely, so the ringleaders reasoned.

Further down the alley, traders offered pirated DVDs in glossy packaging. I spent hours browsing. I may have been buying as well — who wants to say in print — but mainly I read the counterfeit blurbs. The pirates carelessly copied material from the Internet (*Troy* starring Brad Pitt became *Tory*) and, rather magnificently, they substituted English-language reviews for the puff prose of the movie studios. *Man on Fire* starring Denzel Washington was advertised with the proviso, "No amount of plastic surgery can save the plot or the creaky ending." Wim Wenders, the enigmatic German filmmaker, was practically defamed. A blurb said, "One might argue that the 'time you lose it' comes for every director, but the case of Wim Wenders is extreme. It's as if he completely forgot everything he knew about cinema and started all over again only to get sloppy results."

Moving yet further down the warm and stuffy alley, past the fake watches and the five-dollar Gucci bags, one entered the dark heart of the market. Here, everyday misdeeds mixed with something more severe. Men in sports jackets stood around with no merchandise in sight. What they sold was elusive. It needed to be ordered and custom-made. They sold the most original among counterfeit products — identities. One man offered bank statements, another pension papers, yet another passports. There were lookouts at both ends of the narrow passage and sellers seemed ready to disappear in an instant.

I sat down on a stone step below a shuttered gate, a thin stream of brown water running alongside. Having tied and retied my shoelaces several times, I leaned back. My perspective was that of a child — my eyes were at hip level. I watched as embossed papers of sovereign design changed hands, listened to the rustle of banknotes being counted, and heard the echoes of police sirens hurrying elsewhere. If all free markets were guided by Adam Smith's invisible hand, it seemed to be particularly well hidden here.

After a few minutes I got up and approached the sellers. I wondered what if anything I might be able to get. I spoke to a man who had taken off his shirt and hung it around his neck like a towel. "Are you a student?" he asked. I said I wasn't. "You should become one. I've got student passes and diplomas." I nodded. For less than twenty dollars I became a doctoral student in rocket science. The seller handed me my pass, a red booklet with a university crest. It became a useful complement to the laminated picture of me shaking hands with President Jiang.

I listened in when the seller moved on to customers standing beside me in a tight knot. Their accents were strong. I could barely make out what they were saying. Most of them sounded like recent arrivals in Xiamen. It seemed they were still adjusting their identities. They had come to the market to buy documents that would allow them to apply for permanent residency. The city government had certain requirements, including secondary education and property ownership. A few pieces of paper sufficed. With the first step toward reinvention completed, the migrants then settled in Xiamen.

✍

While Lai languished in a Canadian detention cell, awaiting his asylum hearing, more information about his case became public. Some was published by the Chinese government to bolster its request for extradition. But most appeared in newspapers in Hong Kong and on websites, giving details

Beijing was less keen to publicize. Lai was linked to several high-ranking Chinese officials. One was Ji Shengde, the head of military intelligence. He was sacked, that much Beijing admitted, after which he disappeared from public view.

Another was Jia Qinglin, the party secretary of Beijing and former leader of Fujian province, a man with a neck so thick it swallowed his jaw. He was a protégé of President Jiang Zemin and about to be made number four in the Communist Party. His wife was the deputy head of Fujian's provincial trade board. She had allegedly known Lai well enough for him to give her thirty million yuan, something she denied. In an effort to fight back, she invited a television interviewer to her home. "I don't know this Mr. Lai," she said, exquisitely coiffed. "Before foreign media published reports about his company I never even heard his name." The interviewer did not ask how the deputy head of the provincial trade board could not have heard of the biggest trader in the province. Nonetheless, the Jia family's links to Lai were causing severe strains in the government. There were reports that Jia faced dismissal, which would have been a severe embarrassment to his mentor, the president. Eventually, Jia was persuaded to divorce his wife to distance himself from Lai and show contrition. Divorce papers were filed at the civil affairs department of the Beijing municipality. But a few months later, when Jia had consolidated his position, he and his wife denied ever having split up. Asked about the divorce, she said, "The allegations are totally groundless. I have been married for forty years and my husband and I have very good relations and a happy family."

Another high government official linked to Lai was Li Jizhou, the number two in the public security ministry. He controlled China's borders. In his case, Beijing was more forthcoming with information. Li was officially accused of corruption and cut loose. Apparently, there was just too much evidence. State media reported he had helped Lai to import cars by the thousand. Lai's helpers had driven them across the border from Hong Kong without so much as showing an identity card. Lai was furthermore able to import a favorite car for himself, a black bulletproof Mercedes that President Jiang had used on July 1, 1997, when the former British colony reverted to the mainland. Lai had paid $1.5 million for the car and brought it to Xiamen with Li's help.

A picture was emerging of Lai's cooperation with members of the government, but it was still incomplete. How did these men interact? Had they all been to the Red Mansion? I hungered for still more answers. Then one day I got lucky. I was in the counterfeit market by the train station. The traders there had little to say about Lai, but some of them sold books that might. Spread out on thin pieces of cloth on the ground were all manner of remarkable texts — dissident literature, uncensored versions of western classics, true crime stories never reported in the official media. There were risqué bits of historical writing like the gloriously traitorous chronicle of Mao's personal life by Li Zhisui, his doctor. The shoddy paperback, its cover a faded photocopy, was not only banned but toxic. According to Dr. Li's writings, Chairman Mao would have felt quite at home in Lai's Red Mansion. "Most of Mao's young women had been innocent young girls when they first came to him," Dr. Li wrote. "Over the years, I saw the same phenomenon repeated. After being brought to Mao's bed, they would become corrupted."

In the same biography section were also countless western bestsellers. Some had been purposefully mistranslated. Bill Clinton's autobiography was amended by underground publishers to increase its appeal. In the Chinese version, the former U.S. president confessed a childhood interest in Chairman Mao, and recalled telling his wife to "shut up" over his affair with Monica Lewinsky, which "did not affect" their marriage.

Other books were not just mistranslated but entirely made up. A follow-up to the Harry Potter series was published as *Harry Potter and Leopard Walk Up to Dragon*. A Chinese author masquerading as J. K. Rowling drenched Harry in sweet-and-sour rain, transformed him into a hairy dwarf, and stripped him of his magic powers as he battled the forces of evil in the shape of a dragon. When I first saw the book, I called Ms. Rowling's agent in London, who said, "We take this issue extremely seriously and are looking into the matter urgently." I wrote about the Potter book for the *Times,* and later Clinton's doctored autobiography. From then on I made a habit of browsing the wares of the underground booksellers.

Their books were of poor quality — spelling mistakes, coarse paper, loose or missing pages — but the industry was highly efficient. Sellers said there were thousands of underground presses churning out anything that made a profit. To limit the political risk, books were split into bundles of a few pages each. The bundles were printed on different presses and then collected for binding. More underground books were sold in China than officially sanctioned ones, they said.

Perhaps it should not have come as a surprise then when I found, in the true crime section, four newly published books on Lai. The covers were flimsy and the typeset smudged. Pictures showed Lai surrounded by young women against a black background. On the back it said the recommended retail price was thirty-two yuan, but they sold for a quarter of that, about a dollar each. I bought all four and asked Kim to go through them for me since my Chinese was not up to it. Every day she read out a few passages in translation. At first my purchase seemed disappointing. Some passages were copied from official reports; others appeared in duplicate. The counterfeiters had copied each other. But over time the material improved. Kim focused on passages about Lai's private life, which seemed to delight her. She rolled around on our fake leather sofa in the living room, reading and giggling and scratching her shaven head. "This guy is so earthy," she said.

A chapter titled "Just for Fun" described Lai's friendship with a well-known folk diva. Dong Wenhua was the Chinese answer to Dame Vera Lynn, the "forces' sweetheart" who serenaded British troops during World War II. Dong warbled patriotically at military galas and the annual Spring Festival show on state television. Alas, she had also sung for Lai at the Red Mansion, so the book's anonymous author wrote. One evening, a drunk Lai offered her ten million yuan if she took her clothes off, and Dong earned her money. There was no supporting evidence, but it was a fact that Dong had disappeared from public view after Lai's flight. (Three years later she returned to state television as if nothing had happened.)

Another story had Lai propositioning a Chinese film star in the lobby of a Beijing hotel. The woman brushed him off but he followed her and offered her money. She ignored him. Eventually he pulled a large bundle of dollar bills from a bag, which finally got her attention.

Stories such as this were most likely myths, but the material on Lai's business was remarkably detailed and well informed. It explained his smuggling in the context of China's excessive import duties, which stood at up to 100 percent during the 1990s. High tariffs were meant to protect state-owned manufacturers from foreign competition. But they also made goods much less affordable. The government reinforced import restrictions by only allowing state-owned companies to become importers. They alone were issued import licenses. To get around this hurdle, Lai bought licenses from some of the state-owned companies. He wasn't the only one in Xiamen or Fujian doing so, although undoubtedly the biggest. Officials turned a blind eye as long as they could share in the profits. The books depicted Fujian as a sort of Guatemala of China, a banana republic where the local Communists played the role of United Fruit Company bosses of the 1920s, extracting all they could from the economy, regardless of the long-term consequences and the impact on the political system. Among those singled out in the books was Jia Qinglin, the presidential protégé. He was said to have visited Lai at the Red Mansion. A picture showed them standing side by side. But apparently Jia was only given a meal — no Miss Temporary for him. Lai was careful not to jeopardize his relationship with Jia's wife, the provincial trade official.

Another senior government member was also a regular guest: Li Jizhou, the deputy minister for public security. At the mansion he was introduced by Lai to a Ms. Yang, formerly a public relations manager at a foreign trade company. After Li expressed an interest in her, Lai hired her as a full-time mistress. "If you can make the minister happy you can have everything you want," Lai told her. And she did. "She was not only pretty but also gentle," an author calling himself Huang Jie wrote in one of the books. "Li was so well served that he forgot his home and his duty. He stayed with her for three days and didn't take part in any official meetings, lying that he was ill."

Kim was howling. She slid down the sofa and then off it. "A romance novel," she said, "a political romance novel."

Two of the books also claimed Lai had been in contact with one of his worst enemies, Zhu Rongji, the fire-spitting, take-no-prisoners prime minister who had said Lai ought to be executed more than once. Zhu resented the drain on his budget caused by Lai's smuggling. Yet Zhu too had visited Lai in Xiamen. The books recounted a meeting between the two a year before Lai's flight. Under discussion was a one-time tax payment in exchange for an amnesty. A sum of $125 million was mentioned. Though vast, it was only a fraction of Lai's profits. The books differed on who had proposed what and who first sought out whom. But that the two men would even consider such a deal was extraordinary. It suggested the entire government, not just a few corrupt ministers, had long known about Lai's business. One book quoted Zhu as telling Lai, "You owe one billion yuan in taxes. Pay now, stop smuggling, and that will be the end of the matter."

༄

When I went back to the market by the train station, once more exploring the cloth sheets on the ground piled high with counterfeit wares, flipping through loose-leaf pages filled with smudged type, I found under dusty piles another set of books that I thought were just as telling about Lai as the last four. They never mentioned him by name. They were in fact written before Lai was exposed as a bigtime *yeji*, or night trader. But their content, as well as the author's biography, spoke to Lai's inner state more eloquently than anything I had heard over the years.

The books were called *The Operator* and *Living Dangerously* and *Please Don't Call Me Human*. They were novels written by Wang Shuo. As I read them, in English translation, I came to think of Wang Shuo as Lai's alter ego. Both men were born in 1958, the year of the Great Leap Forward, a time of immense fervor. Many of their contemporaries were given names like Guoqing (National Day) and Shiqing (Tenth Anniversary — of the People's Republic in 1959) and Aiguo (Love the Country). In their teens, during the late Cultural Revolution, they witnessed China's falling out of love with ideology. Following Mao's death in 1976, with no hope of getting a decent education, Lai and Wang became *yeji* traders. Both imported television sets illegally — Lai in Fujian, Wang in Guangdong. Wang eventually left the business world and devoted himself to writing. But his language and his fictional characters stayed put. He wrote about cheats, womanizers, and freeloaders — survivors of China's ideological overindulgence who approached the post-Mao era with a mix of old-style fervor and hard-earned cynicism. He called them *liumang*, or rogues. Mostly his *liumang* lazed about, drank beer, and played cards. But what they did they did to excess, and when they encountered the state they sought to defraud as well as to corrupt it.

In one of his books Wang described a group of *liumang* looking for true Communist believers to act as teachers of Marxism for some nefarious money-making scheme. The *liumang* have great difficulties finding teachers. Eventually they hear of underground Communists meeting covertly in Beijing. All of them, it turns out, are patients in a mental hospital.

Wang's *liumang* used the same language as the people I met in Xiamen's nightclubs and underground markets. They called each other *gemen'r* (brother) and *jiemen'r* (sister). The gang leaders were *dage* (older brothers), their followers were *xiongdi* (younger brothers), and their criminal associates were *haohan* (good guys).

These labels — implying swagger and familial bonds stronger than the state — had been in use since *The Water Margin*. As well as ensuring their survival, Wang added a few modern names to the literary record. Crooks siphoning off gasoline from cars were *youhaozi*, gas mice. Common thieves were *foye*, Buddhists. Roadside moneychangers were *huangniu*, yellow oxen.

Wang, furthermore, delighted in parodying the language of the Communist Party and its obsession with correct forms of address. In a fictional *ganxiexin*, a formal letter of appreciation, he thanked one party leader on behalf of the residents of a small alley for defending them against another party leader:

> Respected wise dear teacher, leader, helmsman, pathfinder, vanguard, pioneer, designer, bright light, torch, devil-deflecting mirror, dog-beating stick, dad, mum, granddad, grandma, old ancestor, primal ape, Supreme Deity, Jade Emperor, Guanyin, Bodhisattva, commander-in-chief: You who are busy with ten thousand weighty matters each day, long suffering one, bad habits die hard, and overworked to the point of illness done too often can be habit-forming, heavy responsibility speeding through the skies, powerful and unconstrained, staving off disaster, and helping the poor dispelling the evil, and ousting the heterodox, you who eliminates rheumatism, cold sweats, strengthen the yang and invigorate the spleen, the brain, who are good for the liver, stomach pain relieving and cough repressing, able to cure constipation.

The letter continues in this vein — pure and glorious subversion.

It didn't go unnoticed. In 1996, after selling more than ten million books, Wang Shuo was banned by the government. Counterfeit markets were now the only places to buy his books, earning Wang not a penny in royalties.

Responding to the ban, he said, "The real *liumang* in our China are the officials."

14

ROCKET CADRES

Fujian Public Security Review, Second Copy,
Serial Number 581

> Lai is a national famous entrepreneur. He is fat. His nickname is The
> Monk Who Pleases Many. Once he was secure as a mountain and al-
> ways saw green lights. How capable this person was, and how danger-
> ous. But he made a big lie without reddening his face. He must be
> found. All policemen are mobilized to block up land and sea. Remem-
> ber, you can wear out iron shoes in fruitless searching, and yet by lucky
> chance you may find what you were looking for. He is doomed to de-
> struction. The sword of law is pointing at Lai. The instruction center of
> the Public Security Ministry has ordered his arrest. Participating are 41
> municipal-level organizations, 36 provincial-level organizations, and 15
> national-level organizations. With sufficient theoretical and organiza-
> tional preparation, the relevant departments will maintain normal or-
> der. We will calmly seek truth from facts. We will not be misled by ru-
> mor or exaggerated claims but support the official propaganda. And
> always worry for bad elements infiltrating organizations. Sometimes
> dragons mingle with fish.

THE OFFICIAL ACROSS from me was reading out aloud. He held a stack
of papers in one hand, and rested the other on his government-issue plas-
tic-wood desk. Both were twitching. The official was taking a considerable
risk. Anyone caught like this faced an uncomfortably uncertain future. So it
was just as well he put the papers back in his desk after translating them
slowly enough to be copied down in a notebook.

Little of what official China wrote was meant for the eyes of outsiders.
Not only politburo documents but lesser papers too were classified, even

surveys done by forestry bureaus and casualty reports from mine disasters. They were deemed state secrets unless written especially for publication. All except propaganda was internal, or *nei bu*.

During the hunt for Lai, now long over, thousands of *nei bu* documents had been sent to government offices across the country. They usually arrived in locked caches used to transport circulars and advisories, neatly folded and numbered. Some were high-level *hongtou wenjian,* or redheaded policy papers, with title characters written in flagpole red. Others were more practical in nature, and on occasion could sound less than sober, like the one read out by the official.

Bo Ming, as I will call him, was an assistant to a bureau chief in a Xiamen government department. He was tall and his eyes were constantly searching. His desk stood in an ill-lit alcove in a corridor crowded with chairs, files, and banners ("Serving better tomorrow"). When I first met Bo Ming, I was hoping to interview his chief. I wanted to ask him about Lai — stalled and frequently stymied, I thought it seemed like my best option. I would approach the authorities instead of evading them. Standing at Bo Ming's desk, I made my request. It was cursory and vague but it did mention Lai and the delicate issue of smuggling. Bo Ming pointed across his desk toward an open door. The office behind the door was empty. His chief was out but I could wait, he said, and pointed at a chair.

From where I sat down my view fell on a postcard atop a shelf behind Bo Ming's desk. It was the only spot of color in the vicinity. After I stared at it for a while Bo Ming passed me the postcard. *J. W. Turner,* said the back, *Slavers throwing overboard the Dead and Dying — Typhoon coming on ("The Slave Ship") 1840; Oil on canvass.* White-skinned corpses floated in a brown sea, churning but still reflecting a sun that was about to set behind inflamed, swirling clouds. In the midst of this, a spindly twin-mast ship traveled in a vortex of light. Order and reason abandoned, it headed for the intense chaos of nature.

The postcard had been sent by a woman in Belgium. It was a thank-you note following a business trip to Xiamen. "I would like to go to Belgium one day," Bo Ming said in confident English when I handed back the card. He had traveled abroad before, but only in Asia and America. He was about my age, I guessed, and asked him if he was busy today. "No," he said. "My boss is not here." He leaned back in his chair, the first time since my arrival. "Why don't you come back another day."

When I did, a week later, the chief's door was open once again and the office behind it empty. I sat down in the same chair and settled in to wait. It was warm and the air still. A gently humming air conditioner brought no respite. Then the clock on the wall above us ticked over to eleven thirty. The corridor filled as if a rush-hour train had arrived. Men and women of working age jostled along. A few minutes later they were gone again. "The same every day," said Bo Ming. "The start of lunchtime." He lifted his arm. Indignantly it cut through the warm air. "It's their most important appointment of the day."

I returned to see Bo Ming every few weeks. Usually sitting by his desk, I could see through the open door into the chief's empty office. But even when the door was closed and the chief might have been in, I simply sat with Bo Ming for a while and then left again. I knew if I ever actually met the chief I would have no excuse to return. I was beginning to enjoy these visits, the curious inner life of a government office on display. Its pace was measured by the lunch hour and the passing of women in aprons carrying hot-water bottles. At steady intervals they topped up teapots filled with tired leaves. No meeting started without them, and few phone calls were important enough not to be interrupted. The ritual made the place human, despite the drumroll regularity.

From my seat by Bo Ming's desk I watched tea ladies walk by, thermoses swaying, and looked up at the postcard of the Turner painting. I sometimes wondered why the Belgian woman had chosen it. At first I thought the title *Slave Ship* might be a veiled political comment. But the longer I sat there, the more I came to see it as something much smarter, a reminder that chaos — a typhoon in this case, not uncommon along the southern Chinese coast — awaited even those holding on tightest.

There were other pictures along the corridor too, mostly black-and-white images from China's past. They hung in glass display boxes and showed stacked corn bundles during bumper harvests, neat lines of Mao enthusiasts on Tiananmen Square, model workers receiving their awards, choreographed columns of tanks on parade duty. Order was the theme in each one. Yet in their overstatement they also hinted at the opposite. Every propaganda picture showing dutiful organization contained a mirror image of chaos. Failed harvests, violent zealots, ridiculed heroes, tanks crushing protesters. Anyone who knew the unofficial version of history could see them too.

During one of my visits to the office, Bo Ming offered his own thoughts on the subject of order and organization. He was looking through a large bound folder on his desk, placed on top of a stack of unopened letters. Pointing at a spot near the bottom of the page, he turned the folder around for me to see. "Down there is my name," he said. "And that's everyone above me." He pointed at a long list of two- and three-character combinations, the names of higher-ranking colleagues. The list was steep and craggy like a looming rock face. He looked up and said, "I took this job because my parents said it would give me a lot of security."

"And it's true?"

"Yes. I don't worry for anything."

"I see. How long have you been here?"

"Almost ten years."

We both gazed at his cluttered desk, an inventory of boredom.

"This folder — it's not really part of your work, is it?" I said.

"No."

Bo Ming referred to his colleagues as yes-men, *sansunzi,* and to his boss as a *huojian ganbu,* a rocket cadre who will soon be promoted away. His department was a distilled water unit, *zhengliushui yamen,* meaning it paid a low salary and no bonus.

Sometimes colleagues stopped by Bo Ming's desk. Amazingly, even among themselves, they spoke the meaningless language that they used to fob off citizens asking for licenses and other services. *Yanjiu yixia,* we'll study the matter, they said. Or *kaolu yixia,* we'll think it over. In rare cases, when they meant to say yes, they'd go as far as *wenti buda,* the problem's not so big. But more often they said no, in equally noncommittal terms: *butai fangbian,* not too convenient, or *youxie kunnan,* there are some difficulties. It allowed them to reverse their decisions at a later stage, should they have misjudged the politics of an issue.

Few of the officials were curious about my presence. They looked up briefly when they saw me, then trotted on. There was one exception. A man with a whip-drawn parting in his hair who worked in the foreign affairs department came by one day. He talked with Bo Ming about a trade conference and then said to me, "You might know what is the best way for our trade promotion." I made a few meaningless remarks about the importance of the free movement of goods. "Exactly," he said. "Our China is the same as your foreign countries. The free market is no problem for us."

I nodded.

"You live in Xiamen?" he said.

"Not really."

"I thought I saw you in the International Trade Ocean View apartment building near Number One Wharf, no?"

"Oh, it's possible." I was stunned. How would he know? But before I could say anything more the conversation had moved on.

Apart from that one moment, I always felt welcome in the office. I thought I was beginning to understand how it worked. I sensed a confidence I had not felt before in China. Not smug or defiant, but unconcerned with being "found out." There was nothing to find out about me. I was in the office by standing invitation. In no way had I misrepresented myself or why I was there. I could not be sure about the attitudes of other officials. I didn't know what to say to them or even when to speak. But with Bo Ming something like friendship had developed. He could have curbed my visits. He had plenty of opportunities, but instead he asked me to perform little tasks for him. When he left his desk once to go to a meeting I tended his phone. Nobody in the building had voice mail. During lunches or meetings, the task was either delegated or calls went unanswered. That day, Bo Ming was expecting an important overseas call, so I sat by his desk while he was out. When the phone rang and the callers were Chinese I said, "He's not here at the moment."

During my visits, the subject of Lai and his smuggling sometimes came up. I would tell Bo Ming about my research and the people I met. But I asked few specific questions of him, and he didn't query my interest. Then, more than two years after our first meeting, and without prompting, he pulled a bundle of *nei bu* documents from his desk. Leafing through them, he said they were about Lai. "Are you still interested?"

"I am."

"Too bad I can't give these to you."

"I understand but. . . ."

"But perhaps I could read from them," he said. And he did.

Lai is a black hand that has to be stopped. Abrupt measures will be taken against him. Lightning speed is the essence of the art of war. All relevant departments are working from the angles of their circles. Battle will be done one by one. Every measure will benefit each other. Let us not come back naked.

Bo Wen's translations injected levity into what were no doubt dreary paragraphs. He jumped from one document to the next, occasionally looking up as if to ask "more?"

A reporting letter has been received. The letter has seventy-four pages. It is written by a person close to Lai. This is an educated person. But his name is a special knowledge. It is signed A Group Of People With Justice. But we know it is just one person. The letter tells of the smuggling by Lai in great detail. It is seventy-four black pages. . . . It is case number one. It is worthy of many billions of yuan. All special passes to access the parking lots of government and Communist Party work units given for the cars of Lai are cancelled immediately.

I wondered why Bo Ming was helping me. Was he at liberty now that Lai had reappeared in Canada? I told him there was no quid pro quo. I could offer him nothing more than to tend his phone. He said he remembered all along why I had come to his office. "Better to ask me than my boss."

I couldn't be sure that the material he read to me was genuine, but I could see little reason why he would want to dupe me. It was possible he acted on instructions from superiors to pass on favorable information. Yet the documents were not especially helpful to the government (though even less so to Lai). They did, however, make plenty of local officials look silly, deceitful, and incompetent. That perhaps was what motivated Bo Ming.

He asked me which documents I was most interested in. I said I wanted to know more about how the government took control of Lai's empire, including the Red Mansion. Over the next few months, he occasionally read out documents from behind his desk. Most of them were from 1999 — the year I first came to China — and covered the time around Lai's disappearance. I took notes and checked them against other sources, including reports from the Xinhua state news agency, Canadian immigration records, web postings, and the books I had bought near the Xiamen train station. I found few discrepancies. Names and descriptions matched. For the first time, a full picture emerged. Taken together in equal measures with the other reports, the documents told the story of an elaborate game of hide-and-seek, triggered by a single act of betrayal.

꿍

As the record tells it, among the most regular visitors to the Red Mansion were high-ranking military officers. They were untouchables in the Chinese legal system — immune even to its minimal standards of criminal justice — and that appealed to Lai. He frequently invited senior officers to meet "Miss Temporarys" and struck up business relationships with the officers' children to channel money to their families, all in the expectation of slipping under the protective shield of the military.

It was thus that Lai met Zhu Niuniu, the ne'er-do-well son of a former deputy commander of China's 31st Army from Xiamen. Niuniu had, by all accounts, a highly volatile temperament and was ill prepared for a career in business. As a teenager, his father had hung him upside down on a parade ground and flogged him to punish him for a lack of discipline. But a decade later Lai found a use for him. Together they set up a trading company. Lai provided the capital and Niuniu acted as manager. For a few years, the company participated in Lai's smuggling racket, but eventually it collapsed, despite significant revenues. Niuniu had been skimming money, it turned out, to gamble in the casinos of Macao. Desperate for more money he started borrowing from Lai as well as signing IOUs in Lai's name. He also borrowed from other Lai associates. In total Niuniu owed ten million dollars by early 1999. "He was in a very difficult situation," one *nei bu* document said. "The vice of gambling held him tight."

To escape his debts, Niuniu tried to capitalize on his military connections. He threatened to expose Lai's smuggling unless he was paid off. All of his creditors were involved in smuggling, he reasoned, hence they all had an interest in appeasing him. To prove he was serious, he wrote a seventy-four-page letter that set out everything he knew. It began, "Respected Prime Minister, with your backing I will have the courage to tell the full story." He went on to list hundreds of illegal transactions including, for credibility's sake, the details of one of his own smuggling ventures, a shipment of seventeen containers filled with cigarettes. He sent the letter to Lai, who had someone in his office read it. After lengthy negotiations, Lai gave Niuniu twenty-five thousand and said there would be no more. Angry, humiliated, and fearful of his other creditors, Niuniu decided there was only one way out. He would actually send the letter. If his creditors were arrested, he would be debt-free.

The letter was forwarded by a friend in the military to the Central Discipline Inspection Commission, a shadowy branch of the Communist Party that investigated failings among members. The commission received hundreds of such "reporting letters" every day: villagers complaining about land-grabbing officials, contractors railing against bribe-seeking government departments, sacked workers decrying corruption at state-owned enterprises. Most of the letters were deemed too insignificant to merit action by the center. But not Niuniu's letter. The sums involved and the amount of detail in which he described the smuggling caught the investigators' attention. It mentioned specific amounts of *huise shouru* (gray income) and *waikuai* (outside money) in particular *hei dian* (black accounts), and listed which *guandao* (officials involved in profiteering) received which *zha yao bao* (explosive package, meaning illegal gift).

The investigators requested analyses of the letter from other government departments. "The National Customs Bureau looked at the data and said it was real," according to one *nei bu* report. Another stated, "Comrades from the Public Security Bureau tell us some of the people named in the letter have been investigated before." Having checked the seventy-four-page letter, the Central Discipline Inspection Commission tried to contact Niuniu. He had not signed using his real name but given an email address. The investigators sent a message asking him to call, which eventually he did. After negotiating a plea bargain, he revealed his identity and handed over further information. Armed with detailed shipping charts and lists of suspects, the investigators then met a group of politburo members on April 20, 1999. They agreed to set up a special task force, naming it "4.20."

In his novel *Midnight's Children* Salman Rushdie wrote, "420 has been, since time immemorial, the number associated with fraud, deception and trickery." Little was known about the politburo's literary habits. Maybe they did read Rushdie.

Lai, of course, learned of the 4.20 investigation almost immediately. His government contacts passed on reports, some of which appear to have been exaggerated. Lai believed at the time the task force had twelve hundred investigators, when it had about half that. By the middle of May, Lai was seriously concerned. He was sleeping badly and said to lack energy. Some of his government contacts stopped returning his calls and even the Red Mansion was losing its popularity. The resident women left one by one as news of the investigation spread. Eventually Lai decided to act. He halted his most visible construction projects, such as the eighty-eight-story tower, and diverted smuggling ships away from Xiamen. He also burned incriminating documents and transferred cash abroad through the *fei qian* underground banking system.

By the end of May he felt he had secured his position and his spirits revived. He befriended a stewardess and began an affair with her. Relying on a promise by Lai to finance her university education, she quit her job and saw Lai almost daily. A few weeks later, however, in mid-June, she found her life turned upside down once again. Government investigators were asking her uncomfortable questions about the man who was supporting her and who was suddenly gone. For on June 13, a delegation of investigators had flown from Beijing to Xiamen to begin their work in earnest. Uncertain of the risks involved in entering rebel territory, they had surrounded themselves with a large security force. Soldiers and policemen stood guard wherever they went. The arrangement had tipped off Lai and he fled to Hong Kong.

Having come no closer to Lai than his spurned mistress, the investigators soon returned to Beijing. They were reprimanded severely and the politburo decided to put its most experienced investigator in charge. Liu Liying was the sixty-eight-year-old deputy head of the Central Discipline Inspection Commission. She had a round, plain face with tightly bound hair. It was a face known across China. Four years earlier she had successfully prosecuted Chen Xitong, the former party secretary of Beijing. She sent him to prison for sixteen years on embezzlement charges. A news magazine article about Liu Liying said, "If Hollywood were making a film of her life story, she would be dressed to kill in sleek black leather, handcuffs clipped to her waist."

Liu Liying had risen to the post of chief hatchet woman of the Communist Party soon after the Cultural Revolution and the death of Chairman Mao. She helped to prosecute the Gang of Four, conducting long and difficult interrogations of Mao's feared wife, Jiang Qing. Her prosecutorial zeal went beyond the merely professional. Liu Liying had been in the same position as Madam Mao not long before. During the Cultural Revolution, which she referred to as the "ten years of turmoil," she was repeatedly imprisoned herself. She had been deemed guilty of upholding outdated cultural norms such as law enforcement. She and her family were tortured by Red Guards, and her husband and both her parents died as a result.

Interviewed decades later by the official *Legal Daily* newspaper, she said, "There were no laws then. We still don't know how many people were persecuted to death in the mass campaigns. An important lesson is that some people availed themselves of loopholes because the legal administration in the country had no power. So when I came back to work [after the Cultural Revolution] I had a strong conviction. We must guarantee the authority of the party's rules and the country's laws. We must be upright and above flattery. We must enforce the law strictly. Only then can we maintain the glory of the party and win the trust of the people."

The frankness with which Liu Liying talked was as rare as it was admirable. The great twentieth-century crimes committed by the Communist Party — the Great Leap Forward, the Tiananmen massacre, the Cultural Revolution — were never examined in Chinese schools or newspapers. To protect itself, the party refused to allow anything more than cursory accounting.

And yet Liu Liying's suggestion that the excesses of the Cultural Revolution were due to loopholes in the legal system was laughable. Her revered Chairman himself had started the "turmoil" and encouraged chaos and violence. Beyond these blind spots, however, Liu Liying was genuine. During the five-year period covering Lai's flight and the 4.20 investigation, her commission indicted 840,000 people for graft and expelled 130,000 corrupt party members. Lai had a worthy adversary at last.

After his flight to Hong Kong, he stayed in touch with contacts in Xiamen by phone. The situation seemed to calm down after a few weeks, he thought. No further visits by 4.20 delegations were reported. So on August 9, he decided to return, albeit carefully. He entered the mainland at the notoriously lax border in Macao and traveled overland to Xiamen. Avoiding the Red Mansion, he met with associates one by one and paid staff salaries for the first time in two months. Alas, his presence was discovered when he made phone calls to known sympathizers in the city government. Investigators in Beijing who monitored their phone lines quietly alerted Liu Liying, who assembled a new delegation to go to Xiamen. They arrived within forty-eight hours but Lai — tipped off once more — was already gone.

Investigators later reconstructed his escape based on the confession of his driver, Xu Minxiong. Xu was told by Lai on the morning of the eleventh to swap the armored Mercedes for a less conspicuous car. Then he picked Lai up at a highway exit near Xiamen and together they made the ten-hour journey down the coast to Shenzhen, the city bordering Hong Kong. At the port in Shenzhen Lai hired a speedboat and, avoiding all border controls, entered the former British colony where his wife and three children were waiting. A few days later, fearing extradition to the mainland, they flew to Vancouver on tourist visas and began a new life.

In the meantime, Liu Liying set out to unravel Lai's network. She told officials in Xiamen anyone who had received less than forty thousand from Lai would be pardoned if he returned the money and cooperated. Soon the first few started turning themselves in, fearful of Liu's reputation. Others were caught by chance. One was found to have stuffed his office couch with bank notes. Another was detained after his wife was found at a border crossing with a hundred thousand dollars in her handbag. Yet others revealed themselves unwittingly. Lan Pu, the deputy mayor of Xiamen, was overheard on a tapped phone line talking about tapping the lines of 4.20 investigators. He was soon arrested. Another official was observed making a donation of fifty thousand dollars at a temple to buy divine protection from the investigation. He too was detained.

Liu Liying and her investigators received hundreds of anonymous notes from Xiamen residents keen to denounce one another. They were known as *dianzi,* squealers. In a city where few had lived for more than a few years, there was little loyalty. And not much memory either, so some seemed to hope. City officials voided Lai's honorary citizenship in September, pretending it was never awarded.

Soon, hundreds of officials were facing Liu Liying in interrogation. They were usually asked to come to the Golden Swallow Hotel, where they were escorted to a room and their drivers sent home. Anyone who failed to turn up voluntarily was presumed guilty and put on a police search list. "All fugitives will be dealt with severely," one *nei bu* document said. Slowly Liu Liying unpicked Lai's net. Among the detainees was Big Head, the boatman whom Andy and I had met. The official record of his interrogation read:

TIME: from 13:31 to 16:49, November 19, 1999
PLACE: Golden Swallow Hotel, Xiamen
INVESTIGATORS: Huang Yubin and Yang Jianwei
NOTE-TAKER: Wang Saiyu
INTERVIEWEE: Zhuo Wenhui
SEX: male
AGE: 32
ETHNIC ORIGIN: Han Chinese
PROFESSION AND PLACE OF WORK: self-employed crewman

The document quoted the investigators as asking Big Head the most leading of all questions: "Are you aware what illegal activities you were involved in?" Big Head dutifully listed the specific dates and times when he had delivered fake customs documents to Lai's ships arriving in Xiamen. Apparently without hesitation he recounted the names of people involved as well as their mobile phone numbers, dozens at a time. Satisfied with their handiwork, the investigators then came to the question Andy had also asked. Why was he called Big Head? His head really wasn't that big. "When I was a little boy," he told them, "I used to have my head inclined to one side. People gave me the nickname because of that and it stuck."

Liu Liying's first major breakthrough came when her investigators tackled the Red Mansion. They failed to find much useful documentary evidence, but they apprehended the manager who had overseen the hiring of the "Miss Temporarys." Looking through pictures of local and regional officials, the manager identified regular guests. Hundreds of them were detained.

The main breakthrough in the investigation, however, didn't come until Liu Liying — having held back a while — hunted down Lai's brother Shuiqiang. He had quietly taken over what was left of the family business. Not living in Xiamen but in Shaocuo, the ancestral village, he expected to be safe. Eventually though, an arrest warrant was issued. For a while, Shuiqiang hid at the movie studio, the one modeled on the Forbidden City in Beijing. When investigators spotted him there, he escaped in a high-speed car chase back to Shaocuo. He hid in the villa with the green glass roof. When police reinforcements arrived, hundreds of neighbors surrounded the villa, acting as a human shield. The ensuing standoff lasted several days, and in the end, investigators negotiated a deal with Shuiqiang. He was promised leniency in return for his cooperation. Without revealing his betrayal, he talked the villagers into abandoning their protest, and then led investigators to the garage where he had hidden his brother's armored Mercedes. For the next few months Shuiqiang lived in a deluxe suite at the Golden Swallow Hotel and persuaded thirteen more members of the Lai clan to turn themselves in. Those unwilling were arrested, often after a prolonged manhunt.

It had been around this time, I now came to see, that I first heard about Lai Changxing. I had been traveling in Fujian on reporting business. Police were deployed all across the province looking for 4.20 fugitives. Hence my encounter with officers in the hotel lobby, where they questioned me about an obscure businessman and then drove me to the airport. I had stumbled right into Liu Liying's work. I was glad to confirm this, but more than anything I was stunned it had taken me so long.

15
THE VICE-MINISTER

Xiamen Airlines Flight MF 8101, Xiamen to Beijing

THE LOUDSPEAKER was directly above my seat. It came to life. I knew every note of the song they played before takeoff. I had flown this route dozens of times. In the seat next to me sat a Chinese man. He said he worked for an engineering company. We talked for a while, then I went over my notebooks. I was still wondering why Lai fell out of favor. Could a single act of betrayal have been enough? His government contacts had protected him for so long. What changed? In the end it came down to one thing. The government was a black box. Nobody knew what went on inside. Even experts didn't pretend to. There were always rumors but no way to confirm them. Official announcements were useless. Calls remained unanswered. Very occasionally though, and I mean very occasionally, a small door opened. Someone somewhere agreed to talk. In my case, this someone was a vice-minister in a second-tier government department. Sometimes he agreed to see me. Other times he didn't. I could not quote him by name, but I was spared the platitudes commonly used by officials.

When I arrived in Beijing I contacted him once more. Within a week I received an invitation to dinner. The instructions were familiar. A car would pick me up at my office and take me to a hotel in the city center. There, a second car would be waiting, which would take me to a private courtyard on the outskirts. The vice-minister had explained this was a security measure. "Neither driver will know the entire route. The first only knows where you came from, the second only where you went."

Having been dropped off by driver number two, I walked through a gravel-filled courtyard built like a monastic retreat. The walls were plain gray, the earth raked with grooves running in parallel like high-tide marks on a beach. In places they bent around clutches of gently rustling bamboo, and I felt a sense of calm much like stepping from a European market square into a dimly lit cathedral.

The vice-minister was waiting by the door. His hair was thin and his hands soft, his face perpetually flushed but never sweaty. His demeanor fitted that of a priest given to divine confidence rather than righteous anger. He took my hand, shook it, and briefly showed me examples of painterly calligraphy, the same he had shown me the last time. "These are passages I copied from ancient texts," he said. Then he rolled up the scriptures and put them down on a wooden table.

From an anteroom we walked into a small dining area shielded by latticework dividers. A table had been set for four. As usual, the vice-minister was accompanied by a note-taker, while I had a translator with me. She wrote down what the vice-minister said and repeated in English the parts I didn't understand. Above all it saved me having to take notes.

The four of us sat on low stools around a low table. The vice-minister asked what I had been working on recently. I mentioned Lai's name.

"Canada can be very cold if one is used to the warm climate of Fujian," he said.

"So you think Lai will come back?"

"I hope."

"But you are not sure?"

"The matter is decided by a Canadian court, is it not?"

"Yes."

"Then I cannot be sure."

But what about Lai's helpers in the Beijing government? I described what I had heard and read about Li Jizhou, the number two in the public security ministry, what Kim had called a "political romance novel."

"It's correct," he said. "Li has had some irregular relations. He helped with the smuggling of thousands of cars. But he helped more than just Lai. There were other smugglers too."

"And where is Li now?"

"Not in the government anymore. *Fensui le.*" *Fensui* meant to smash, a verb often used to describe what Mao's successors did to the Gang of Four.

"But he was a vice-minister like you," I said.

"There are many vice-ministers. About three hundred in total."

"And Jia Qinglin?" I knew I was going a little too fast here. But it seemed to work.

"He is no mere vice-minister."

"But he too knew Lai before he went to Canada?"

"I believe so. He was the party secretary of Fujian. It was his job to know all the big figures in the province."

"But not to take money from them."

"No."

"He had a wife though?"

"Yes."

"She still is his wife, is she?"

"Yes."

"They were not divorced?"

"Only briefly."

"It must have been difficult to annul the divorce."

"Comrade Qinglin is like a son to President Jiang. A father has to look after his son."

There was a pause in the conversation while he whispered to his note-taker. It seemed he wanted the last answer kept off his record. Or perhaps he was creating a pause to move on to a new topic, yet I still had a query on Lai. I described the meeting between him and Prime Minister Zhu, the one where they discussed a cash-for-amnesty deal. I wasn't sure how the vice-minister would react. This was a serious allegation against the prime minister, whom I knew was his ally. I stumbled through the story, sounding like a lapsed believer in the confessional.

"That's interesting," the vice-minister said, "but I am not sure it's true." I mentioned the source of the story. "I think you should not believe all you have read," he said, "but the books you describe are interesting. I have read similar ones myself. Actually, some are published by state-owned publishing houses — under a different name of course. Not all, but some." He said some of the Lai books sounded like they came from official sources. Especially the material on public security vice-minister Li Jizhou. "He admitted to all his links with Lai. The details could not be published in an official newspaper." The vice-minister suggested it would be an embarrassment. But if the contents became otherwise known it would be very useful in the immigration case against Lai in Canada.

While we talked, dinner was served. Small plates appeared. Preserved cucumber. Marinated beef slices. A thousand-year-old egg with capsicum. The dishes were served individually. As we finished one, the next would appear. The waiters worked like croupiers, dealing cards from an unseen deck.

This form of dining is known as imperial. It had developed over centuries at the emperor's quarters in the Forbidden City, where cooks selected the best bits from every regional cuisine, devising a menu spanning an empire, from Korean kimchi to Vietnamese spring rolls. Yet it has destroyed what is most enjoyable about eating in China, the carnival atmosphere where everyone shares food from overflowing pots. Imperial cuisine is a sit-down dinner of nothing but canapés. Dish after dish comes and goes, many of them opulent. But there is no choice in what you eat. Plates are served in preordered sequence.

"The material in those books reflects badly on Lai," I said, after yet another little platter had been whisked in and out again, "but I wonder whether they don't make the government look bad, too."

"Really? How?"

"It is no longer in control of the country."

"The country out of control?"

"Maybe not out of control, but not the opposite either."

"Foreign journalists like yourselves like to remind us of the troubles of 1989, the student demonstrations. Would you not say the government is much more in control now?"

"Yes."

"Are students now not much more interested in finding jobs than making trouble? Are the workers not much better off now that they work in private companies in greater numbers?"

"Yes. But the government needs to create ever more jobs and economic growth to keep them happy."

"And it is doing so. Every year new industries are opened up and new opportunities are created."

"But with every opening a loss of control goes along."

"Does it really?"

"In 1989, Lai could never have done so much smuggling."

"You are right." The vice-minister paused as more plates with ever smaller portions arrived. We might still be hungry by the end of the meal, I thought. "Smuggling damages the economy," the vice-minister said. "President Jiang himself has said so. He wrote in the margins of an official report on the Lai case, 'If we don't control smuggling we'll lose our party, our state, even our heads.' But that was after Lai went to Canada."

"And before?"

"Before, the situation was not the same. You have to remember the

1990s. The number one aim for the government at the time was entry to the World Trade Organization, which would lower tariffs for our exports and create more wealth and jobs."

"What does Lai have to do with it?"

"He was already doing a lot of trading on those much better terms."

"Are you saying Lai wasn't such a bad thing? That he actually helped the economy?"

"Oh, not at all. It was terrible what he did. Many other companies made losses because of him and many people were made unemployed."

"But there is a *but?*"

"Some people in the government thought it was too early for China to enter the World Trade Organization. The benefit to our country would be to get lower export tariffs. But we would also have to reduce our import tariffs, and that meant more competition from foreign companies."

"But if Lai and others were already trading with foreign companies at lower tariff rates anyway . . ."

". . . in that case, lowering import tariffs would not really be such a big concession."

"Lai was useful."

"Perhaps."

"But if Lai was useful, why then take him down and hound him out of the country?"

"Well, once the World Trade Organization entry was agreed, he certainly wasn't useful anymore. You will remember he fled around the same time as the entry negotiations were concluded in 1999."

My head felt like a swivel chair placed on a carousel. The vice-minister had taken a case of criminal justice and turned it into Communist Party catechism, his dialectic logic straining the laws of gravity. I presumed what he was trying to sell me on was this: a few bad apples in the politburo had been close to Lai, but overall the party was strong. So strong, in fact, it could play Lai like a puppet, using him for its own purposes, and then discard him. Oh, all was well on the reform path. The party knew how to loosen controls without losing control.

☙

During the long months when I was in Beijing rather than Xiamen, I worked out of the *Times* China bureau. It was located in two small rooms in an imperial park that the paper rented from the son of a general. He had no official permission to rent out public property, but who was to argue with the son of a general? When I arrived in the mornings, I saw pensioners hang birdcages in the trees along manicured lawns and perform calisthenics. I would walk through the park past the inevitable slogans ("Liberate your thinking") to a large wooden gate and enter a sixteenth-century courtyard framed by red walls. In the middle stood a regal stone table where a shuffling caretaker dropped off the mail. I could see him from my desk off to one side of the yard.

One lunchtime, soon after my dinner with the vice-minister, I left the bureau and crossed the park. The calisthenics crowd was gone by now, replaced by a gaggle of old men tugging at kites. At the park's north gate, I turned onto a busy street that ran past the North Korean embassy. From there, it was a ten-minute walk to a squat office tower across the street from the gray building housing China's foreign ministry. On the tower's fifth floor, overlooking the ministry's east gate, was a Sichuan restaurant, my destination.

For forty-five minutes I watched cars with diplomatic license plates pass below the window. Then Hu Shuli arrived. She was a rare Chinese journalist who did investigative work. In the past I had met her at her nearby office. This was our first lunch.

Hu sat down across from me with a sigh so loud and resonant it sounded like a laugh. Her frizzy hair was disheveled and the cuffs on her blouse unbuttoned. Her large eyes fell shut for a moment, then doubled open again. "Sorry I'm late," she said. "The last few weeks and months have been crazy. My magazine came closer to being shut down than ever before." One of Hu's recent stories had exposed a scandal at the Shanghai stock exchange. As a result, the stock market had dropped more than 4 percent and the government was displeased. For a while there had been talk of the magazine being closed. "But now I think we're fine," she said. "I just spoke to our lawyer."

Hu was the founding editor of *Caijing*, a crusading biweekly specializing in corruption investigations. In the last few years it had grown from being a one-woman watchdog to having a staff of fifty. Hu believed graft was a direct threat to China's growth and prosperity. "It holds back reform. It enriches a few at the cost of everyone else." She said calculations by the government's own auditor-general showed that 20 percent of the national budget was misappropriated every year. In her magazine she quoted a respected economist at Tsinghua, China's top university, saying that 80 percent of officials were corrupt.

Issue after issue Hu exposed bribery cases, earning her the sobriquet "China's most dangerous woman." She was able to do so despite draconian press restrictions. How? She liked to point out that her position matched that of the Communist Party. Officially, it too was fighting corruption. Growing public resentment was undermining the party's legitimacy. Hence, Hu's work was tolerated as long as she confined herself to financial scandals and stayed away from politics. "An impossibility, of course," she said. "In China, everything is political."

Hu flicked through the menu. "*Ma la zi yu.* I like that name. Hot and numbing tiny fish, that's what journalists are." Hu was a passionate reporter. "I just love scoops," the fifty-year-old had told me breathlessly at our first meeting. Yet her work made her prey as much as hunter. Corrupt officials pressured her. Some threatened to sue, others demanded "self-criticism sessions" styled on the Cultural Revolution. Hu grinned at the thought. As a young woman she had been a Red Guard. "It's funny sometimes how my work reminds me of the past."

Hu said she never doubted her eventual choice of career. She became a journalist shortly after Mao's death, following in the footsteps of her mother and grandfather. She joined the *Workers Daily*, a stalwart party paper that turned out to be an invaluable training ground. As a pro-government reporter, Hu covered the 1989 student protests on Tiananmen Square (which were as much against corruption as they were for democracy, she said). Hu came to sympathize with the students, and yet she had to restrain herself. For a while the paper had wavered, then it toed a hard line. She learned how far the system might bend and at what point it was advisable to back off. This training went some way to explaining why she had avoided the fate of many equally enterprising colleagues who were now in prison. (China jailed more reporters than any other country.) "I am really very lucky," she said with a pinched smile. "So much corruption, so many good stories. It would be a shame to be in prison and miss out on them."

Occasionally Hu picked up a few "hot and numbing tiny fish" with her chopsticks, swirled them around in a chili sauce, and ate them. Mostly, though, she talked. "You have to know where the line is. You can go right up to it. You can push a little, but for goodness sake don't cross it. Where is the line? You can't see it. You have to feel where it is."

Hu took manifest pride in her mastery of the system, but even she blundered sometimes. On one occasion, she had to pulp an entire issue of her magazine when she realized just how offended government officials would be. "It's better to stop yourself than be stopped by others," she said. "I don't want them to think they can bully me."

"But why do they allow a magazine like yours at all?"

"The higher-ups aren't stupid. They realize they have a problem — as long as there is one party with absolute control and no independent watchdogs, there will be massive abuses of power. Of course, they could have real checks and balances, but an independent media and judiciary would probably end one-party rule. So they tolerate people like me, hoping it might curb excesses."

Regardless of her moral aspirations, Hu was not above using an occasional trick to help her cause. A few years earlier she tried to list the magazine on the stock exchange. She was told media companies were banned. Not a problem, she said, and turned the magazine's advertising department into a separate marketing company that was then listed instead. "You can't be too literal in China," she said.

After finishing our food, I asked Hu about the Lai case. Of course she had followed it. But was she going to run a story about him in the magazine? Why hadn't she already? It sounded like her type. "Here is the problem," she said. "You have to be quick in a situation like this. You have to move before the government makes up its mind. At the beginning you can write almost anything. If you get complaints you say you didn't know the subject was sensitive. But now it's too late. Now there is an official policy. We were too slow. We were busy with our own problems." Her voice sounded sour and her face looked tired. She didn't enjoy saying she had missed a story.

"You've lived in Xiamen, right?" I asked, remembering a previous conversation.

"Yes, for a while in the 1980s. That makes it even worse."

I explained what the vice-minister told me. Did she agree? Had Lai been played? Why *did* he fall?

"There are two views," she said. "One is Lai grew too big. His business became too powerful and his smuggling too expensive. The leaders could no longer overlook him. They felt threatened. No amount of bribery could change that. The other view is what you described. Lai was useful for a while. He helped to unblock a logjam. He nudged things along." She paused for a moment. "These two views are really one and the same. Officials tolerated Lai, whatever the petty reasons." A smile spread over her face. "Then they turned on him."

∽

A few weeks later, I went from Beijing back to Xiamen. I was flying on this route a few times a month now.

I was seated next to a gentleman in a suit. The skin on his hands and face had the meaty gloss of cooked aubergine.

Waiting for takeoff we conducted a convivial and sometimes honest conversation.

"American?" he said.

"Yes," I lied. "How could you tell?"

"You are quite tall."

"And you? From Xiamen?"

"Yes." He put on his seat belt. "Have you been before?"

"Yes, once," I said.

"You enjoyed it?"

"Wonderful place. Charming. And very safe, I believe."

"Very."

We were silent while the plane took off. Then he said, "You have business there?"

"A little."

"A local partner?"

"Sometimes."

Below us we could see the ocean and the steeplechase mountains that separated Beijing and Xiamen. I took out a folder with recent interview notes and started reading. My neighbor kept looking over. After a few minutes I put my notes away.

"What do you do?" I said.

"I work for a chemical company."

"Do you have a business card? You never know when you might need a chemical company."

"Sorry. I forgot. But my surname is Lu."

While we talked, the crew performed a routine common on flights operated by Xiamen Airlines (yes, Xiamen had its own carrier). The head steward conducted an onboard auction. Passengers were invited to bid for airline merchandise and seats on future flights. Junior stewards were positioned up and down the aisles to signal bids to the front. Enraptured passengers paid more than the face value for tickets to seemingly random destinations.

I watched the auction, but Mr. Lu would not be distracted.

"You are in the chemical business, too?" he said.

"Plastics, actually."

"American plastics are the best."

On my flight from Xiamen to Beijing a few weeks earlier the same Mr. Lu had sat next to me. A coincidence perhaps. But how odd that he would not even acknowledge we had met before, in fact, had had a conversation. Parts of his résumé were different now. He worked for a chemical company, not an engineering company, but he was the same man. He was, of course, under no obligation to tell me whether he was a chemist or an engineer. Maybe he enjoyed the charade as much as I did.

"How is the local football club?" I said after we touched down.

"Terrible. They lost again."

"But isn't that the club once owned by Lai Changxing?"

He nodded. A little too quickly, I thought. Then we lost sight of each other in the arrivals lounge.

Driving into the city, I thought back to a recent occasion in Beijing. Arriving at my desk one morning I had found the cables on my computer changed around. The modem wire was rolled up in a coil, the power cable unplugged, and the printer attached to the wrong port. I thought the cleaning lady might have been in overnight. Then I lifted up the computer to fix the mess and found a piece of paper. On it was my office address, written in an unfamiliar scrawl. At the time, I ignored it, refusing to draw the obvious conclusion. But when I thought of it now, I was overcome by the wish never to find myself next to another Mr. Lu.

Correspondents in China mostly affect an air of nonchalance when it comes to surveillance. We protect our sources fiercely. But in personal interaction with the authorities we prefer humor, however uneasy. The thought of being followed is absurd, and often the reality is too. Once, driving in Beijing, I noticed a black BMW with tinted windows behind me. When it was still there twenty minutes later I stopped and got out. The windows of the BMW were half rolled down. I could see four men in suits. Politely, I asked for directions to the Temple of Heaven, which they gave me.

The temple park was a wonderful place for an afternoon outing, and all the more enjoyable if you could watch grown men crouch in the bushes. I walked around in the cold for a few hours and then went to a nearby Starbucks café. Having bought myself a warming coffee, I got four more for the men in stained suits at the neighboring table. Starbucks could be awfully expensive, even if your work involved driving a BMW. I toasted them. It had been a good day for everyone, I hoped.

I sought out situations like this one rather more than I probably should have. I liked the frisson. At least I had liked it. My encounter with Mr. Lu on the plane changed that. What had been convivial at the time no longer seemed so now.

The next day I went to a tobacco store near my apartment. The store sold mobile phone numbers without checking identity documents or registering names. I bought a handful of numbers at twenty-five dollars each and began to switch between them every few days. Yet my anxiety continued and I talked to my friends. Andy began to worry too. He created a new email account for himself, registering it in a made-up Spanish name. When I dropped him off at his dorm he now insisted on walking the last few blocks. Kim was less concerned. She said our landlord charged us a pretax rent and didn't ever give us a receipt. "It means he doesn't pay tax," she said. "And if he's not paying tax he won't have registered us with the police. We'll be okay."

Kim suggested a parlor game. The three of us should make up new identities and print them on business cards. We appointed ourselves executives of a furniture company. Andy was chairman, I was president, and Kim "chief test sitter, sofa division."

Deception and secrecy are second nature in Xiamen. New lives are enjoyed but not yet trusted. Rules — currently defunct — might be reinstated later. Past backlashes are not forgotten. New identities can collapse as quickly as they have been created.

16

LAWYERS

Karaoke Room No. 22, the Shaoshan Club, Xiamen

AFTER MONTHS IN detention in Canada Lai was still waiting for his asylum hearing. He asked, through his lawyers, to be transferred to house arrest so he could be more comfortable. The immigration authorities turned him down, saying he might never come back. His lawyers contacted a private security firm and worked out a plan under which Lai would be kept under surveillance in a locked apartment. They submitted the plan to the authorities, who once again turned him down. Lai and his lawyers revised the plan and he pledged to spend twenty thousand dollars a week on round-the-clock security guards. All telephone calls and all visitors would be screened. Finally, against the wishes of the Canadian government and after renewed delays, the immigration authorities agreed. Lai and his wife were allowed to swap their detention cells for what Chinese media described as a "luxury" apartment in the Vancouver suburb of Burnaby. It was said to have a nice view as well as two bedrooms, which the Lais shared with three security guards. They were not allowed out — they were, however, able to receive visitors. Restrictions applied but still, this would be my best chance to meet and interview Lai. I called his lawyers. They asked for a fax with questions. I sent one from the office of a friend in Xiamen. Then another. No reply. I checked with the friend every day. No reply from Vancouver.

༄

It was past midnight. The dancers had just finished performing in a one-time show dressed up as vehicles. Boxy costumes covered their backs and cotton bumpers and battery-powered headlights adorned their chests. In the finale of the show, a solitary traffic warden appeared onstage. For a moment, he calmly marshaled imaginary traffic, then hundreds of dancers rushed toward him. The warden waved his arms and trilled a whistle in vain. A studiously scripted traffic chaos ensued. Headlights and bumper chests collided. As a display of sexual anarchy it managed to be both grotesque and coy.

The dancers received more flower rings than they had expected and that's what they chose to remember of the show. Recent talk of leaving Xiamen and going home was shelved. It was in jest that they now argued about what was worse: to have a paying lover or none at all. Xiao Wang said, "When I go over to their table I look at them funny, like this . . ." She cocked her head and puffed out her cheeks. "They usually pick someone else." She fiddled with an extrawide watch strap on her arm. Andy had seen her take it off once. Her wrists were marked with cuts and cigarette burns, some recent. "I get very angry sometimes," she said.

The next day I accompanied the dancers to a hair salon. A row of reclining chairs faced a mirror and an overhead television. None of the dancers needed a haircut. They came here whenever they could to look at magazines with pictures of young women who'd had plastic surgery. Rather than hiding the fact, the pictures flaunted it. Two pictures in particular caught everyone's eye that day. In the first, a woman stood next to her slightly taller mother. In the second, the daughter was the taller one. The pictures were taken a year apart. In the meantime, the daughter had been operated on. Surgeons broke her shins and extended them with metal pins, growing her by three inches. With muscles lengthened and new skin grafted onto her legs she was able to walk tall.

The dancers, who came up to my shoulders, passed the magazine around as if valuable contraband. They leaned in close, peeked, and straightened up again, facing a simple fact. Tall women got better jobs — in private companies as well as the government — and better men. Gone were the days when beauties were diminutive and hobbled around on tiny bound feet. Everything tall was in fashion. Tall buildings, tall women, tall tales. The dancers could accept that, yet they rebelled against being relegated. Trailing each picture in the magazine with their fingers, they shopped for inches. It might take a year, cost thousands of dollars, and cause terrible pain, not to mention the bore of having to learn to walk again. But three inches were three inches.

Dilinor went outside to smoke a cigarette and I followed her. "Without you we would have stayed at home today," she said. "We have a *dui zhang* [team leader] who lives with us. He is responsible for our discipline. He only allows us to go out during the day if it's with guests from the club. If we become friends with them, they will come back to the club."

"What happens if you go out alone?"

"A few days ago I told the team leader I needed to go to a pay phone to make a call. I stayed out for half an hour, shopping for a pair of shoes. *Ha!* Later I told one of the other girls. When she did the same, the team leader locked her out for the rest of the day."

Dilinor looked through the window of the hair salon. Her friends were animated but soundless. Dilinor considered their fates one by one. Xiao Wang had sad hooded eyes. With money from the club, she hoped to pay for an operation that opened up her eyelids. Next to her was Ding Xiang, the shortest. She received almost no flower rings and dreamed of becoming a policewoman. Then Maria, the most successful. She recently visited a wedding studio. A rich guest would marry her, she said, and her dress needed to be ready. By her side, Zheng Zheng, who liked to wear black pinstripe. Any money she earned was instantly converted into clothing. "It makes her mad," Dilinor said, "how everything is for sale in Xiamen and she can afford so little."

～

I went to the office of my friend who sent the faxes to Vancouver. He had chosen the name Laura in addition to his three Chinese characters. "I know it's a woman's name," he told me when we first met. "But I wanted a name nobody else had."

I checked a pile of faxes in Laura's office. Nothing from Vancouver. I had been to Lai's ancestral village and his private bordello, but his two-bedroom apartment in a Canadian suburb was out of reach. How could that be? I sent another fax.

～

Maria had a keen sense of form. During lulls in conversation, she spoke up to avoid embarrassing silences. And then kept talking. She liked attention but never demanded it. She waited for it to come to her, and usually it did.

Maria was seventeen when she came to Xiamen, and the first — and so far only — of the five dancers to have a regular patron. She called him her boyfriend, and sometimes her husband. He was a married lawyer in his thirties and a regular at the club. Lili had pointed Maria out to him when she first appeared onstage. Since then the lawyer had sent her flowers most nights. Yet she never left the club with him. Instead, they met in the afternoons to shop.

On her eighteenth birthday Maria invited Andy, Kim, and me to a party in one of the club's private rooms. Off to the side a door led to a balcony overlooking the auditorium from where guests could watch the stage show. Another door led to a squat toilet. The walls were papered with imitation French drapes and lampshades stood around like scarecrows. With the lights set to dim and a disco ball on the ceiling sparkling gamely, the room was festive in the manner of a department store at Christmas.

The birthday party started with an awkward ritual. The lawyer who was paying for it sat on a sofa with his guests, which included two judges and a partner in his law firm. Lili sat down with us and called a dozen dancers into the room. They lined up against a wall. She suggested picking companions for the evening now rather than waiting for the show. We could send flowers later. The lawyer pointed at Maria — even she had to do the lineup. The lawyer's partner picked Xiao Wang. The two judges asked for dancers from another team.

For the next hour, the lawyers and the judges huddled in a corner, saying they had a case to work on. Then the judges left with their dancers and didn't come back.

During the show, the lawyer sent Maria forty flower rings. His partner sent Xiao Wang two. Xiao Wang called him a *ci gong ji*, a porcelain rooster, or miser.

Afterward, the dancers once again talked about leaving the club. They said they were not earning enough. A bid to negotiate a fixed salary with the club management had failed. They were told that times were hard. Business had slowed after the departure of Lai and the economy was in trouble. People had less money for entertainment. Some guests might even fear being tainted by association with the Lai case. Police had come to know of Lai's fondness for Miss Temporarys.

It didn't help when the dancers protested that they did not want to be Miss Temporarys. They wanted to be dancers. They had had enough of the *dan fei,* solo fliers or businessmen without a wife, of the *hua lao tou,* flower heads or dirty old men, of the *ban can fei,* half-cripples or men shorter than five feet six inches who desired tall women, and of the *can fei,* cripples or men under five feet three inches.

The dancers were learning what Lai must have come to realize long ago. The boomtown promise was often an illusion. To leave family behind and travel across the country was only the beginning.

⌇

When the third fax to Lai's lawyers went unanswered I called their offices in Vancouver again. A secretary said they were busy. In any case, Mr. Lai was not giving interviews. It didn't sound like he had been consulted on the matter.

I called the offices of Chinese websites that had correspondents in Vancouver and was given a few numbers for them. One correspondent suggested getting in touch with the Reverend Moses Cheng. He acted as an unofficial go-between for Lai. Reverend Cheng had been allowed to visit him and his wife in detention, and continued to do so now. Apparently the Lais were preparing to convert to Christianity in their guarded suburban apartment.

I called the reverend, using an anonymous mobile phone number I had just bought at the tobacco store. "Mr. Lai is keen to be baptized," said Reverend Cheng. "He and his wife are seeking comfort in prayer."

"What are they praying for?"

The reverend thought for a while, then he said, "Mostly, they want to learn about forgiveness."

As for me meeting Lai, he sounded encouraging. Lai was having problems with his lawyers, but he could help. I should call back.

⌇

For as long as anyone can remember, correspondents in China have been assigned official minders by the foreign ministry. This is less sinister than it sounds. The minders are civilized people, usually young women. Some of them imply that they personally do not think it necessary to monitor us. One more rule, they seem to say, what can you do? My minder called me on the phone a few times after I arrived in China. She pointed out certain "mistakes" in the *Times.* One time she complained about Taiwan being referred to as a "nation," but she never demanded a correction. Then she stopped calling altogether. While Lai was in hiding I did not hear from her.

But now that he was in Canada and his asylum hearing loomed something changed. The quibbling started again. I received complaints about headlines and photo captions, even after telling her they were written in London. Then someone from the ministry's security department took over. The trigger was a trip I took together with a German colleague to the border with central Asia, incidentally the region where the five dancers came from. There we witnessed, by chance, a group of Chinese Muslims being led off to execution by police officers. A picture I snapped of the condemned as they passed us in the street — their hands tied and signs hanging from their necks proclaiming their crimes — appeared in the *Times*. When I returned to Beijing, my mobile phone rang within minutes of the plane touching down. I was told to present myself at the foreign ministry immediately. When I turned up I was led into a room with half a dozen armchairs arranged in a circle. "What is your intention?" a senior member of the security division asked, and then answered himself. "You have evil intentions. You are trying to sow discord among the ethnic groups of China." His face was bulbous, his voice booming. "Have you read the regulations for foreign journalists?" I had. "But you have broken the regulations. It is *hen bu ying gaide,* inappropriate, and *meiyou daolide,* unreasonable," he said, unable even now to free himself from official language. Then he made a thinly veiled threat. "Would you like to continue to work in China?" I was too stunned to answer. Perhaps he was not expecting me to. "This type of reporting will stop or your situation will get much worse."

At the end of the meeting I picked up my coat from a plush armchair and walked out. I was already beyond the door when my interlocutor came running up behind me. He plunged an arm into my coat and pulled out a lace doily. It took me a moment to realize what it was. The armchair where my coat had rested had been covered with white doilies. I must have picked one up by mistake. I was about to apologize when I saw him holding up the doily above my head in a gesture that seemed to say, "Not only a liar but a thief."

As soon as I got home I called my German colleague. He had reported the same story in his paper. Did he get this kind of reception from the foreign ministry? No, he said.

Within a few weeks, I received another official summons, this time from the Public Security Bureau. I was asked to present myself at their headquarters, entering by the rear door. When I turned up I saw hundreds of dust-covered bikes leaning against the back wall. Did they belong to people who went in and had not yet come out again?

At the door, I was met by two uniformed officers who led me to a windowless room. They came straight to the point. Had I been in touch with Wang Dan, the exiled dissident? Yes, I said. I had exchanged emails with him — but not yet published a story (so how did they know?). Was I aware, they said, of the rule requiring foreign journalists to ask for official permission to interview Chinese citizens? "Yes," I said. "But there is a problem. Wang Dan has become an American citizen." The officers waited for me to go on. "In future," I said, "which government department should I ask for permission to interview Wang Dan?" They whispered among themselves. Then the more senior of the two said, "Beijing foreign affairs office." I thanked them for their advice and found myself back by the dusty bikes.

I told colleagues about these encounters yet found it hard to admit to them I had been frightened. They had never been warned about emails. So we laughed. The rules being applied to us were unfair. Why care? My unease, however, persisted. The worst of it was not knowing why I was being called in. Lots of correspondents were in touch with Wang Dan. The police knew that. I wondered if the real reason was Lai. The officers never mentioned his name. Yet it was the only rationale I could think of. I wondered whether I should leave Xiamen, but in the end I didn't. I might as well have left China.

༄

Maria's boyfriend, or "husband," was a man of substantial size. His basketball-round torso tugged at his belt as if on a leash. By comparison, his head appeared to suffer neglect. The hair on top was thinning and stubble grew in nomadic patches on his chin. He had been a working lawyer for a decade and enjoyed what he considered a good life. "Chinese are already free," he said. "We can say whatever we want as long as it's not published." When I confessed to being a journalist he made me promise not to use his real name. He suggested calling him Mr. Liang, or Lawyer Liang, as the usual form of address went.

Lawyer Liang was a man of routines. Each day unspooled for him like the last. He came to the club in the evening between eight and nine and stayed until midnight. The next morning he got up around seven and went to his office. "Then at twelve o'clock I come here," he said. We were sitting side by side in a massage salon, our backs resting in reclining chairs, our feet propped up on stools. On a low table between us sat plates of fried noodles, provided free of charge. While we ate, masseuses worked on our feet. First they bathed them, then they kneaded the soles. Soon, Lawyer Liang was fast asleep. His masseuse — he had the same one every day — said, "He always sleeps." When the massage was done, she woke him. "See," he said, "I take a nap like this and I'm back at my desk at three. In the evenings I am never tired."

He put his gray socks on. In the parking lot we got into his car, a green jeep with tinted windows, and drove to his office. On the way I asked about his business. He said, without prompting, that he earned one million yuan a year ($120,000). "Half of that I spend on entertaining important people. I pay for everything out of my own pocket. All lawyers finance their own contacts. It's like university education in your country — an investment. No firm pays for it and you can't deduct it from taxes. You have to pay yourself."

"And it's worth it?" I knew what I was fishing for. Lawyer Liang had previously told Kim and Andy that among his clients were some of Lai's more distant associates.

"Business is very good," he said. "There are so many cases resulting from Lai Changxing."

"And you have clients like that?"

"Of course."

"Any big names I might have heard of?"

"Perhaps not. My clients are not very interested in journalists."

There was a pause in the conversation. Then I said, "How did your clients find you?"

"They didn't find me. I found them. Courts suggest lawyers to defendants. I happen to have friends at the intermediate court and they recommended me. That's the easy part. The problem is not getting in trouble. If officials don't like how you defend a client, they throw you in prison, along with him."

He said many lawyers were their own best clients. The idea that counsels should be independent was slow to arrive in China. Until 1992, all lawyers were officers of the court and wore uniforms. Even now, they were expected to ultimately serve the state. To underline the point, lawyers could be imprisoned when their clients perjured themselves. There were about a hundred such cases every year. The state, wary of seeing its power eroded by legal reforms, in effect placed lawyers in the dock alongside defendants. The safe choice in a sensitive case was to accept the prosecution's case and meekly plead for leniency. Only a tiny percentage of cases did not end with a conviction. There was one exception, however. Money could make the system work properly and deliver a semblance of justice. Wealthy clients were able to insist on a genuine defense if they paid extra. The rest of the time, it just wasn't worth it for the lawyer.

"I've bought a house in Australia," Lawyer Liang said. "If anything happens, that's where I'll go."

"But not yet?"

"No. I'm careful."

I thought of the routines that would be disturbed by a move to Australia, but he seemed remarkably unconcerned.

We passed the five-star Golden Swallow Hotel on Southern Lakeside Drive, the twenty-eight-story tower once taken over by government investigators and turned into a detention center for defendants in the Lai case. Lawyer Liang stopped his car across from the hotel. The pink and white building was set back from the road. Evenly spaced windows gave it the checkered appearance of a chessboard.

"You went inside?" I said.

"Yes."

"What was it like?"

"Eight people in one room. Crowded, but convenient for investigators. It's always like this. They like to prevent sleeping. If people stay awake for a few days it's easier to make them confess. Only some people, the most cooperative, are allowed their own room. But they have to pay for it."

"And they do?"

"Yes, if they have the money." Lawyer Liang restarted his car and pulled onto Southern Lakeside Drive.

"Your clients — guilty or not?" I said.

"Guilty."

"And are they treated fairly?"

"When the interrogations are finished, everyone has to sign a piece of paper saying they have not been tortured."

"What happens if they don't sign it?"

"I always tell my clients to sign. You have to be predictable to the investigators and the court. That's your only chance. If the court can trust you, if they know how you will behave, you get better treatment. I recommend my clients always follow a set pattern of behavior. If you call someone Officer Zhang the first time, keep calling him that. If it was Director Zhang, stick with that. They like to think they know you and control you. When they do, I can start discussing how to get a better sentence — usually in a nightclub."

It was just before three o'clock and we had arrived at Lawyer Liang's office. He parked in his usual spot. Men of habit self-evidently disliked surprises, but that didn't mean they were unprepared for them. Lawyer Liang's numerous routines appeared to be more like acts of fortification. "*Boluan fanzheng*," he liked to say, "bring order out of chaos," a phrase that Mao's successors had used to end the Cultural Revolution in the late 1970s.

⁓

When I called the Reverend Moses Cheng in Vancouver again, he sounded gloomy and less sure of his mission. Lai was having problems, he said. He gave no details but a few days later Canadian media reported Lai's bank accounts were frozen. Apparently Beijing had traced part of his assets to the Caribbean and put pressure on the banks there. As a result Lai could no longer afford to pay twenty thousand dollars per week for live-in security guards. After three months out of detention he and his wife were forced to return to their cells. Furthermore, the immigration authorities heard claims that Lai was in contact with a local Chinese triad gang, the Big Circle Boys, possibly to launder or transfer money, but there was no proof.

⁓

I rented a wooden junk for the afternoon and invited Kim, Andy, and the dancers to go on a trip across Xiamen Bay. At the club there was rarely time to talk now. Everything was overshadowed by the need to earn flower rings. The dancers turned up at No. 1 Wharf, saying this would be the furthest they had been from the club since their arrival. Soon our junk passed Gulangyu. Container vessels rose on both sides, houses along the shore receded.

Zheng Zheng was wearing her favorite pinstripe suit. She told me she received close to a hundred flower rings per month now, but she still wasn't happy. She resented management's adding someone new to their team. Nana, who had already been in Xiamen for three years, was taller than Zheng Zheng and a more accomplished dancer. "She has three boy-friends, except she doesn't call them boyfriends," Zheng Zheng said, her voice hovering between disapproval and envy. "Maybe I should leave." I took out my camera and suggested taking a picture. Zheng Zheng asked Andy to sit next to her. She slunk down low in a blue plastic chair and draped Andy's arm around her shoulders.

When Maria saw us she too wanted her picture taken. Her face looked brittle. Someone called out, "You look different today." Without moving a muscle, she said, "Yes, more beautiful." When we sailed back to No. 1 Wharf a few hours later I asked her if she too planned to leave the club. "I don't, but Lawyer Liang wants me to. He said he would prefer me to live by myself and he offered to pay for an apartment. The team leader keeps making problems for us. He won't allow me to see Liang after the club closes."

That day was the last time I saw the dancers. They stopped performing at the club soon after and then disappeared. "I don't know any details," Lili said, raising her hands as if to protest innocence. "It happens all the time." Kim tried to call them on their mobile phones and eventually, months later, she got through. "It started with Zheng Zheng and one other girl leaving the club," Kim told me. Once the dance team was too small to perform, the rest were laid off but still hopeful. Then Maria vanished. The remaining dancers heard Lawyer Liang had rented an apartment for her, but Maria never turned up. She double-crossed him. Having received money from him to become his official mistress, she ran off with the team leader. They had secretly been a couple all along, which explained why Maria never saw the lawyer at night. Maria and the team leader stayed in Xian in north China for a while. Then she returned to her parents alone, taking with her what was left of Lawyer Liang's money. She was now selling lottery tickets. There was no reinvention, it seemed, without betrayal.

The other dancers eventually left Xiamen as well. They returned home, they told Kim by phone, although some were making plans to leave once again, perhaps try another boomtown. They might ride the four-day train again to escape the confinement of home. I half-expected Kim to report en-counters with witch doctors and headhunters, how the dancers had battled pits and nets while listening to the hoots of parrots.

17

The Gambler

No. 3 Dock, Shekou District, Shenzhen City,
Guangdong Province

Almost a year after Lai had been detained in Canada, his asylum hearing was finally scheduled. Evidence would be presented and witnesses heard, at the end of which he would either be deported or given permanent residency in Vancouver. The hearing was to become the longest in Canadian legal history, stretching everyone's patience, but all I knew at the time was I wanted to be there. Locked away since his luck ran out in a Niagara Falls casino, Lai would speak at last. That seemed a good reason to travel to Vancouver. On my way there, I decided, I would follow in his footsteps — drive down the boomtown coast as he had done, cross over to Hong Kong, and fly from there instead of Beijing.

For the first part of the journey I hired a driver on a street corner near the Red Mansion. Seeing what Lai had seen on his departure, and surrounded by his physical legacy, I hoped to pick up his ghost. It was raining when we set off, and when it rained in Xiamen the streets were filled with wet hollows. Rain mixed with sand from building sites in fathomless potholes, ground into the tarmac by all-night lorry traffic. Beyond the streets there were bigger holes still. Vast craters dug by construction crews gaped from unseen depths. For every shiny new tower, there was a project that had failed or run out of money. Swampy construction graves lined the road, none bigger than the one for Lai's eighty-eight-floor tower. We passed the site on the way to the Haicang Bridge and found ourselves on an empty coastal highway, where my fugitive spirits soon soared. A few cars were creeping along uninterrupted by tollbooths and green brush dotted tidy hillsides. If this highway promised anything, it was easy passage, a clear run. After a few hours we stopped in Shantou for lunch, as Lai had done. Fish head soup and tofu, according to the *nei bu* record. I marveled at his calm. Even the threat of arrest could not disturb his appetite.

A worker in a stained shirt sat down next to us at a roadside restaurant. "Have you used a computer?" he asked. He was being friendly.

"Yes," I said.

"Still using the first one?"

"No."

"Then we've probably seen it here." He grinned. His teeth were black. They were stained from drinking the local water, he said.

In 1980, Shantou had been one of the original four Special Economic Zones, along with Xiamen. Earlier still, Shantou had been an East India Company station and a treaty port known as Swatow. It was built on a headland jutting into the South China Sea, making it a natural port. Today its quays were put to unusual use. Rather than exporting goods like most places along the coast, Shantou was reimporting them. Every day, ships unloaded holds filled with wrecked computers. Keyboards, monitors, and printers, many of them produced years ago in neighboring cities, were transferred to backyard stripping centers. Frayed stickers and scribbled notices hinted at erstwhile users:

S.A. Italia
There for you. Guaranteed.
Denver, Colorado
Company property. Do NOT remove.

Thousands of black-toothed workers squatted among the scrap, removing microscopic layers of precious metals hidden in the electronic circuitry — gold and copper mostly. Seated on conked-out monitors, they broke apart casings, stripped cables of their coating, and collected motherboards in buckets. Then they melted down their loot in roiling brews of cadmium, phosphor, lead, and quicksilver. Unwanted leftovers were poured into the Lianjiang River in between two jetties.

After a lunch that mixed garlic with heavy metals, we went back on the highway. The hills rose higher on both sides now. Temples with spiky red gables squatted on tufts of green. I barely noticed them though. I said to the driver I would do anything to avoid the fate of the men with black teeth.

"Anything?"

"Just about."

"Well, don't get caught."

Arriving in Shenzhen at sunset I checked into a hotel. My room was decorated in varying shades of brown, even the minibar. It contained Scotch, bourbon, cognac, and Coke but no water. After dinner I visited an art gallery. It was showing oils painted by local artists. I doubted Lai had come here on his trip, but he would have appreciated the exhibition. It showed paintings soon to be shipped off to western department stores. They were done by a group of young workers who had sought to escape industrial drudgery. At a local art college they learned to copy old masters. Without ever leaving China, they churned out remarkably faithful Provençal landscapes, Dutch still lifes, and South Sea idylls in volumes large enough to fill shipping containers. Their work was labeled van Gogh, Renoir, Gauguin and earned them more than the old masters ever made.

On the street outside the gallery I met Wu Zhonghua, who was picking up an order sheet. He wore his hair long and his mobile phone clipped to his belt.

"Every painter has a special area," he said.

"Portraits, impressionism . . . ?"

"No. Heads, legs, shoes. Only a small part of a painting."

"And the rest?"

"Colleagues do it. Everyone works together."

"So what do you do?"

"Legs, mostly for Picasso paintings." He took a dance step sideways that was awkwardly cubist. "I have worked on sixty thousand Picassos so far. That's more than Picasso ever did, and I am only thirty-four."

Shenzhen is the mother of all boomtowns. In two decades it has grown from a sleepy checkpoint on the border of British-ruled Hong Kong into a city of five million people. Its container port is the world's fourth largest now, it has China's only stock market outside Shanghai, and it dominates global markets for toys, shoes, and untold other goods. Opinions differ why Shenzhen had surpassed other boomtowns like Xiamen that were already functioning cities in 1980. Some say it is Shenzhen's proximity to Hong Kong and Guangzhou. But neighboring Zhuhai, the fourth of the original Special Economic Zones, has been equally privileged, and yet it lags far behind. Others explain Shenzhen's success as flowing from its lack

of history. It had started clean. It has never been marked on a map of imperial China. No emperor visited, nor Mao. But does that matter? Millions of
migrants flooded into the city, bringing with them the past. Shenzhen is as
Chinese today as anyplace ancient.

The next morning I went to one of Shenzhen's lesser port terminals.
Lai had hired a speedboat here to slip over the border to Hong Kong. He
had the contacts to do so. I did not. Passing turbid fish farms and exhausted
dredging fleets, I walked down a line of docks. Rounding a headland, I
spotted a cluster of tents. When I approached I was met with gauzy stares.
Men with wrinkled skin sat on overturned crab crates. They were mending
netting by hand and spoke in low murmurs. One stirred a cackling wok. I
said I was looking for a ride to Hong Kong by boat and asked if they were
fishermen. One nodded. So could I get a ride with them? They shook their
heads, then continued stitching their weedy netting.

I walked along the seafront. The mustachioed captain of a docked mo-
tor junk told me he was heading the other way, up the coast. Further along,
the hollow-eyed bridge of a rusting Russian freighter loomed out of reach,
gangways and ladders having been pulled up. In the next bay, a thin woman
in her nineties laid out squid to dry on a concrete wall. Cheerfully she directed me toward the regular ferry terminal with its passport checkpoint.

When I had already given up and was walking back to the coastal road
I realized my mistake. There was perhaps no greater reservoir of criminal
energy in China than taxi drivers. They violated traffic rules even more casually than party secretaries. I stopped the first one coming along. A "private crossing" to Hong Kong? He would do his best, he said, with pieces of
fried rice stuck to his pointy chin . . . if I hired him for the day. I did and we
took off. For three hours he drove me around the container docks, a stretch
of coast as far removed from a South Sea idyll as could be imagined. Metal
boxes eight by forty feet dominated all aspects of life. People filled them,
hoisted them, ate from them, slept in bunks between them; some even
turned the broken ones into homes. Most of the road traffic was container
trucking. Every job was linked to the conveyance of containers.

In this craterscape my driver went from taxi stand to fry kitchen to car
wash to negotiate on my behalf. For about four hundred dollars, it turned
out, one could cross the border illegally on a sampan. The trip was shorter
than I had expected, about fifteen minutes to reach the northern edge of
Hong Kong. From there one walked a few miles to a bus stop and then rode

into the city. I thanked the driver and directed him to take me to the regular checkpoint. Waiting in the car I had changed my mind about the crossing. I wasn't on the run. If I were caught, even I would have little sympathy with myself. I could resist scratching this itch.

When I arrived in Hong Kong I checked into the Mandarin Oriental Hotel, a posh colonial leftover. I doubted that spackled wood veneer and engraved hunting prints were to Lai's taste, but I found them a welcome change.

For dinner I went to Ah-Yat's, Lai's favorite restaurant. I had found no record of his last meal before going into exile. But if he'd had one, it would have been here. Chef Ah-Yat, the owner, was a friend of Lai. Once he had flown to Xiamen by charter plane to cater a banquet at the Red Mansion. His small restaurant in Hong Kong's Causeway Bay specialized in abalone, a rare shellfish. Regular helpings cost two hundred dollars, with specials going for up to eight hundred dollars. When Chef Ah-Yat came to my table, he was wearing fogged-up glasses and carrying a white plate with two mollusks. They were the size and color of cow livers. "These abalones are so big you need a knife to cut them," he said proudly, wiping his glasses on his white apron. "They're like steaks." I hoped he would stay and talk a little about Lai, but he turned around and hurried back to the kitchen. He was stewing two hundred more abalones in pots with ham and chicken. They had to cook in broth for a whole day to take on flavor, he said in parting. Fresh from the sea, abalone tasted of nothing at all.

ᔕ

I arrived in Vancouver after a twelve-hour flight. Having crossed the international dateline mid-Pacific, it was now a day earlier for me. But it felt like going forward several decades. Government records, strictly controlled in China, were suddenly open to the public. I could delve into the files prepared for Lai's hearing and see what chance he might have of avoiding deportation.

I learned that his fate would be decided by two judges from the Immigration and Refugee Board, a panel independent from the Canadian government. It presided over an exceedingly generous system. Any refugee persecuted "for reasons of race, religion, political opinion, nationality or membership in a particular social group" could stay in Canada. The board sought to extend special protection to people who faced "the possibility of torture, risk to life, or risk of cruel and unusual treatment or punishment" if deported. The acceptance rate was about one in two, or up to thirty thousand refugees per year. In the Vancouver region they were mostly Iranian, Latin American, and Chinese. Cases were decided after hearings lasting a few hours. Yet in Lai's case four months had been scheduled. More than twenty witnesses would be heard, after which the board would review written evidence filling an entire room.

The core issue was this. Did Lai's actions flow from political beliefs and contacts, however loosely defined, or was he a common criminal? China's government was almost as much on trial here as Lai. It had quickly grasped this. In the run-up to the hearing, it denounced Canada as "a haven for criminals." Lai's flight was part of a wider problem. An estimated one thousand officials accused of major financial crimes had gone abroad. Among them were two managers of the Bank of China who embezzled five hundred million dollars and a vice-mayor who took thirty million dollars in bribes. They all claimed to fear persecution.

❧

After reading through refugee board records in my hotel room for several days, I went to a government building in the center of Vancouver. I took a lift, walked along a carpeted corridor, then took another lift to a cozy federal courtroom. As I approached a set of double doors I heard Chinese voices. The sound was both familiar after years in China and unexpected, this being Canada. I could feel again the initial draw the case had had on me, the sudden violence with which it pulled.

The courtroom was filled with Chinese reporters. They chattered among themselves, a beehive of activity, vying for seats and a first glimpse of Lai, who had yet to arrive. I sat in the back and listened to them. Most expected Lai to be deported. They assumed the Canadian government would see to it, mindful of the importance Beijing attached to the case. The reporters talked in small groups, standing in between their western colleagues. Bits of English, Mandarin, and Cantonese floated above them in excited dissonance, like an orchestra tuning its instruments before the arrival of the conductor. Then their cadences converged. The double doors opened and a man walked in.

"Lai Changxing?"

"That's him."

His stride was slow yet jaunty. He seemed to measure each step as if setting foot for the first time on the shores of the New World. He waved to the Chinese reporters. Then he looked up to the ceiling, taking the measure of the room where he would face the accusations of the Chinese government. The room — more wood than marble — was to his liking. He smiled and sat down.

Lai had been brought in under guard from a detention center. He was dressed in a green jumpsuit open at the neck and baggy all over. Glancing around, something seemed to preoccupy him, something specific. He stared in one direction, then turned as if double-checking. It wasn't the piles of legal folders or the observers in the back. No, he was examining the suits worn by the lawyers around him. Their flannel linings and crisp ties contrasted markedly with his appearance. After one more admiring glance at a freshly pressed jacket draped over a chair, he leaned over to his lawyer and whispered in his ear. Then he got up and walked out of the courtroom as if he were a mere bystander or at most an idle witness. The doors of the courtroom flapped open and closed again. Some twenty minutes later he reappeared. The green prison suit was gone. Instead he wore a pair of black trousers and a black jacket over a collarless white shirt, missing only a cummerbund and bow tie. He nodded at his waiting lawyer, his chin dipping slightly, signaling he was ready now for the curtain to go up.

David Matas, Lai's lawyer, seemed confounded by his client. He was fifty-seven years old and Canada's leading human rights counsel. He had hunted Nazi war criminals, observed Third World elections, worked at the Canadian Supreme Court, attended UN General Assemblies as a member, and written books on the Holocaust. A man of clear moral distinctions, he saw Canada's destiny as a haven for the persecuted. He was, however, not an experienced performer in criminal cases, nor was he a China expert. Lai had hired Matas only three weeks earlier after firing his expensive criminal lawyers when they demanded to be paid for work done so far. They declined to fight for the satisfaction alone of opposing tyrannical government.

When the hearing began Matas rose to his feet. His head was bare like the steppes of his native Manitoba. His large glasses covered his cheeks and brows like a protective shield. In his opening remarks, he laid out the case he was hoping to make. "In a general sort of way, and this deals with the facts of the case, it's our position, first of all, that Mr.. Lai is guilty of nothing and this is — the evidence against him is essentially evidence extracted through fraudulent documents, fear of torture, the — or threats of the death penalty, that it's a fabricated case." Matas was a friend of long sentences and had an almost German obsession with subclauses. "Secondly," he said, "our position is that if you feel he should have done something wrong, then if you balance the wrong that he may have done against the danger that he faces, that balancing test comes out in his favor, that the wrongs that he is even accused of doing pale in significance to the fate that awaits him in China."

Matas's preparation for the case appeared to be cursory. Many of his facts came from recent news articles. "I was just reading in the *New York Times* today or yesterday that . . . ," he said, and, ". . . since April, according to the *New York Times*, there's been over one thousand executions in China."

His argument was basically this. Lai would not admit he was a criminal, but all the evidence said he was. So the defense would both challenge the validity of the evidence and reach beyond it, appealing to Canada's tradition of support for the vulnerable. Lai was not accused of violent crimes, Matas pointed out. And yet if sent back to China, Lai faced the death penalty, and who would want that on their conscience?

Lai was next to Matas, listening to a whispered translation. He sat straight-backed and was seemingly alert, his eyes darting back and forth between the judges from the Immigration and Refugee Board. His facial muscles moved to indicate, what, agreement or comprehension? A nod was followed by a sideways tilt of the head as if weighing something. Then his head would roll back silently as if to say, "Ah, now I get it."

Occasionally, Lai would interrupt Matas. Early on, he insisted on correcting a recital of biographical details. Matas, momentarily muted, consulted his papers, a jumble of folders and notebooks. Then he suggested moving on. Lai demurred. "I am afraid if I don't tell the whole story it won't be clear." For the next hour, Matas was forced to consult him point by point. During a short break in the proceedings the two men conferred.

"Why didn't I know about this?" Matas said.

"I told you."

"Well, if I had known . . ."

Matas was Lai's only lawyer, and he was trying to build his case as he went along, on the fly. The other side, by contrast, had plenty of expertise and manpower. The person in charge was Canada's immigration minister, Elinor Caplan herself. She invested in the case the full might of the sovereign, drafting in armies of government lawyers and diplomats to work out every conceivable argument for deporting Lai. He was described as a Chinese Mobutu straight from the heart of darkness — the cars, the mansions, the absurd corruption and anarchy. He did not deserve refuge. Referring to both Lai and his wife, one of the minister's lawyer said, "They are guilty of smuggling, fraud, tax evasion, and bribery. They left China because they feared prosecution, not persecution."

What the government lawyers omitted to say was that Canada's national interest was at stake here too. Three months after Lai was detained, the Canadian prime minister had visited Beijing. His hosts made it abundantly clear that trade relations were dependent on Lai's swift return. Canadian investments in the world's fastest-growing major economy might be condemned to wither if . . .

After that, Ottawa's lawyers set out to build the case against Lai in close cooperation with Beijing. Documents were shared, delegations exchanged, and Canadian diplomats joined Chinese investigators in interviews with imprisoned Lai associates to find evidence of his guilt. One of the interviewees was Lai's brother Shuiqiang. He described the smuggling operations in detail in exchange for a promise of leniency. The government lawyers thought they had strong evidence. But this being Canada, not China, news of how they obtained their evidence soon leaked out. Matas pounced. He said the Canadian government was the beneficiary of torture, or at least the fear of torture. Less cooperative Lai family members had suffered in detention. "There is some direct evidence around torture of family members," Matas said.

He won the support of the judges, who allowed extensive discussion of government tactics. One aspect in particular exercised them. Did Canadian law not protect anyone facing the death penalty? The government said the law did not apply in Lai's case. The Chinese had given formal assurances that Lai would not be executed on his return. They had written a "diplomatic note" to that effect, signed by the Chinese ambassador in Ottawa. (Just the week before the same ambassador had said, "Blood has to be paid with blood. Death has to be paid with death," criticizing the Canadian legal system for being too soft.)

Matas pounced again. He said Beijing did not actually write the note.

It had come from the pen of the Canadian foreign minister. In the service of the national interest he had turned ghostwriter, composing the note guaranteeing Lai's life, and then obligingly handed in his work at the Chinese embassy for the appendage of a signature. The foreign ministry in Ottawa did not deny the charge. Nor did the embassy. For the first time, the case against Lai was looking dented. But did Lai know it? It was hard to tell. During hours of lawyerly back-and-forth, he sat rigidly composed. He said nothing but smiled whenever he heard his name mentioned, which was often.

∽

After a week of preliminary arguments it was time for Lai to take the stand. He became more animated, nodding in all directions as if to greet those who had made the special effort to see him. He was determined to justify himself, he said. Reluctantly, Matas had gone along with his strategy. They would attempt to counter allegations of bribery not by denying them but by insisting the flow of money from Lai to officials was legal. They started with the charge — utterly ludicrous to Lai — that he bribed Li Jizhou, the number two in the public security ministry.

Soon, though, Matas ran into problems.

"Was there any money that changed hands between you and Li Jizhou?" he asked.

"Yes." Lai drew out the single syllable, dipping his head for emphasis, then picking it up again as he finished.

"Tell us about that."

"There was one million yuan. It had something to do with his wife," Lai said, then he waved his hand as if to dismiss the point.

Matas insisted. "Did the money go to his wife?"

"The money was not handed over by me personally. A friend of mine in Beijing handed it over."

"To whom, to him or his wife?"

"His wife."

Matas looked like he was already regretting this line of questioning. "Was there any other money that went to Li Jizhou or his family?"

"Yes. Another five hundred thousand dollars. It was mailed to the United States."

"And who in the United States were you sending it to?"

"Li Qian. That's Li Jizhou's daughter."

Lai was looking at some notes in front of him as if searching for the names of further recipients of his largesse. Hurriedly, Matas moved on. "Okay. So, also, was this money a loan or a gift? Loan or gift?"

"Loan."

"Okay. Many — well, let's not list them all, but in a general sort of way, who is the sort of person you would lend money to?"

"Some are government officials. Sometimes, I would borrow money from somebody. So when people came to me for money, I would also lend to them."

"Always?"

"Yes."

"Anybody who asks?"

"Yes. Yes. Unless that person does not have money. Because if that person has money, he would also lend to me."

"Okay," Matas said. He flipped through some papers, then wrote a note to himself. "But the government officials and the business people that were borrowing from you, how did you decide whether or not to give them a loan?"

"I would see what they had to say, whether they were reasonable or not." Lai lifted up one hand, then the other to underline the distinction. His hands rose and fell, mimicking scales. Given his minimal education, he must have been familiar with employing substitutes for vocabulary, but the gesture did not come across as helpless. He used his hands like someone who enjoyed expressing himself in front of an audience.

"Okay. And what do you consider reasonable?"

"If it's a rare circumstance such as for family, then I will lend them money."

"And what's unreasonable?"

"If somebody wants to blackmail me with official power. I don't like that."

"Okay. What, if anything, did you want in return for these loans?"

"I just wanted the money back." Lai curled his lips in mock indignation at what the question implied.

"Anything else?"

"No."

"Did you ask these government officials to do anything for you?"

"No."

"Okay. All right. You'd lend money to government officials for their families if they needed it. You didn't want any — you wanted the money back but you didn't want anything for your business." Lai nodded. Matas stared at him. The lawyers on the government side shook their heads, perhaps pitying their colleague.

He tried again. "You weren't in it for favors, so why were you doing it?"

"Just basic principle of being a human being. Borrow money, lend money."

"Okay. How do you relate this to being a human being?"

"I just believe that I should do this."

⌇

Lai strode out of the courtroom as if a verdict in his favor had been announced. He grinned, shook hands with bystanders, raised his arms in a victory salute, and undid a few buttons of his shirt while he went down a corridor surrounded by cameramen and reporters. He spun himself into their web so tightly I could no longer hear him, his arms doing the talking once again, his words lost in the microphones. I noticed a tautness and brightness in his face. Early on in the questioning there had been hints of cold calculation, but the longer it lasted the more Lai grew into his role. I remembered his change of clothes, swapping his prison suit for a tuxedo. Lai must have thought himself on a stage. He was performing and wanted the right costume. He was an actor. And not an unsuccessful one, though more so in China where the Red Mansion had been his personal stage.

The scrum around Lai outside the courtroom loosened a little and I joined.

"Are you innocent?" he was asked.

"I am completely innocent. I was given a bad name in the Chinese state media. They have told lies about me. But I believe in Canadian justice. The Canadian justice system will protect me."

"Will you be able to pay your lawyer?"

"The Chinese government froze some of my accounts and I had some problems. But friends have sent me more money."

"From China? Friends from China?"

"More than forty thousand dollars was sent from a bank in Hong

Kong. I have lots of friends in Hong Kong and in China too. They're all types of friends — in business and in government. They send me money even if the Chinese government throws them in prison."

If true, these payments gave some credence to Lai's self-portrayal as a casual borrower and lender. But only some. I walked out of the courthouse. By the door I saw a Chinese man with a hairline inching away from his round face. He was short and dressed in a collarless shirt. "You know him?" I said, gesturing toward the departing Lai.

"Sure."

"You a relative?"

"Am I what? No."

"I just thought you looked alike."

"That may be, but no. I am a Chinese who grew up here." He said his ancestors came to North America more than a hundred years ago as laborers. They worked for a pittance. "At least that much has changed," he said. "Now the Chinese come with enough money to employ Canadians."

On the way back to my hotel, I walked past the old Central Pacific train station, its stony columns and neoclassical façade overlooking a small park. I sat down on a lawn and stretched out. Wasn't this a little like Xiamen? Vancouver too had once been a frontier town by the water. Only a hundred years ago, according to the potted histories on faded postcards sold at the station counter. Vancouver got its first railway link when British Columbia's treacherous Eagle Pass was joined to the continental grid. A boom followed, fanned by robber barons and the Roaring Twenties.

When I got up from the lawn I went to a travel agent. I would delay my return flight. I was hooked on Lai's performance. I had to stay.

༄

Matas thought he was set for a good day in court. He told the judges that a year ago Chinese police officers secretly met with Lai in Canada. "They tried to persuade him to return to Xiamen," he said and showed off copies of their travel documents. This had happened before Lai was detained and China made its extradition request. The officers from the 4.20 investigation team had tracked him down far earlier than anyone had realized. Following negotiations by phone, they met him at a hotel in downtown Vancouver. With them was Lai Shuiqiang, who was promised leniency if he could persuade his brother to give himself up. But Lai refused. He paid Shuiqiang's hotel bill and left. Four days later, the officers and the brother returned home. What was most interesting, Matas said, was this. The Chinese government had gone to great lengths to conceal the officers' identity from the Canadian authorities. Their visa applications made them out to be traders at the China National Pulp and Paper Corporation. In a letter to the Canadian embassy in Beijing, China's ministry of economic cooperation declared the three to be a "trade delegation" and arranged express visa approval. Need he produce any more evidence, Matas asked, of Beijing's talent for fabrication?

Then he called Lai's wife to the stand. Zeng Mingna wore a black leather skirt and her brittle face was hidden behind strands of dark hair. At the start of the hearing she had been taking so many sedatives she regularly fell asleep in the courtroom. She told Matas she did not want to think about the situation she and her family were in. Her mother and her brother were imprisoned in China and her father had been tortured. "Just because he's my father."

"If you went back, what would happen to you?" Matas asked.

"The only solution is death."

"And your children?"

"I can't imagine their future." Then she broke down and sobbed.

I looked at Lai. He sat still.

After weeks of testimony orchestrated by Matas, it was then the Canadian government's turn to call witnesses. Most of them were investigators from Xiamen, flown in at Beijing's expense. They described Lai's smuggling and the work of the 4.20 team. The most stunning part was the videotaped confession of a Lai associate. "I fell for the charms of a woman," said Yang Qianxian, the customs chief of Xiamen and a frequent visitor to the Red Mansion. "I totally lost my principles. This is truly a lesson for life."

The customs chief looked awful. The Chinese investigators denied beating the confession out of him. Nevertheless, Matas was able to score a few points. He showed how they had tampered with evidence, removing a safe from the Red Mansion and then forgetting which room it had come from. Using documents provided by them, he also showed that detainees had been interrogated without proper procedure. Some interrogations had lasted several days without a break. "Is there any case left at all?" Matas called out at one point. But there was. The evidence presented by the Chinese was riddled with inaccuracies but its weight was undeniable. And Matas knew it.

After weeks of arguing over the facts of Lai's life in China, he shifted the focus back to what would happen if Lai were returned there. He called an unimpeachable expert witness. Wei Jingsheng was known as China's Mandela, a four-time nominee for the Nobel Peace Prize. In 1979, the chain-smoking electrician had publicly demanded a move to democracy. Following a sham trial, Wei disappeared into a vast gulag of labor camps and reeducation centers. There he was physically broken. He spent years in solitary confinement interspersed with beatings by fellow prisoners. His body succumbed — his teeth fell out, his heart weakened, he developed high blood pressure, arthritis, and headaches. But Wei's mind refused to give in. He wrote hundreds of letters from his cell addressed directly to Paramount Leader Deng Xiaoping, challenging him to justify such prison treatment. With every letter he mocked Deng's public commitment to human rights. A few months after Deng died in 1997, Wei was put on a plane to America on "medical parole." Now he showed up in Vancouver. Asked by Matas what would happen to Lai if he were deported, Wei said through a new set of front teeth, "For sure there will be no fair trial for him." And what about the promised exemption from execution? "The government of China seldom keeps its promises. I was personally deceived and tricked many times."

In countering Wei's testimony, the Canadian government asked a deceptively simple question: Had there not been dramatic changes in China since 1979? To answer the question, the government found an expert witness whose standing was at least as good as Wei's. Jerome Cohen was a legal pioneer, an American lawyer who had been visiting China for three decades and frequently helped to defend regime critics. "I have no doubt the Chinese government will adhere to the promise with respect to the death penalty," he said, white-haired and clear-eyed. "The Chinese will seek to play this by the book." Would they hinder the work of Lai's defense lawyers during a trial, he was asked? "I don't think so because of the glare of publicity."

Cohen did not appear naïve. He said he doubted Lai would be tortured but added, "I can't be an insurance for the Chinese government." Lai listened to what Cohen said and gave a wordless commentary. He shook his head and buried it in his hands.

⋐⋑

Matas and the Canadian government lawyers presented two achingly different pictures of Lai, neither of which rang true. In his closing statement,

Matas said that Lai was a law-abiding Chinese citizen persecuted because of his links with the political elite. Some of his associates had been involved in a power struggle inside the government and lost, he said. As a consequence, people like Lai were hunted down and persecuted. This was no mere criminal case. "It's about as political a case as you will ever see," Matas said. When he finished speaking the judges barely looked up. Matas was the anti-Lai. He had no talent for showmanship. His delivery was polished but aimless. Nobody doubted he believed every word he said, but the words were amorphous, congregating in irregular shoals.

The Canadian government lawyers scoffed at Matas's closing statement. Lai was a "greedy criminal" who should be sent home to face justice, they said. Overwhelming evidence showed he had illegally amassed hundreds of millions of dollars. "Mr. Lai was the head of the largest smuggling enterprise in Chinese history," one of the lawyers said. "Mr. Lai committed these crimes to make money for himself and these are serious non-political crimes."

I was no Sinologist but it seemed to me both sides missed the point. Lai was a criminal as well as a political target. Nobody in Xiamen doubted he was a smuggler. Yet that was not why he left. His backers in the government had been sacked and a political decision was made at the top to no longer turn a blind eye. Instead of acknowledging this, the Canadian government stuck by Beijing's official line that Lai was a common criminal. By insisting no politics was involved, it consistently undermined its own case. It came across as blind to reality. And it left all the political ammunition to Matas.

The Canadian government was saved by the fact that Matas didn't know what to do with the ammunition. I was no more a lawyer than a Sinologist, but I could see no sense in insisting Lai had broken no laws in China and was victimized in a nebulous power struggle. Lai was a criminal. He was guilty. It was undeniable. But look at the crime scene. That's what Matas might have said. The crime scene was not the Red Mansion or some dockyard. The crime scene was the political environment in which Lai had to work, where rule-breaking was the rule, where only men like him could truly prosper. To obey the law of China's post-Communist jungle was to ignore it. With Lai in Xiamen, the local economy had grown by more than 20 percent a year. When he left, the rate dropped to zero.

In my mind, I saw Matas standing in a grand courtroom and I stood right next to him, forcing words into his mouth like cough drops. In this version of events he was more of a tub-thumper than he really was. He would cry, Who is responsible for this mess? Not Mr. Lai. No, the government. Then, after fingering his oversize glasses and patting down the last few hairs on his head, he would call an expert witness, someone who knew the universe Lai had inhabited. The expert would explain that China's economy was a gymnastic blend of authoritarian controls and anarchic privateering, and point out that Beijing had deliberately created this environment. How? By not guaranteeing private property rights and failing to make government business transparent, and by drawing few clear policy lines and tolerating official extortion rackets. But — so one of the judges might ask — why do such a thing? How could Beijing possibly benefit? Milord, it benefited tidily. Beijing was afraid of the entrepreneurs and their ambitions. Men like Mr. Lai were accumulating fortunes and with it political power — power that made them independent and dangerous. To rein in the entrepreneurs, Beijing played favorites. Men like Mr. Lai were offered tax breaks, land deals, and sweetheart contracts. In turn they were expected to renounce their political ambitions — and hand out cash and cars and women. Academics had a name for this: state capitalism, a system where the government combined economic freedom with a firm hold over private businesses.

The Matas of my imagination plowed on. He called a second expert witness, this one familiar with the thinking inside the Chinese government. He — for there were few women Sinologists — testified that Beijing pursued an offensive strategy, not just a defensive one. By leaving the rules of the game unclear it boosted economic efficiency. How? Here was an example. Throughout the 1990s, China charged very high import tariffs. Foreign-made cars cost double the western price. Beijing had already signaled that it was prepared to lower tariffs, but only if its trade partners followed suit. And so the partners negotiated. For thirteen years, they haggled over the terms of China's entry to the World Trade Organization. In the meantime, China desired ever more foreign cars. The economy was booming. And this was where the crafty Mr. Lai came in. Instead of paying the high official tariff on imported vehicles, he paid a lower, unofficial "tariff" directly to customs and military officers who controlled the shipping lanes and dockyards. The result was that market prices in China for foreign cars dropped and more people could afford them. The same happened in almost every other market, benefiting the whole economy. China had had it both ways. It maintained a strong negotiating position in the trade talks, yet also benefited from cheap imports: fuel, electronics, and cigarettes, for example. But then, in 1999, Beijing agreed to terms for entry to the World Trade Organization and Mr. Lai's position collapsed. He was no longer useful and fled. Until then, however, Beijing had not only tolerated gray areas like the one in which he operated, it had practically mandated them.

The expert witness finished and headed out. It was time now for Matas's closing statement. But this time around he would have real fire. *Corruption? Bribery? Smuggling?* I heard him say. For Beijing to indict Lai for such crimes was shameless. Beijing had brought this on itself. It bore the moral responsibility. Its own actions were to blame. Free markets and free thinking had not undermined public morality in China. No. Mao and the Cultural Revolution had. Corruption was merely a symptom. The real disease was a system of government that granted unlimited power to officials. A good deal of corruption could be eliminated overnight simply by taking away what officials had to sell — their arbitrary control. There lay responsibility for corruption, not with citizens subject to the whims of officials.

Though exhausted by his passion, Matas reached for a copy of *The Wealth of Nations* by Adam Smith and quoted a passage that said a smuggler was a person "who, though no doubt highly blameable for violating the laws of his country, is frequently incapable of violating those of natural justice, and would have been, in every respect, an excellent citizen had not the laws of his country made that a crime which nature never meant to be so."

The courtroom would rise in spontaneous applause, hands flying above Matas's head. Except, the room was now filled with a new audience. There were hundreds of students. They ringed Matas in adulation. Eventually, though, a Canadian government lawyer pushed them back into their seats. Standing over them, he jeered. "Listen to the old saw that a little bribery greases the wheels nicely," he said, "that red tape economies worked better with baksheesh. Anyone who has recently been to Moscow knows better." He quoted an article on Russia in the *London Review of Books*. The writer, Edward Luttwak, had written that organized crime groups "resist the excessive concentrations of economic power brought about by government corruption . . . They are, in effect, competitors which use physical force, usefully, to offset monopolistically market power in a lawless country." The lawyer then turned away from the judges and faced the students. "Anyone want to move to Moscow? See what useful physical force feels like? All right. Let's not turn China into thuggish post–Soviet Russia then. The Chinese know how messy things can get, and they want to clean up before it's too late. We should support that and help them build a rule-based, civilized society. Because let's face it, we're stuck with them. They're not losing power. Either lend them a hand tackling their cancer or face it coming over here."

18

The Gambler II

Table 12, Imperial Chinese Seafood Restaurant,
355 Burrard Street, Vancouver

The Chinese nation would undoubtedly be better off if Lai were
punished in an effort to deter others. And so would all of us who bought
Chinese sneakers, televisions, and toys. But did that justify sending him to
the labor camp hell endured by Wei Jingsheng?

The judges from the Immigration and Refugee Board said it would
take them a while to decide. First they had to sift the evidence. In the meantime, they released Lai from detention on a $50,000 bail bond. The judges
reasoned he didn't have the money for a further flight, one that would be
increasingly expensive as China pressed countries around the world to aid
his capture or suffer trade penalties. They allowed Lai to move back into his
guarded condominium in the suburb of Burnaby. But he had to observe a
nighttime curfew and could not visit casinos. He was also banned from associating with local triads — the *shetou* or snakehead travel agents of the
Chinese underworld — just in case he found a country willing to take him.

Seeing Lai in court had made me want to interview him even more
than before. I watched him dazzle the judges with theatrical gestures, or at
least try to. He acted out what he must have thought an asylum seeker
should look like. Far from being meek and haunted, he presented himself
as a wronged but important man, an equal to the government persecuting
him and hence worthy of protection. By the end of the hearing he was
treating the security officers in the courtroom as part of his entourage
rather than as captors.

From a Canadian journalist I got a phone number for Matas. I called him and asked for an interview with Lai. He said I should contact a Chinese-Canadian woman called Sandra, who acted as his legal assistant and translator. I called Sandra and told her I was writing about Lai. "I'm sorry. Mr. Lai will not give an interview," she said. Chinese officials didn't say sorry when they turned you down, but the tone was the same. I thought of just turning up in Burnaby and ringing Lai's bell. But as far as I knew there were still guards.

I called Sandra back. I explained I had spent time in Xiamen and the village where Lai was born. This seemed to make her even less willing to allow the interview.

A week later I called her a third time.

"There are many things Mr. Lai cannot talk about," she said.

"Like what?"

"I can't tell you that."

"Perhaps the situation will change after the verdict is announced?"

"I can't say."

In the end Sandra agreed to a short "meeting" with Lai, rather than an interview. She would be present to monitor the interview. Three days later she picked me up in a car on a street corner in Burnaby. She was about fifty, brittle, and heavily made up. Together we drove into an underground parking garage below an apartment building. We took a lift to the seventeenth floor. She rang a bell.

When Lai opened the door, the muscles around his eyes played a silent symphony. They rose in uneven sweeps and bobbed in staccato. His temples followed a beat behind, twitching left and right and then together. He appeared to be rousing himself, as if he'd just left bed. One hand worked the belt buckle on a pair of black chinos and the other tucked in the fringes of a black turtleneck. His eyes were bloodshot and small. The stubble on his chin was almost as long as the hair on his recently shorn head.

He was looking about his age, forty-four, but he did not look like the Lai from the hearing. I had imagined someone taller, more imposing. In the courtroom he had been far away, making it difficult to judge his height. Standing up close now, I towered over him. He was barely five feet tall. His shoulders were hunched and his hands knitted together. Nothing about his physical bearing suggested the lyrical countenance of a tragic hero or a human devil as variously suggested during the hearing. To have expected anything else was, of course, naïve. But secretly I had hoped for little red horns.

"Please," he said in English, "welcome."

"You have a comfortable home."

"Very comfortable." The apartment was a far cry from the baronial follies he had inhabited in China. We were standing in a carpeted living room. Lai pointed at a forty-eight-inch television, one of only a few furnishings. "Television," he said in English, and then, "telephone," gesturing toward a combined phone and fax machine. There was a short pause while he seemed to search a mental dictionary. "Tah-ble."

"Oh, yes. A table."

A longer pause. Finally, he said "television" again.

I nodded. "It's a big television."

"I am learning a little English," he said, switching to Chinese.

"So, you're hoping to stay in this country?" I said. He looked at me. The sentence had come out as a question. Of course, he wanted to stay. The real question was, would he be allowed to? "Well, at least you're no longer in the detention center," I said.

"It's good to be out. I can eat with my children." He pointed to the open kitchen at the back of the room. Dirty dishes and take-out containers sat on a counter, the smells of yesterday's stir-fry still in the air.

"What confuses me," he said, "why do Canadians not have separate kitchens? In China, we don't cook where we eat."

"Not enough room."

"Oh."

He closed the plywood apartment door and snapped a lock shut.

"So you cook yourself?" I said.

"Not very often. I am not familiar with cooking. In China, I ate in restaurants."

"And in the detention center?"

"It was terrible. Western food. But now I am gaining weight again. You know they called me Fatty Lai in China?"

"I heard."

"Yes. So my situation is good now."

We walked from the door into the living room. I said I had been to his hearing and learned a lot about him, especially his links with Li Jizhou.

"You think I am guilty?" The question stood between us for a moment like someone squeezing through a crowded bus door, then he continued. "It was a very long hearing. Canadian justice is very careful. In China, they would have finished in a day. And, you know, afterward. . ." He tied an imaginary rope around his neck. Then he went over to the sofa and flounced down. I sat across from him, on a chair at the dining room table. Sandra sat next to me.

I turned my chair away from her to face Lai and said, "I can understand how a business as big as yours would have had many important government contacts." The sentence was written out and underlined in my notebook. It was to be my opening. It conveyed a certain sympathy, I hoped, without signaling wholesale approval. But Lai was preoccupied. He had found three remote controls on the couch. Trying to tell them apart he pointed all three at the television. He could barely read the keys. Each remote was covered with a layer of milky bubble wrap. Like many of his countrymen — keen to protect new purchases — Lai had chosen not to remove the factory packaging.

"Is that television from China?" I said.

"Should be, should be."

The television sprang to life. Then a stereo — that was the second remote. The third seemed to belong to a home trainer in the next room, which now began to beep. Lai put the remotes away. "You know," he said, "I had a Mercedes. It belonged to President Jiang Zemin once. It weighed five tons, but the steering was smooth. I also owned many buildings." He pointed at photographs on the gray wall behind him. They showed highrises in Xiamen. I recognized some of the ones he had built. I asked if he missed home. "It's difficult to say. In the beginning I thought my problems would finish quickly. After one or two months I'd go back. I thought I could wait and then return, so in the beginning I never thought about missing China, and I also talked to people there on the phone."

He opened his palm and showed me a small mobile handset. "I was careful at first," he said. "I hardly talked to anybody. But then I became bored. I started calling friends. I also called my relatives. I heard what had happened. I heard about my brother Shuiqiang. He made a deal with the government. Later, I talked to my brother directly. I knew the investigators were listening. Then I thought I might as well talk to them too. So I did. I complained to them about the arrest of my parents-in-law."

Lai had a way of telling his story that was both clumsy and vivid. His stabbing, rollicking delivery was more like sports commentary than after-the-fact narration, but he spoke more quietly now than in the courtroom.

"You were not worried the investigators would find out where you are?" I said.

"No. I always used a mobile phone registered in the United States."

"But still they found you . . ."

"Yes."

"And they offered you a deal to come back."

"Yes. But, you know, it's too early for that. The same people are still in charge in Beijing."

"So you hope to go back one day? Of your own will?"

He thought about this for a moment. Then he said, "Canada is a very developed country. It has good opportunities for business. Take this building. It is called The Crystal. Eighty meters tall. Twenty-six floors. It has very good quality. Much better than what I built in China. So I will learn a lot here. I will do some business. After I am finished with the hearing. You cannot do business under curfew. But afterward, I will be involved with the Canadian real estate. It will bring me big money. Real estate is always a good business. Land stays the same size."

"And China . . ."

"Maybe I should not say this before the judges make a decision . . . but China is my home."

Sandra interrupted. "Perhaps it would be best to wait."

Lai nodded. "I can also invest in Chinese real estate from here. The Crystal is a very good model. It should be built in every Chinese city. I will organize this. I still have partners. Xiamen will get it first. Then Shanghai. It will make a big change. There are so many people in China. They all want to live in a place like this. China has a big future."

Lai's voice was faltering. Invoking China's bright future, he sounded like a government flack. He might have been right about China, but he would not be part of that future. Even he must have realized that was a reinvention too far. Whatever the outcome of the hearing, he would not be riding in presidential limousines again.

Lai stood up from the sofa. He put his mobile phone down on the table and went to the next room. The home trainer was still beeping. Lai turned it off. In the meantime, Sandra went out to make a call. While we waited for her, Lai walked up and down in the room. "This here is borrowed," he said. "Television — borrowed. Stereo — borrowed." Almost nothing in the apartment belonged to Lai. He tried not to sound downcast.

"I have many friends in Canada. They gave me these things. It is a good situation."

When Sandra returned, Lai sat down. Their relationship was both intimate and formal. She was his Mandarin translator vis-à-vis Matas. She was also his border guard and confessor, poised between sin and sin. He'd had nobody like this in China.

"How did you get to know so many officials?" I said. "It can't have been easy."

"The government holds a lot of ceremonies and the private businessmen were always invited. You exchange business cards with officials. So you meet more and more. Your circle widens."

"Did it take you a long time?"

"Listen, I don't have a very good family background. I had to do things step by step, by myself. That's how people came to respect me. I never fussed about big money. Instead, I would tell someone: Oliver, I trust you, do this for me, I need this done. And when people made mistakes I had them come to me. We discussed the problem. They would see I was reasonable. I looked after them."

"In Xiamen, some people believe you had a favorite saying: I am not afraid of officials — I'm only afraid of officials who don't have a hobby."

"I think at this point," Sandra said, "it would be best to stop and wait until the judges make their decision. Then we can continue the discussion."

Lai demurred. He said, "If I had really been a briber and a smuggler I would not have kept my money in China. If someone breaks into your house to steal, he doesn't leave his wallet behind." Lai's face was flushed. He reached into his chino pocket for a pack of cigarettes. The pack was bright red and a picture of the Gate of Heavenly Peace was printed on the front. Chungwa brand, imported from China.

"Please, Mr. Lai," Sandra said. She didn't want him to smoke in the room. He walked over to the main window. It stretched from floor to ceiling, but only the panel closest to the floor could be opened. Lai sat down on the knitted carpet and opened it. He blew out smoke through a narrow gap. He crouched down there, clinging to the window frame, while Sandra and I sat at the table. We could see suburban Vancouver lumber past seventeen floors below him. Pickups on wide boulevards, mountains in the distance. It was difficult to imagine Lai ever becoming part of this landscape. He had changed identity before, but he had little left now.

Still he tried, no matter how lonely or forlorn. He had his old tricks. "Do you smoke?" he said. "Let me give you some." He reached into his pocket and pulled out a second pack. It was red like the first, but a different brand. "Yuanhua," he said. "My company made these in China. I designed the logo myself. That was more than five years ago. We sold millions." He turned the pack over in his hand a few times, then extended his arm. "I have only three of these left. Take one."

〜

At the end of the meeting I knew I wanted to see Lai again. I had come close to finding the original, the Chinese Lai. There had been glimpses of him, yet he was still obscured.

As we left Lai's apartment Sandra told me I could meet him again but not alone. I would have to go through her. "Make another appointment," she said. Yet while she had been out of the room an hour earlier, Lai had given me his mobile phone number. He had scribbled it in my notebook. He was no good at writing words but his numbers were fine.

I called him the next day. I told him I wanted to write a book about him. I wanted to ask him about his upbringing in Shaocuo, for example. Would he have time to meet? He said he'd think about it. When I called again twenty-four hours later he sounded unenthusiastic. After a pause, I suggested having dinner together.

"Where?" he said.

Before calling him I had asked at my hotel for the best Chinese restaurant in town. I told him the name.

"*Hao, hao, hao,*" he said. "Good, good, good."

I should have known. A book meant little to him, but a Chinese restaurant was a temptation. It was the closest he could get to home now.

The next evening, as I waited for Lai on a street corner, I found myself hoping food would unlock his previous incarnation. I also hoped he would come alone.

"No Sandra?" I asked when he arrived.

"She is always making problems. Like a wife. Don't miss the curfew, she says, let me help you."

Lai was fine on his own. All over Vancouver he could order food in Chinese, even file his taxes, if he paid them. Near his apartment was Chan's No. 1 Chinese Language Tax Accountancy. We ate dinner at the Imperial

Chinese Seafood Restaurant. The large dining room was a favorite with wedding parties. The tablecloths were starch white, as were the wind-whipped crests on Burrard Inlet outside.

Lai was dressed in a black suit and a blue collarless polyester shirt. The shirt was covered in tiny, crenelated stripes. I had time to study them while he spoke to the waiters in dialect. Like him they were from Fujian. Lai's voice was deeper than I remembered. It rumbled like a speeding coal train, occasionally pitching up with clacking laughter, then returned to a *rat-tat-tat uh-tat-tat.*

The waiters said hardly a word, and when they tried to hand Lai a menu he refused. Instead he asked them to bring out uncooked produce for inspection. A live fish. Some shrimp. A lobster. They went off to the kitchen. In the meantime, Lai buttonholed Chinese at the next table. How were the scallops, he asked? And the squid? Lai was a familiar figure from restaurants back in Xiamen — the overbearing guest. Before dinner had even been ordered he harangued his table and everyone in the vicinity, toasting to make himself heard. And, amazingly, others joined in.

I had once heard someone describe Ken Kesey, the author of *One Flew Over the Cuckoo's Nest,* as having "transactional charisma." People fed off him and he off them. Lai had something similar. His charisma was like dog-gerel — clumsy and ridiculous but irresistible.

The waiters came back to the table with a tray of seafood. Lai told them he wanted to see more. They returned to the kitchen, cajoled into showing us everything they had while keeping other guests waiting. They came out again and again. I hoped they were taking notes. Lai had what every one of them would need to open his or her own restaurant one day. He could bend wills to do things neither needed nor wanted.

At last, Lai finished ordering and settled in his seat. I said I was interested to hear his explanation for what happened to him in China, not what his lawyer said during the hearing, but his own version. Why had his business crumbled in the end?

This was the sort of question Sandra dreaded. She thought Lai might incriminate himself further, but his response was flimsy and defensive. "The government randomly rounded up people and accused them of smuggling. Those people then accused me of smuggling to save themselves."

"Really?"

"Yes. Many people in Xiamen were jealous of me. Let's say you're a businessman and I'm a businessman. I do well — you're unhappy. So you accuse me of smuggling."

I tried again. I asked about his last few months in China. What happened? He said he quarreled with his brother Shuiqiang over business interests. He also argued with his wife. She had returned to Xiamen in early 1999 after years of living separately in Hong Kong. It was difficult being together again. And then there was Changbiao, his brother in a wheelchair, injured in a fight in a nightclub around that time. So much happened at once, Lai said.

Was he surprised by his downfall?

He said his friends told him he was in trouble and should leave. But he only listened to them when it was almost too late. "Anyway, why should I leave?" he said. "I'm innocent."

I wasn't learning anything new. Lai was repeating testimony from the hearing, and eventually I stopped asking. How much better to slow down and enjoy the thrill of sitting across from him after chasing his ghost for so long. I listened, taking in no more than a few words at a time. Lai called Chinese officials *kongtiao*, air conditioners, since most of them did about as much work. Officials who harassed him were *gundaorou*, hard meat to chop, a term he also applied to Canadian government lawyers at the hearing. His bank accounts were his *fan wan*, or rice bowls.

Lai's language was a compelling mix of old and new, though neither entirely stable nor particularly coherent. He seemed to carry his whole complicated past with him in his vocabulary. Other people did too, sure, but rarely in such stark relief.

When our food arrived I realized Lai had not ordered a single dish from the regular menu. Everything was one-of-a-kind, a chef special, an ambitious request, an impromptu creation, and perhaps in some cases a misunderstanding. Shrimps were served with lychees, scallops came with persimmon, sea bass was covered in isinglass and tangerine peel, thorn berries accompanied the taro yam, and galangal was draped over a type of intestine. At once Lai lifted up one dish after another to show them off to the neighboring table. "Normally this is not available in Canada," he said and ordered waiters to bring additional plates. He filled them with generous portions for our neighbors to try. He himself ate very little. He was busy ladling food onto plates with a porcelain spoon and passing them over. The neighbors complimented Lai on his imagination. They would never have dreamed of ordering such things, they said. That, I thought, must have been what people who encountered Lai in China had felt too.

Then, when I had already given up on hearing from Lai himself about his situation, he began to recall life in Shaocuo, his hometown, as I had suggested on the phone. He talked the way people do when they look at photo albums. He would happen upon a mental snapshot, enlarge on it, point fingers at details, smoothing out wrinkles and dog ears, flick back to a previous image, compare adjoining ones, how different they were, were they not? — contrasting before and after, borrowing from one to illuminate the other, all the while overlaying them with a voice many years older, turning a record that had once been no more than a series of random moments into a singular past, all without applying a shred of reflection or analysis.

To me, all his pictures had one thing in common: hope — hope invested cautiously in his teens and twenties, and then crushed with merciless routine from above. One of his pictures was of a fallow patch of land near Shaocuo — surrounded by trees and frequently flooded — where Lai's father had tried farming methods not approved by the local commune. He expected to gain higher yields. When the commune found out the land was confiscated — not because private land use was still illegal in China then, but because it was starting to show results — "My father was quite sad," Lai said. Another picture was of the primary school he had attended, an earthen structure a few miles from Shaocuo where teachers used bamboo canes to point at cotton bed sheets inscribed with simple characters and numbers. A hundred or more children would sit around each sheet, repeating after the teacher. Lai went to the school for a year. Then it was closed down in the Cultural Revolution.

The one picture conjured up by Lai that was already familiar to me was of the enterprise he started in the 1980s before moving to Xiamen. I had heard about it from his relatives in Shaocuo. With initial trepidation and only after losing his job as a blacksmith, Lai had set up a "gang of one." To his own surprise, it was a great success. He earned more than the rest of his family together. Soon though local officials came asking for gratuities. When he refused, they beat his sister so severely she went to the hospital. Bruises and cuts covered her arms and torso for weeks. After that Lai never refused another official. Indeed, he forced money on them whether they wanted it or not. The attack on his sister seemed to release all the fervor stored in him during the Mao years and all the cynicism it had bred. He sprang back in a burst of recklessness and risk-taking.

How much of this picture was family myth and how much true reflection I could not say. Lai was clever enough to come up with a convincing back story, but could he coordinate one with his relatives? Given his hasty departure, I thought it unlikely. In any case, this was context, not justification.

Oily plates covered our table when the food was finished. Lai looked around for waiters to clear them, but could see none. They had already forgotten his earlier lesson.

Eventually one of them turned up.

"Where were you?" Lai said. "Screwing a chicken in the back?"

"Apologies."

"And your colleagues?"

"We are busy tonight."

Lai was enraged. His neck had disappeared. His shoulders had risen up to his chin and his short arms were snapping open and shut like a pocketknife. Once the table had been cleared he said, still visibly angry, "I don't like the food here."

"Should we have gone somewhere else?"

"I like food that is simple. This is not simple."

"Like what?"

"*Zhou*. Rice gruel. In Xiamen, my guests always wanted fancy seafood. It gave them face. So I would order it. I would sit with them. I would eat a little. But not so much. I would go to the kitchen after the meal. I would ask the cooks to make me some *zhou*. Then I would eat it in the kitchen." Lai was delusional. The owner of the Red Mansion an ascetic? Or was he? Perhaps there had been nobody to show him how to enjoy the more intractable fruits of his empire.

"You know what I want to do now?" he said, sounding calmer. "I want to go to a casino."

"A particular one?" I said, having heard of Vancouver's Chinese back-room parlors.

"Oh, it doesn't matter."

I paid and we walked out of the restaurant. A strong wind came off Burrard Inlet.

"The problem is this," Lai said. "I'm banned from going to casinos."

"You lose your fifty-thousand-dollar bail bond if you do?"

"Yes, I think so."

"Might be an expensive evening."

"Yes."

We were standing on the street and I asked him about his visits to casinos in Niagara Falls when he first came to Canada. He liked slot machines, he said. All you had to do was wait. You were guaranteed to win as long as you didn't leave your machine. If you took a break, even a short one, you might miss the payout. But the Canadians had a trick. Their men would use plastic coin cups, you know, instead of going to the toilet. They could stay by their machines all day.

When we said goodbye I wondered if I should express hope of meeting again in China one day. It all depended. He would have to win asylum here first, a gamble. Then, at some later stage, he would have to make a deal with Beijing, an even bigger gamble. Perhaps he would try. The rootlessness of exile was not for him.

When he walked off it was around ten, an hour into his curfew. He hailed a taxi and got in. The taxi stood at the curb for a short while, long enough for him to explain in poor English that he wanted to go to a casino. Then it took off.

19

THE OFFICER

Room 512, Xiamen Hotel, No. 16 Huyuan Street,
Xiamen

MY HOST WAS called Officer Wen. Wen Yanhong. He introduced himself outside the Xiamen courthouse with elaborate courtesy. Officer Wen worked for the Public Security Bureau, so his business card said. Early in our conversation he had stopped himself midsentence as if remembering something important. From a wallet inside his suit he retrieved a card and passed it to me using both hands. He was a short man and if he'd had any inclination to bow he would have disappeared from my view. He asked if I would be available to go to the Xiamen Hotel with him. It was around midday and I hoped he meant lunch. When I agreed, knowing even then refusal was pointless, he summoned a car with his raised hand. A blue Audi pulled out nearby. It was driven by another officer, and at the hotel there were a few more in the lobby. Instead of heading for the dining hall — serving a dish called "Buddha Jumping over the Wall" according to the room service menu — we took a lift to the fifth floor and walked through a door held open by another officer. Officer Wen looked through my bag and found my digital camera. To own one was no crime and he never suggested it was. But neither did he give a reason for canceling lunch. He just asked me to wait in the room a while.

A southern Chinese children's rhyme said if you tear off the tail of a gecko it grows another. Xiamen had plenty of geckos, but did anyone ever get close enough to their tails to try? Not me. I was only watching. A three-inch gecko was running across the ceiling. It was brown and limber and we were playing a sort of game. I would tap my knuckle on the wooden headboard and the gecko would stop. Perhaps it was looking at me upside down. I couldn't tell. Its eyes were the same color as its gnarled skin. Then after a minute it would go on further until I knocked again. In short bursts it headed away from the bathroom door, past the kettle and the complimentary tea bags and the sachets of instant coffee, and finally behind the room service menu (which offered unknowable dishes such as "Sun rising from the east mountain" and "Phoenix-tailed prawn bowl"). Then the gecko was gone. I waited. *Cheat. Come back or I really will tear off your tail.*

I stretched out on the bed. I knew there was a line connecting these comfortable and clean sheets to everything that had happened since my return from Canada. But it wasn't I who had drawn that line. I had only watched, like the gecko. And often not even that.

When government investigators opened up the Red Mansion to the public, I had stayed away. It was easy to resist, admittedly. The place was no longer the same. The investigators had put up self-congratulatory notices: lessons to be learned from our successful work. The mansion had become an anti-corruption museum with visitors filing through rows of marble-tiled saunas and brocade massage rooms. The investigators hoped to invoke the timeless connection between luxury and evil, trying to shove Lai into the crooks' gallery of Saddam Hussein, Nicolae Ceauşescu, and Imelda Marcos. After their various downfalls, the masses had inspected their households and found much to revile. Saddam's golden fixtures, Nicolae's pet dogs grown obese on steak while the country starved, and of course Imelda's shoe collection. Exposure of their extravagance had made them human. Their myths collapsed. Their hold on the imagination faded. But not in Xiamen. Quite the opposite. The more people saw of Lai, the more excited they became. Crowds at the Red Mansion grew day by day. Travel agents started advertising its splendors. Hotels in the city filled up with entrepreneurs flying in to take notes. Then, a few weeks after the grand opening, the Red Mansion, the "Graceland of Graft," was abruptly closed down again. The government, despite having won physical control, was losing the battle over Lai's public identity.

I didn't see any of this myself. I only read about it in the official media. The *China Youth Daily* said the museum had failed in its mission to educate the people, and its editors did their best to rectify the mistake. Once unmentionable, Lai was now becoming a staple of state propaganda. Newspaper articles listed his crimes, as did officially sanctioned books. A twenty-five-part television miniseries was planned, portraying the mansion as a period drama palace full of scheming eunuchs and concubines. The anti-Lai propaganda also included coverage of the show trials of hundreds of his associates in Xiamen and three other cities. The evening news carried footage of judges, often retired military officers with little legal training, reading out sentences (the really incompetent judges were given rehearsals the day before). The accusing news cameras panned across the courtroom and focused on men in prison garb with recently shorn heads. They provided confessions and nothing else. Within days, official reports on the trials were sent to party organizations across the country with the order to "study" them. The study sessions were again filmed and shown on the evening news. It was a Maoist steamroller campaign. Despite all the evidence to the contrary, it seemed China had hardly changed at all.

Admittedly, I was watching from afar. I had come to press less and less hard. I contented myself with just being around.

During the weeks and months after Lai's hearing in Canada, I did nothing more than walk around the colonial district by the docks. I searched in the colonnaded alleys for new slogans ("Life is precious, be careful!") and visited my favorite bakery, buying doughnuts filled with pickled vegetables. The price varied from day to day, depending on the owner's mood and my willingness to talk. The most I paid was five *yuan*, the least was two. Then one morning the bakery was closed. The next day its front was boarded up. I asked a neighbor what had happened. "No more bribes, no more business," he said. The bakery's license had run out and officials were refusing to renew it. They were afraid to do anything while the investigators and propaganda cameras were around. Officials had always lacked "motivation," the neighbor said. You had to give them a little money to get things done. But not even that worked now. It was a common complaint. Xiamen's economy was collapsing on its feet. No building applications were approved, no companies founded, no jobs created. Bank accounts were frozen, prices for imports rose, investors stayed away, nightclubs stood empty. The trials of Lai's associates made defendants of everyone. The city was under siege. What had risen so quickly and confidently proved to be fragile. It fell apart easily. Its ardor turned to impotence. One push from above and the sap froze. With no communal history to fall back on, no ties older than a few years, no common identity, Xiamen began to unravel.

Yet not everyone was cowed by the might of Beijing. I saw a group of protesters by the gate of the Intermediate People's Court one day. They were relatives of one of the defendants, Yang Qianxian, the customs chief, who was being tried as a Lai associate. They said he was being made a scapegoat. His superiors had been involved with Lai as well. They were the truly guilty parties and should be punished, but Beijing loathed to admit how high up the rot went.

The relatives were there most days and police at the court gate left them alone. One relative held up a picture of the customs chief in his uniform. The others ate rice and vegetables from small plastic containers. They were noticeable mostly for their studied calm. They did not shout or jostle. They sat on the ground in a tidy line along a fence, behind them a courthouse proclaiming omnipotence, fifteen stories high, covered in white bathroom tiles and with an entrance encased by mirrored glass confronting arriving defendants with their own reflection.

I spoke to a woman in her fifties who introduced herself as Auntie Yang. She wore a loose-fitting cotton dress and an oddly colorful clip in her white hair. "You are tall," she said.

"Would you like me to sit down?"

"Not necessary, not necessary."

She said the family had written a letter to the court, listing the customs chief's many achievements, including his tireless service to the party. They were trying to deliver the letter but nobody at the court would take it, she said. After exchanging phone numbers I left. A few days later I called Auntie Yang and arranged to visit her at home. She was cleaning her living room when I arrived. "I'll be finished soon," she said, and swept the floor from the edges to the center, filling a dust pan and carrying it to the furthest corner of the room where she left it. "The dust has to stay put for another week," she said. "Then I carry it out the back door, not the front. Good fortune leaves by the front door."

"Good to know."

"Yes. You should always carry it, not sweep it, or a close relation will be swept out of the house."

"Has that happened to you?" I was thinking of the accused customs chief.

"Oh no," she said.

I asked about her detained relative more directly.

"We heard he was arrested as soon as it happened," she said. "He was interrogated. He was asked many difficult questions and he was never allowed to sleep and he was beaten, but still he wouldn't admit what he didn't do. Then they also arrested Zhang Lin, that's his wife. Her health is not so good. They interrogated her too. But she knew nothing. To punish her they forced her to sit on a block of ice. She was there for days. When she was finally let go, her legs were dead. She is paralyzed now and sits in a wheelchair. After her husband heard this news he changed his mind. He signed a confession. He also signed a paper calling for his own death as punishment. Of course, he would normally never write such a thing. He must have felt very alone."

"Did he not have a lawyer?"

"I don't know. Should he?"

"Well, yes." Defendants had a right to a lawyer even in China. The legal advice they were given may be perfunctory, but defendants did have a right to it.

When I visited Auntie Yang again a few days later I brought her a copy of the Chinese criminal justice code that enshrined a defendant's right to a lawyer. I also gave her a membership list of the Xiamen legal association. It contained the names of about forty lawyers. "Just choose one," I said. It was a small step to pass on the two documents, and entirely legal. Both were public and easily available. No authority was defied or resisted, no rule broken in spirit or the letter. And yet, I knew this was a departure. I was no longer just watching.

ᔕ

The gecko was back. It walked the ceiling, waving its snappy tail in mocking salute. Was it chewing on something, the twitching leg or severed wing of another resident of this room, one I had not been aware of and whose existence the hotel management would have denied? The sideways sun was coming through the window. It caught the gecko on the wall above the bed. It looked translucent. I knocked on the headboard. It stopped.

When Officer Wen found my digital camera he deleted everything on it. He was smart, smarter at least than they used to be. He knew how easy it was to restore images on a memory chip. Only by taking new pictures on top of the old ones could anything be deleted permanently, digitally. So he took seventy-nine pictures, aiming indiscriminately around the room. I didn't object. The pictures would be a useful record. One showed the blond wood frame of the bed, cracked at the base, another the wide-open safety deposit box, yet another the wavy net curtains. When he was done he handed me back the camera and left me alone in the room.

With the gecko sitting in the sun, I picked up a brochure from the nightstand. It showed the red seventeen-story hotel façade outside my window, the parking lot sloping down to a main road, cars passing. "Xiamen Hotel is an ideal place for the guests from home and abroad to stay in. Located in the center of Xiamen city with convenient communications, 2km from the Passenger Port, 3km from Xiamen Railway Station, 10km from Gaoqi International Airport." That really would be convenient. I read on. "Surrounded by beautiful gardens, Xiamen Hotel has 8 luxurious buildings with 480 rooms . . . The Chinese restaurant with elegant furnishing caters local flavor food and continental dishes prepared by famous chefs."

It would seem I was in good hands. My hosts had put me up comfortably. Four-star hotels were their facility of choice. They could ask questions first, and then decide what to do. Rented rooms had none of the gravity of a holding cell. Who would not be comfortable here? All could still be downplayed and explained away later, ensuring them against a change in the wind, a yet-to-be-unearthed fact, a higher purpose only known to superiors. They used vague language that committed them to nothing, saying my actions were inappropriate, *hen bu ying gaide,* or "very not should be." They were no freer than their prey. They could of course sow confusion and fear with arbitrary detentions, but they too were unsure of the boundaries. What should be deemed a threat to the state, what newly legitimate? They were struggling to adapt, reinventing themselves just like the citizenry, or at least trying.

～

The green-on-black clock face on the nightstand showed 18:14 when Officer Wen returned. He placed a chair in the middle of the room and sat down. A mock baroque mirror was mounted behind him on the wall. Framed by gilt, I could see the back of his head. It was as flat as his face. Through his cotton shirt I could see the outlines of thick-cut ribs.

"What were you doing at the courthouse?" he said. "Were you meeting someone? At what time?" Speaking softly, he asked a long list of questions. He wasn't reading from notes but he sounded like it. Slowly his questions moved on from the courthouse. Why had I gone to the ancestral village of

Lai Changxing? What was my interest in the replica Forbidden City built by Lai? He seemed to know quite a bit about my time in Xiamen. But most of his information was either wrong or incomplete. He asked if I had stayed at an apartment in a certain compound and met a contact at another. I had never heard of either.

Eventually Officer Wen went back to asking me about the family at the courthouse. "Was it the wife you were meeting?" he said. "Do you know her? She is ill at the moment and cannot receive visitors, do you understand?" I was relieved he didn't mention the aunt. He didn't seem to know I had visited her. But I still had to answer his other questions. With true cooperation we could solve this problem together, he said.

Officer Wen was the product of a system that prized confessions above all else. Interrogations were meant to end with one, as they had for Lai's associates. Admissions of guilt were often the real aim, not the extraction of information. In most cases, the detained had been convicted before they were even caught. All that was left was to settle their punishment. They could win leniency with a public show of contrition, a widely publicized confession. Having cast doubt on the official writ they were asked to help restore it. Confessing was the only sensible choice for them. But my situation was different. Not once was I asked to admit guilt. Officer Wen's instinct may have pointed in that direction, but the closest he came was an admonishment that I should have sought official permission to interview Chinese citizens, referring to a rule we both knew to be defunct.

I held back questions of my own. How much longer would this take? I settled on giving answers honestly as far as I could. For a while it worked. When I was asked to name a contact I would say it was against the rules of my newspaper to do so and that I had no choice but to follow the rules. Officer Wen went on. After a while he said, "Please answer the question."

"I wish you would ask me different questions."

"Later, later."

"I met Lai Changxing recently."

"What?"

"I met him in Canada."

"What is the relevance?"

"It's highly relevant. He is connected to everything you've asked me."

"There is no relevance."

"Have you met him?"

"What? No."

"He lived in Xiamen for many years."

"This is not relevant. Please answer the question."

∽

I was tired and hungry when Officer Wen left the room at 20:22. He said he would order dinner for me, and half an hour later room service arrived. A waiter set down a tray on the bed and the smells from under the plastic lid woke me with a jolt. I felt like a mouse poking out of her hole and finding assembled on a mousetrap not just a glistening cheese cube but also some charcuterie, fresh tomatoes, several slices of whole grain bread with New Zealand butter and a glass of white wine. I entertained the idea of refusing dinner. Not that I was going to do it. No mouse ever did. But I wanted to prolong the moment, the sheer, slow pleasure of it. I knew once I had lifted the lid I would be consumed with blind, senseless greed. Time would collapse in on itself and become knotted in a ball until every last bit of food had disappeared.

But then, when I finally did lift the lid and filled a plate bearing the hotel's name and tasted the first few bites, my spirits faltered. I was in no way disappointed with the food. Officer Wen had ordered well. There was a pork dish and a fish dish, a green vegetable in a steamer as well as a bowl of noodles, which the waiter said could be refilled, a cold cucumber dish and a melon soup, a diced chicken, baked shrimps, and a glutinous rice ball for dessert. This was a fine meal. But it felt odd eating alone. In China eating is an event. It is enforced socializing. Food is designed for groups. Ordering a proper meal for one is ludicrous. The portions are too big. Dining alone means overordering and wasting food, like I now did.

I thought of all the stories in Chinese newspapers I had seen about food. If eating is a metaphor for life, it is also one for harm. With no private gun ownership, food poisoning is a popular way to murder here. Most days there are grim news stories about gangsters lacing porridge with rat venom, spurned wives serving insecticide breakfasts, and rival restaurant owners spoiling each other's ingredients. Where outright malice is absent, greed and haste work just as well. Factories pump toxins into fishing grounds, counterfeit milk powder kills newborn children, and unsanitary fowl farming triggers global flu pandemics.

∽

At 21:47, Officer Wen came back into the room with a colleague who sat down on the chair by the gilded mirror and prepared himself to take notes on a preprinted form. Officer Wen remained standing and waited a moment. Then he said in a formal, declarative tone, "We are from the Xiamen Public Security Bureau. I am Wen Yanhong and this is my colleague Liu Darong. We are here to ask you some questions. We welcome your cooperation. Everything you say will be written down and read back to you later." He asked me for my name, overseas address, place of work, date of birth, my parents' and siblings' names, and my passport number. The latter I could not remember and said so. Officer Wen turned to his colleague, hunched over his form, and read off my passport number from a piece of paper in his hand. Then he asked me the same questions about the courthouse as before, but bundled together, giving a heavy hint of what he expected to hear — answers honed by us earlier, their passage having been eased, making this a mere formality, so he seemed to suggest. "You were visiting the Intermediate People's Court, right? There you hoped to meet someone. Can you please state who you were going to meet?" When this line of questioning didn't produce the desired result, Officer Wen switched to repeating questions. But he didn't just repeat the questions I hadn't answered. He also repeated ones that were not in dispute. Who did I work for? Why had I come to China? When did I first visit Xiamen? Who did I work for? It was tiring. Eventually Officer Wen stopped and asked his colleague to read his notes out loud. When he was done, the colleague asked me if this was a fair representation of the conversation. I said it was. What I didn't say was that I objected to the questions being littered with names of people who had done no wrong.

The note-taking officer pulled a small metal box from his pocket and opened it on the bed. It contained a sponge sodden with red ink. "Please put your finger on here and then on the bottom of the report," he said. Officer Wen stepped up to the bed and closed the metal box. "That won't be necessary," he said to his colleague. Turning to me, he said, "You can just sign your name."

I shook my head. It was all I could do not to burst out laughing. A red finger print as a signature? Asking me for my overseas address and my parents' names? Were they really saying "Watch out, we know where you live"? I wanted to share this moment with someone. I looked up at the ceiling but the gecko was gone.

The Public Security Bureau — the official name of the police in China

— was in no way to be taken lightly. It could create darkness at noon, make detention seem like a relief for those who heard it rumored for weeks, hold out hope like an executioner's rope. But none of this applied to me. I was no associate of Lai. I tried not to laugh.

〜

At 23:07, the two officers left the room. A few minutes later, Officer Wen returned alone. "Let's go to the hotel bar," he said, as if we were on a business trip together. I picked up my bag to take it down with me. He didn't discourage me. In the hallway I saw two junior officers. At the mezzanine lobby above the reception Officer Wen ordered beer for us. I seated myself so as to look toward the front door, where I hoped to be heading.

We toasted.

"At the end of my first year in China," I said, "someone asked me how long I had been here. I told him it was about a year. A year, he said, so you are well-acquainted with China. That's very true, I thought. Well-acquainted was how I felt. Familiar but not intimate. Now that's changed."

Officer Wen said, "I would like to give you some advice. It will be best if you sign the report of our conversation."

"I understand."

"No, I don't think you understand." He pulled a folded copy of the report from his pocket. "The trials of the helpers of Lai Changxing are almost finished. Everybody wants to go back to a normal situation."

"I am ready to go back to a normal situation. In any case, I am not on trial."

"Of course, you are not on trial."

"It feels like it."

"You are not."

We went upstairs to Room 512 again.

I folded back the bed sheets and lay down, wide awake. As a teenager I had been an occasional shoplifter. Mostly I stole books. At the time, I told myself these were acts of fair redistribution. But if I had asked my parents I am sure they would have bought them for me. Then one day, an alarm went off as I walked out of a small independent bookshop. In my bag I had three books I had not paid for. I started running, quickly leaving the shopkeeper behind. Around the next corner I slowed down. A minute later, a police van pulled up alongside, inching forward, having been summoned by the shopkeeper. I started running again and the van followed at a steady pace, neither overtaking nor falling behind. From his rolled-down window one of the officers said, "Just stop . . . there's no point . . . okay, keep going for a bit." Eventually I did stop and the officers found the books in my bag. They drove me to the nearest police station and led me to an empty cell. Without so much as taking my name or asking me why I had lifted the books, they locked me up. The cell was clean, the walls white, a sink in one corner. I sat there with nothing to do and no books to read. I imagined the officers outside saying, "Stupid middle-class boy." Then after a few hours they let me out. They didn't charge me or call my parents or even speak to me. They just showed me the door.

Whenever I bought books now, waiting for the cash register queue to inch forward, I thought of those officers. I could recognize boundaries and perhaps even live with them, even if it had taken me longer than most. But somehow that was not enough here. My situation in the hotel required more, a gesture of cooperation. I had to play along, or at least seem to be.

In the morning, I told Officer Wen I really could not sign his record of our talk but I was prepared to sign something else, something I had written myself. He shrugged as if to say, "Let's see what you come up with," and brought me an official notebook. In it I wrote a thank-you note, saying he had been a wonderful host and how much I had enjoyed our conversations. I mentioned in general terms that we had talked about Lai's ancestral village and the replica of the Forbidden City. Then I wrote that China was one of the freest countries I knew, evidenced by our free-ranging discussion. I was trying to butter him up, but there was also a personal truth in there somewhere, though not a universal one. I had enjoyed an unexpected sense of freedom over the last few years. Every trespass had felt like a minor triumph. In a country where much was nominally forbidden yet frequently tolerated, this was a cheap thrill (and wearing off now). Still, Officer Wen didn't know that. I ended the note by saying, "I am sad to leave your wonderful city. However, I have a flight to catch to Beijing." I hoped he would be appeased.

When I was done I handed in the notebook and waited in the room. I was exhausted. However juvenile I might still be, real adolescence had been pressed out of me. An hour later Officer Wen came back. With a casual smile he gave me my hotel bill. One night's stay, one room service meal. Five hundred sixty-four yuan. "I got you a police discount," he said. "The normal rate is much higher."

EPILOGUE

Private Dining Room No. 18, Shuyou Restaurant,
Huzhong Street, Xiamen

OUR DINING ROOM, one of many along an upstairs corridor, was filled
with the smell of food. Half a dozen steaming plates rotated on a lazy Susan
in the middle of the table. Here came more. The water duck furiously en-
crusted with red pepper corns and cinnamon sticks rolled around; the
dried jellyfish, its diaphanous mass harpooned and puckered with chili oil;
the pig liver, chopped with precision and hidden under star anise; the black
fungus lolling in pea starch like someone who had spent the last three
weeks in a hotel pool; the bruised collision of mixed vegetables in rice wine
vinegar; the shins and shanks of what must have been a sturdy line of
lambs, their marrow extracted and mixed with minced ham on a separate
plate; the bean yam with cornflower; the pork suet, whose vicious spice and
monstrous heat are said to have been remarked upon by an albino prince in
Sichuan; and among them all, as a toast to abundance and a belated fare-
well, a bowl of plain boiled rice.

"I might have plastic surgery," Lili said while ladling food onto my
plate.

"You?"

"I found a good doctor."

Sitting at the table with us were two men she had brought along. One
was a watch-strapped, leech-faced entrepreneur, the other his assistant.

256

"Be sure not to forget the eyes," the entrepreneur said. "They are the most important part for a woman. The eyelids should be double-folded. And wide open."

Lili excused herself from the table. She said she had to make a call. Holding her mobile phone she left the room.

The entrepreneur turned to me. "You are the foreigner who met Lai Changxing?" he said.

"I think Mr. Lai's met a lot of foreigners."

I recounted my meetings in Vancouver. In Xiamen, Lai was passing ever deeper into the realm of myth. He now lived on a vast estate called the Blue Mansion overlooking the Canadian Ocean — was that true? No, I said. He was involved in business again, the gem business? No, not at the moment. He had a Canadian girlfriend? Not that I knew of.

"I saw a picture of him with a young woman on the Internet," the entrepreneur said, "and they were walking in front of the Canadian Palace of Justice. She was a pretty Chinese, but more modern than our girls."

"She might have been a translator."

"Good thing he speaks no foreign languages."

Lili came back to the room, but immediately she excused herself again. She said she had business to attend to.

Without glancing up at Lili, the entrepreneur asked me, "You think Lai will be returned to China?"

"It does look that way, doesn't it?"

A verdict had finally been announced. Lai's asylum bid was denied by the refugee board. He was a "common criminal," it ruled. Lai was appealing against the decision and new hearings were scheduled. But his situation was bleaker now than before.

"He won't last long if he comes back," the entrepreneur said.

By now the trials of Lai's associates in Xiamen were over too. More than six hundred had received prison sentences in China's biggest criminal case and fourteen were condemned to die. They included a vice-mayor, a regional police chief, the customs chief, the vice-minister for public security, and, apparently, the head of military intelligence, but no senior politburo members. They were protected. Jia Qinglin, the former Fujian boss whose wife headed the provincial trade commission, was promoted to number four in the Communist Party. Half the execution orders were commuted after intense string-pulling and the exchange of more money. The rest were carried out. Among the dead was also Lai's brother Shuiqiang. He had been given a remarkably light seven-year sentence, having confessed all and talked some of his relatives into cooperating with the authorities. But after his failure to lure Lai himself back from Vancouver he was found dead in his cell. There were reports of an illness but no autopsy. He was cremated immediately after he died. His family swore he had been bumped off. One of Lai's accountants died in similar fashion a while later.

Lili returned to the dining room. She apologized effusively for her absence. Then she walked back out. Where to? She returned ten minutes later, by which time the table had been cleared. The entrepreneur and his assistant were saying goodbye, promising to show up at the club in a few hours. They wanted to meet the new *gutouqing*, light-boned. The *chaiheniu*, lean country girls. The *jiumi*, alcohol honeys.

I waited while Lili paid the bill. She was in fact paying three bills. She had been conducting three separate dinners in three private rooms along the same corridor, each for a group of clients from the club in the hope of luring them back. None of them knew of the others. To them, Lili had been an attentive if overworked host. She would eat a few morsels, pile food on to her guests' plates, and leave and return, and leave and return, hopping from room to room. She frequently entertained like this. Her absences were rarely questioned, or indeed noticed. She always brought with her companions to entertain each room, usually one of her dancers, or a friend, or on occasion an unsuspecting foreigner.

An unseasonably cold political season was coming to an end. Spring was in the air — and in the restaurants and nightclubs. Xiamen was getting back on its feet now that the Lai trials were over, and the prisons full and senior politburo members exonerated. Thus went the unspoken message of a new propaganda campaign. "Hold high the banner of socialism," read a conveniently vague article in an official newspaper displayed in glass boxes along Xiamen's main roads. "Return your city to its prime position." On the same street, new red banners proclaimed, "Persist in reform and opening up to the outside world."

Little encouragement was needed. Building work resumed, dog ownership soared, and shoeshine boys once again polished stilettos. Ferries at No. 1 Wharf were busier than ever. From Lakeside Drive to Piano Island, from subterranean bars to bamboo scaffolding, economic growth came roaring back. A new specialist spa opened where people could bathe in chicken broth. My favorite pawnshop, a place where one could still find things made more than five minutes ago, was knocked down and replaced by high-rises. Walking down Zhongshan Street one evening I spotted two workers redecorating a wedding studio. After scraping and painting all day, they were setting up a double bed by the window. Next to it was a small black-and-white television. When I walked past the shop again a few hours later I saw them lying side by side, surrounded by white dresses, watching a program about dwarfs.

Across the city, reminders of Lai were removed. His five-ton Mercedes and other possessions were sold at private auction. The Red Mansion was turned into a training center for migrant workers. In recognition of the mansion's history, the act of "sexual bribery" was added to the criminal justice code. Over at the Xiamen customs house, home to many frequent mansion visitors, an all-too-subtle manipulation was carried out on a ten-foot stone statue. The two white lions guarding the front door had long been holding down a fistful of coins with their mighty paws. Masons now chiseled away the coins.

What will become of Xiamen? Fakers and fortune seekers, oddballs and outlaws continue to pour in, harboring desires as vast and treacherous as the waters beyond the shoreline, while officials and businessmen cling to age-old relationships of mutual dependency. The emperor's grain is still the city's favorite dish. And yet despite the resulting injustices, Xiamen is surprisingly stable. It knows few battles between haves and have-nots. Somehow the system works — not least because Beijing still wields a bloody club. But also because Beijing has learned to be flexible. It encourages the raw energy of its subjects, the millions volunteering to be shredded in the gold rush. Most of them, used up, will eventually drop out. But many more wait to replace them. Beijing neither stops nor protects them.

The results of such unfettered industrial convulsion are by now familiar. In her book *China's Plight*, He Qinglian, an exiled chronicler of corruption, writes:

Modernisation does not mean simply that you have a lot of money. Those nouveau riches who have pretty women, fierce dogs, villa houses and nice sedans are barbarians with just the trappings of modernity. If a society lacks a humanistic spirit that undergirds everything, if it lacks a tolerant social atmosphere, lacks pursuits deeper than materialism, then it will be lost. Our path is clear. We should emphasise reforms in non-economic areas, and emphasise humanism to give society guidance, ideals and meaning.

She is right, but perhaps a little ahead of her time. One day He Qinglian may be read as widely as Joan Didion is in America. But before she can defrock the frontier myths that fire up so many Chinese, they want to live them, get rich, and dream of a Red Mansion.

Alas, it is doubtful there will ever be another Lai Changxing. Xiamen has become less opaque since his departure in 1999. Restrictions were scaled back and chances to gather quick billions diminished. Trade is moving to the hinterland. The boomtowns are no longer lone islands of prosperity. Backwaters in the interior get their own high-tech factories, high-rise buildings, private bordellos, and seafood restaurants, even if the majority of Chinese still live on less than a dollar a day. Lai belongs to a dying era: the infancy of modern China's rise, dating from Mao's death to perhaps the 2008 Olympic Games in Beijing.

Still, Lai's memory lives on. Millions followed his example, trying to reinvent themselves — as bosses, as billionaires, as dirt emperors. If any one thing could be said to explain the rise of modern China, then perhaps this: The rush to reinvention freed pent-up energies. Unceasing hunger and boundless enterprise fuel the country's breakneck transformation. Without it, top-down reforms would have fallen flat and China would have stumbled. For three decades, its people have faced immense social change. Ways of life were upended by rapid modernization and most Chinese responded with amazing good grace. They acted with finesse and reason. They did not join violent millenarian movements, nor did they pine for a return to seventh-century spiritual laws. Chinese like Lai took social change as it came, adjusting one life at a time. Sometimes they might feel an inclination to blame others for setbacks, but they rarely act on it.

Setbacks, of course, did occur. The personal makeovers they are undergoing — now common even in remote hinterland towns — have created a new set of problems. For one, most makeovers were incomplete. A past is not easily left behind, least of all in a civilization thousands of years old. But many Chinese try anyway. They play around with identities, mixed and matched, stolen and renamed, and little by little reshape their nation.

Whether they will continue in this vein depends on how much room to experiment they are going to have in the future. Will the government dare to loosen the shackles further? Will it finally confront its terrible past? Will it stop executing more people than all other countries put together? Not a foregone conclusion, but I'm optimistic. Beijing is undergoing its own slow makeover. At the current pace, it will hold another Olympic Games before it holds genuine elections. Yet meddling in private lives is becoming rarer and rarer. For the most part, the government contents itself with watching. Always watching.

A year before publication I told my handler at the foreign ministry I was writing a book. Perhaps I mixed up my tenses, mistakenly suggesting I had already finished.

"Yes," the official said, "I enjoyed the book."

I was too stunned to ask how he might have got hold of the manuscript. I felt faint with surprise.

Later, when he wanted to know what had made me write it, I told him, showily, having recovered my breath, that I was trying to record events of significance. I drew myself up in my chair. There was more to history than wars and revolutions. Then we parted.

China was, of course, compelling. Yet what had interested me from the start was how individuals — far from the forces of history — were transforming lives on their own (even if their ability to do so was often an illusion, a political fiction).

I identified with that. I myself, when I arrived in China, had left behind an unwanted life, a cubicle existence in the Rockefeller Center, escaping office journalism and its obsession with pegs and charts. The summits it dared to climb were inevitably those visible from the foothills. Only now did I fully realize that that was what had preoccupied me. I had been looking for nothing in particular, no new identity. But I had hungered for what was not yet evident, the other, any other.

What I found I'm not so sure. After six years I took a break from the *Times* to spend more time in Xiamen and write about it. I felt at home in the city, a migrant among migrants. I experienced giddy liberation. I also bumped up against the limits of new freedoms, moving from false summit to false summit far out of sight of the foothills. I lived intensely, surrounded by others, but found it hard to hold on to them. They were always moving, and so was I. We belonged to a ghost set, resigned to movement.

Of my friends in Xiamen, only Lili was left now. The teenage dancers were home in Xinjiang, while Fangmin had gone to Guangzhou. After failing to find solitude in Xiamen he decided to start again elsewhere. The last I heard he was trying to set up a two-hour minibus service between Guangzhou and the border to Hong Kong.

Soon after that, Kim and Andy left too. Kim opened a teahouse in an historic courtyard behind the Central Military Commission in Beijing. Andy joined an international newspaper, engaging in the same heated discussions with editors about China that I knew — and he was winning many of them.

On occasion, Kim and Andy came back to Xiamen. During one weekend trip we all went to Lili's club together. "It's busy tonight, isn't it?" Andy said to Lili, looking around the auditorium.

"It is now. But for a while it really wasn't." She said during the 4.20 investigation the club had been empty. One of her colleagues was married to a Lai nephew and another to a customs official. And of course a lot of the guests were part of the city's trading class. It made business difficult. Now, however, the investigation was over, Lili said, and they were fine. The old guests were coming back. One had been in the night before recounting his interrogation. Locked in a hotel room, a metal bucket was put on his head. Officers beat the bucket, but not him, with wooden clubs.

"And you?" Kim said. "Did you have problems?"

"It wasn't so bad." Lili leaned back in her seat. She had a way of signaling she would tell a story that was almost grandfatherly. "One day, the police caught one of my girls with a guest as they left the club together. The girl was accused of prostitution and to save herself she told them about me. So the police came to look for me, but of course I heard about it." Lili shifted in her seat, turning sideways and hitching up one knee. "I left immediately and changed my phone number. For six months I didn't come here. I just played mahjong with friends. When the police couldn't find me, they showed no mercy to the girl. She got seven years in prison. But once her trial was over I knew I could negotiate. I spoke to a friend who had relations with the police. In the end, we settled the case, and I came back."

"And all is normal now?"

"Yes. I'm busy." She said she had set up her own trading company. "I do that during the day and at night I look after officials from the customs bureau here. It's a good combination."

She got up and walked across the auditorium, past cornices and bas-relief panels fixed to private rooms where guests sang along to someone else's tune. One guest, a man wearing an outsize hat, beckoned Lili over. She knelt beside him, hitching up her gray suit just enough to be comfortable.

ᥪᦏ

After more than six years in Vancouver, Lai Changxing's future was still unclear. He waited and waited under curfew in his apartment, while lawyers and politicians argued over the implications of sending him back. Could China ever become a civilized country if the west sheltered its criminals? Would deporting Lai shore up support for the rule of law in Beijing? Or would it validate the current system? Had bandits not played important political roles in China's past, with Coxinga and many others defying the despised Qing rulers?

Eventually, in the summer of 2005, the case wound up in front of the Canadian Supreme Court. David Matas, the human rights lawyer, said Lai would be tortured if sent back to China. Police were certain to force a confession. Assurances to treat Lai humanely were worthless, he said, citing the unexplained death of Lai's brother and his accountant in prison. Matas's arguments were backed by Amnesty International. It warned against "relying on assurances by a state that it will refrain from torture in the future, when it has engaged in illegal torture in the past."

On August 31, the Supreme Court in Ottawa announced its ruling. The judges agreed with the Canadian government that Lai was not a political refugee. "That makes him removal-ready," a gleeful government spokeswoman said. But Lai's battle was still not over. Legally, he could only be deported after another hearing to examine whether he faced "cruel and unusual punishment" at home.

Matas, unbowed, said, "Lai will pursue every legal channel to remain in Canada. The government of China, the president, the prime minister, and the central committee of the Communist Party have all said that he is guilty. And he has not even been charged yet."

Lai himself was not exactly helping his case. He was found in breach of his nighttime curfew. On an evening just before the Supreme Court ruling, immigration officers arrested him as he was leaving a Chinese restaurant at half past nine after attending a birthday party.

The Canadian government welcomed his renewed arrest. It was busy preparing to host the Chinese president on an official visit to Canada. Under pressure from Beijing, it was working harder than ever to deport Lai. The Canadian trade minister sent a letter to the prosecuting lawyers in Vancouver. "This case could have direct implications to [our] future diplomatic and trade relations with the People's Republic of China," he wrote. A copy of the letter found its way to the newspapers.

A month later, after the Chinese president had safely departed with assurances of an imminent deportation, Lai was once again released on bail. Under a new curfew he had less freedom than before. He could go out only between one and three in the afternoon. And he was banned from using mobile phones. The refugee board feared he might try to escape, as he had done in China.

Yet, there was also good news for Lai. The presiding judge at the bail hearing said legal proceedings would likely take a while longer. In the meantime, he told Lai, "What we don't want to see is any more testing of the water."

"I never will," Lai said and smiled.

Then on May 15, 2006, he lost his last immigration hearing and a deportation order was issued. Police detained him the next morning. Matas challenged the order in federal court in Ottawa in a last attempt. Two weeks later, the court ruled — less than twenty-four hours before Lai was to board a plane to China — that he did after all face "cruel and unusual punishment." The deportation order was lifted, pending further legal challenges, and Lai was freed. He returned to the apartment with the large television and the view of the mountains. "I guess this really is my home now," he told me on the phone.

ACKNOWLEDGMENTS

I AM DELIGHTED TO acknowledge the bountiful help I received. Writing this book would not have been possible without three very special women. Sophie Yu was my first — and often unseen — supporter in China; she smoothed my path with uncommon skill and warmth. Barbara J. Zitwer came all the way from New York to Xiamen to sign me up and then sold my manuscript while dancing salsa at a Puerto Rican funeral . . . you are unbeatable. Juliana Liu saw me at my lowest and hosted me in Singapore during months of editing; her love and insights improved the manuscript immeasurably. Thank you.

Anton Mueller at Houghton Mifflin was everything I could have wanted in an editor. He inspired and encouraged me, he saved me from embarrassment and procrastination, and he applied his revision pen with exceptional skill, patience, and imagination. His assistant Nicole Angeloro was a constant source of support. Reem Abu-Libdeh and Muriel Jorgenson sped along production. Eamon Dolan gave generously of his time and wit. Lori Glazer, David Yoo, and Brooke Witkowski worked tirelessly to promote my efforts, as did Bridget Marmion and Sanj Kharbanda (who was able to explain, magnificently, the difference between publicity and marketing).

Eleanor Birne at John Murray and her assistants Ed Faulkner and Helen Hawksfield brought welcome new insights to the manuscript. Gordon Wise was an enthusiastic early supporter, as was Catherine Benwell, his then assistant. Robert Kirby at PFD and his assistant Catherine Cameron worked hard — not to mention Robert's singing — to ensure publication. Carmen Koelz, Dieter Muscholl, and Doris Engelke at Eichborn made me feel at home again in Germany after a fifteen-year absence, and Edith Beleites executed the task of translating an author into his mother tongue superbly.

At the *Times* in London, my special thanks go to Peter Stothard, who sent me to China much to my and everyone else's surprise, Robert Thompson, who kept me there with a mission to explore, and Martin Fletcher, who inspired me above all else. Furthermore I would like to thank: Gill Ross, Christine Sykes, Gerry Taylor, Matt Gibbs, Ben Preston, George Brock, Bronwen Maddox, David Watts, Phillip Pank, Alan Copps, Martin Barrow, Alex Blair, Richard Beeston, Michael Binyon, and Rosemary Righter.

In Germany, my father, Erdmut, read every draft and made countless improvements. My mother, Tini, visited me in Xiamen and welcomed me home when I fled the city temporarily. My brother, Florian, was the one person I knew I could always call on for good cheer. My uncle Heiner encouraged me to find adventure in the mind, and my late grandmother Mila, the soul of inquisition, always journeyed with me. My high school friend Peter Albrecht and his wife, Sandra, were early travel companions to Xiamen. My former high school teacher Klaus Helms found mistakes in my writing as he had done almost two decades earlier. Hans-Wolf Sievert gave me the right advice at the right time, as did Michael Braun.

In London, David Staton was a most generous host and Nikki De Marchi helped out with research. Niels and Cass Bryan-Low endured early wake-up calls and late-night conversations about an obscure immigration case in Vancouver. Hillary Rosner and Phil Higgs gave me shelter in Boulder and instant feedback down a phone line. Adam Jones and Catherine Whitaker sent thoughtful comments and recommendations from Paris. Richard Burn let me borrow from his library in Singapore. Julian Rubinstein warned me of the natives in the New York publishing jungle, Jonathan Turner sent ideas from San Francisco, and Stephen Grant bliss from Panama.

In China, I received help from Xu Xing, Yang Li, Chen Fang, and Inway Ni. I also benefited from conversations with Achim Bosslet, Mitch Presnick, Dan Brody, Rachel DeWoskin, Sabine Eckle, and Buddy Buruku. Maya Alexandri was a terrific reader. Edmund Cheung helped in many unexpected ways, and Arthur Kroeber lent towering intellectual support. Kim and Andy I can't thank enough.

Among my greatest debts of gratitude are also those to colleagues in China. Jane Macartney, Clifford Coonan, and Jim Pringle of the *Times* were wonderful to work with. Michael Sheridan of the *Sunday Times* offered shrewd and timely advice. Bay Fang of *U.S. News & World Report* was a re-sourceful travel companion. David Rennie of the *Daily Telegraph* sounded a warning at the right moment. Richard Jones and Wang Tong brought a lot more than cameras to their photo assignments. Peter Hessler of *The New Yorker* gave invaluable guidance. Andreas Kluth of *The Economist* showed unbridled enthusiasm, as did Karen and Mark Magnier of the *Los Angeles Times*. Alec Sirken of *CBS News* advised me on how to present a book, as did Frank Sieren of *Wirtschaftswoche*. Evan Osnos of the *Chicago Tribune*, Didi Tatlow of the *South China Morning Post*, and Pallavi Aiyar of *The Hindu* critiqued the critiques of others, as did Karen Smith. The re-porting of Mark O'Neil, Jasper Becker, and other writers on the *South China Morning Post*, as well as on the *Globe and Mail*, helped me greatly. Geoff York, the *Globe and Mail*'s Beijing bureau chief, was a patient mentor throughout. James Baer, supported by Henry Chu of the *Los Angeles Times*, offered wonderfully detailed and insightful comments. Brook Larmer gave wise counsel in moments of need, and his wife, Hannah Beech, of *Time* al-lowed me to steal a line from her story about Lai. Harald Maass of the *Frankfurter Rundschau* accompanied my research from the beginning and has been one of its most tireless supporters.

I would furthermore like to acknowledge the debt I owe to the authors of books I relied on. *A Dragon Apparent* by Norman Lewis (London, 1951) inspired me. *Modern China* by Graham Hutchings (London, 2000) I used incessantly; it deserves to become as ubiquitous as Mao's Little Red Book. *The New Emperors* by Harrison Salisbury (London, 1992) still seems like the best introduction to Communist China. For background on Chinese crime I pilfered Bertil Lintner's *Blood Brothers* (New York, 2002). The same goes for Geremie Barme's excellent study of contemporary Chinese culture, *In the Red* (New York, 1999). Going back in history, I found *God's Chinese Son* (London, 1996) and *Chinese Roundabout* (New York, 1993) the most enjoyable of Jonathan Spence's many books. *The City of Light* by Jacob D'Ancona, translated by David Selbourne (London, 1997), is in the same league. Reading up on Coxinga I came across the wonderful *Coxinga* by Jonathan Clements (London, 2004). Except for failing to mention Coxinga, *Bandits* by Eric Hobsbawm (London, 1969) is unsurpassed in its breadth even if Hobsbawm's argument seems even more farfetched today. Lastly, *World Bank Report No. 24169-CHA*, "China: Promoting Growth With Eq-uity," October 15, 2003, which riled me. The report claims the number of

Chinese living on less than $1 a day has fallen to 161 million. This seems wrong. To have $4 per day a four-person family would have to earn $120 per month. Even if one assumes two adults in the family are working full-time they would each have to earn at least $60 (with no breaks for holidays and job changes). That's more than most unskilled migrants make in the boomtowns, and a multiple of the wages I heard about on trips to the countryside. My impression is that the Chinese remain far poorer than statistics show, and their pell-mell striving for betterment will continue for some time.

Beijing
August 2006